TEACHER DEVELOPMENT SERIES
Series Editor: Andy Hargreaves

THE REALITIES OF TEACHERS' WORK

D1227839

THE REALITIES OF TEACHERS' WORK
Never a Dull Moment

Sandra Acker

CASSELL
London and New York

Cassell
Wellington House
125 Strand
London WC2R 0BB

Cassell & Continuum
370 Lexington Avenue
New York
NY 10017–6550

www.cassell.co.uk

First published 1999

British Library Cataloguing-in-Publication Data
A catalogue record for this book is available from the British Library.

ISBN 0–304–32669–0 (hardback)
       0–304–32671–2 (paperback)

Typeset by Ensystems, Saffron Walden, Essex
Printed and bound in Great Britain by
Redwood Books Ltd, Trowbridge, Wilts.

Contents

Series Editor's Foreword

In Britain and Australia, they call it teaching. In the United States and Canada, they call it instruction. Whatever terms we use, we have come to realize in recent years that the teacher is the ultimate key to educational change and school improvement. The restructuring of schools, the composition of national and provincial curricula, the development of benchmark assessments – all these things are of little value if they do not take the teacher into account. Teachers don't merely deliver the curriculum. They develop, define and reinterpret it too. It is what teachers think, what teachers believe and what teachers do at the level of the classroom that ultimately shapes the kind of learning that young people get. Growing appreciation of this fact is placing working with teachers and understanding teaching at the top of our research and improvement agendas.

For some reformers, improving teaching is mainly a matter of developing better teaching methods, of improving instruction. Training teachers in new classroom management skills, in active learning, co-operative learning, one-to-one counselling and the like is the main priority. These things are important, but we are also increasingly coming to understand that developing teachers and improving their teaching involves more than giving them new tricks. We are beginning to recognize that, for teachers, what goes on inside the classroom is closely related to what goes on outside it. The quality, range and flexibility of teachers' classroom work are closely tied up with their professional growth – with the way in which they develop as people and as professionals.

Teachers teach in the way they do not just because of the skills they have or have not learned. The ways in which they teach are also rooted in their backgrounds, their biographies, and so in the kinds of teachers they have become. Their careers – their hopes and dreams, their opportunities and aspirations, or the frustration of these things – are also important for teachers' commitment, enthusiasm and morale. So too are relationships with their colleagues – either as supportive communities who work together in pursuit of common goals and continuous improvement, or as individuals working in isolation, with the insecurities that sometimes brings.

As we are coming to understand these wider aspects of teaching and teacher development, we are also beginning to recognize that much more than pedagogy, instruction or teaching method is at stake. Teacher development, teachers' careers, teachers' relations with their colleagues, the conditions of status, reward and leadership under which they work – all these affect the quality of what they do in the classroom.

This international series, *Teacher Development*, brings together some of the very best current research and writing on these aspects of teachers' lives and work. The books in the series seek to understand the wider dimensions of teachers' work, the depth of teachers' knowledge and the resources of biography and experience on which it draws, the ways that teachers' work roles and responsibilities are changing as we restructure our schools, and so forth. In this sense, the books in the series are written for those who are involved in research on teaching, those who work in initial and in-service teacher education, those who lead and administer teachers, those who work with teachers and, not least, teachers themselves.

Teachers of children in the years before adolescence have a profound influence on their learning and their lives. In primary schools and elementary schools across the world, children spend most of the school year with a single teacher in a single class as members of one community. In their waking hours, they see more of their teacher than they do of their parents. Teaching in primary and elementary schools is without a doubt, therefore, one of the most important jobs in society in terms of its capacity to shape the hearts and minds of our future citizens. Understanding the work of primary and elementary teachers – what constitutes it, shapes it, supports it and undermines it – is therefore an important priority for research, for policy and for practice in education. This important new book by Sandra Acker, *The Realities of Teachers' Work*, provides this much-needed understanding.

As Acker herself repeatedly points out, our understandings of primary and elementary teachers' work are often superficial, stereotypical and one-dimensional in nature. Policy-makers can become so obsessed with neat and tidy reform programmes in teaching strategies or in curriculum content, they can overlook or be oblivious to all the other complex, messy, multifaceted aspects of teaching, working, organizing and caring that are both integral to and unavoidable interruptions to the primary and elementary teacher's day. Other studies have tried to unpack what this work is really like but, as Acker herself explains, most of these studies are based mainly on surveys and interviews, on how teachers report and account for their practice, not on observations of the gritty realities of practice itself. Sandra Acker's eye-opening study is one of the few, the very few, to correct this tendency. In an intensive ethnography of one primary school, spanning several years, she brings to life the difficulty, the dedication, the complexity, the busyness, the messiness, the agony, the ecstasy and sometimes the sheer rib-cracking hilarity of primary and elementary teachers' working lives.

Most school ethnographies are usually conducted by doctoral students and published as their first book, at the very beginning of their careers. Although insightful, these studies are usually also inevitably underdeveloped in their command of the field and their capacity to communicate findings with the intellectual and cosmopolitan authority of someone who has spent many years in their chosen line of study. Few senior academics in education return to the hard graft of sustained ethnographic study. The logic of their careers takes them on to the methodologically less demanding paths of interviewing, survey work and research team management that can be integrated with their mounting academic responsibilities. Sandra Acker has wilfully bucked this trend. Entering the seemingly small world of an English primary school in a country where she herself worked as an academic for many years, she brings to it the insights of her own US biography, and the retrospective insights of experience of education and society in Canada, where she now lives and works. With a long record of research and writing on teaching and on gender studies in education, Acker also brings real intellectual authority to her study and analysis of teaching. Her book is a truly cosmopolitan one, with implications for teachers and teaching in many parts of the world.

The results are powerful, and they are far-reaching in their significance. Thus, while international readers might be amused and occasionally distracted by idioms of English culture and English education from time to time – by references to school assemblies, children wearing their wellies, playgrounds being supervised by dinner ladies, and gossip about parents snogging in the church – and while they might have to endure occasional descriptions of the English National Curriculum and associated educational reforms, it would be a tragedy if these unavoidable idiosyncracies prejudiced people against reading the book and engaging with all it has to offer. American academics and educators especially are often unwilling to entertain or acknowledge any research literature in education that does not emanate from their own country. This apparent academic ethnocentricism is often justified by the failure of writers and researchers in other countries to stand outside the peculiarities of their own systems and communicate their findings in a more globally relevant way. Acker stands apart from this weakness. With her cosmopolitan biography, her intellectual authority, her command of international literature and her experience, she is able to engage with the core issues of primary and elementary teaching on an international scale and with a depth that will transcend the passing vicissitudes of particular reform moments.

The results of Acker's in-depth analysis will be edifying for academics and practising educators everywhere. Acker conveys the texture of the real difficulty and challenge of primary and elementary teachers' work. She shows how teachers' caring orientations and the resource-starved contexts in which they work can convert the virtues of care into the draining excesses of self-sacrifice. She shows how primary and elementary teaching is rooted in gender scripts, but not completely tied to gender prescriptions. While elementary and primary teachers are often portrayed as being isolated and individualized, Acker reveals how closely her teachers work together – not in the sustained forms of intellectual collaboration that academics often prefer as they try to re-carve teaching in their own scholarly image, but in a multitude of informal, snatched but nonetheless serious moments where busy teachers plan and reflect together on their work. Nor, Acker demonstrates, are primary and elementary classrooms and schools as insulated from outside influence as much as they are portrayed – teachers have to deal with constant streams of visitors, and their own work extends to corridors, staffrooms, playgrounds, athletics fields, churches, bus trips, field visits, university seminar rooms, and innumerable other places beyond the boundaries of their own rooms. And while teachers are often pilloried as failing to change, Acker shows how her teachers change all the time in their room arrangements, teaching strategies, curriculum materials, and so on.

Sandra Acker's book on the realities of teachers' work does not gratuitously celebrate teaching and everything that teachers do, but it does honour and bear witness to the difficulty and the dedication of teachers' work. Her book, in my view, is one of the most important, non-judgemental books on teaching of the last two decades. Educators everywhere will learn a very great deal from it.

Andy Hargreaves
Toronto, January 1999

Acknowledgements

Over the years it has taken to produce this book, many folks have helped in one way or another, and inevitably I can name only a proportion of them. The head teachers and teachers who participated in my study must come first, because without them there would be no study. I regret having to use their pseudonyms in this acknowledgement section, but there is no choice. I am particularly grateful to Liz Clarke, who tolerated my presence as a hanger-on at Hillview for so many years that she must have thought she had hired me. As she mentored her staff, she mentored me, and showed me a positive role model of a woman leader. Debbie Stevens gave me her friendship and her insights and patiently put up with my faxing 'urgent' questions when I tried to get the detail of the study pinned down, and she always gave me helpful responses. Both Liz and Debbie read some of the chapters and when they did not recoil in horror, I figured I was all right. All the other Hillview teachers and general assistants tolerated (or even encouraged) my intrusions and answered my questions. The Rosemont staff were just as welcoming and I thank them, particularly Alison Holly, the deputy head teacher. I also owe thanks to the parents, children, ancillary staff and others who populated the schools and my book.

My family deserves more gratitude than I can easily convey. If my parents, Charles and Marjorie Acker, had not been teachers, I probably would not have become so entranced with the study of teachers' work. I have had many conversations about teaching with other teacher-relatives, including my aunt, Rosanne Ehrlich, my cousin, Judy Green, and my sister, Betty Baisden. Friends who are teachers, including Fran Klarin, Duncan Payne, Peggy Payne and Andrée Stock, have similarly enriched my understanding. Thanks also to my other sister, Debi Zolnoski, and my stepmother, Mercedes Acker. My partner, Geoff Millerson, has supported me in every way imaginable. He is equally at home as 'Geoff the chef' or using his sociological and academic background to be a critical friend, reading and commenting on every chapter. Our daughter, Dorie Millerson, has left her primary school years long behind, but still functions as my expert on the student point of view.

There are many colleagues who have discussed relevant issues with me and encouraged me over the years. This group includes colleagues at (or formerly at) the University of Bristol, among them Sally Barnes, Elizabeth Bird, Patricia Broadfoot, Edie Black, Ray Bolam, Beryl Collins, Philip Gammage, Maureen Harvey, Tim Hill, Eric Hoyle, Agnes McMahon, Sara Meadows, Marilyn Osborn, David Satterly and Jackie West. Colleagues from my current institution, the Ontario Institute for Studies in Education of the University of Toronto (OISE/UT), have been similarly supportive. They include Nina Bascia, Kathy Bickmore, Michael Connelly, Kari Dehli, Jo-Anne Dillabough, Margrit Eichler, Grace Feuerverger, Michael Fullan, Ruth Hayhoe, Mary Howes, Brent Kilbourn, David Livingstone, Linda Muzzin, Keith Oatley, Alison Prentice, Dorothy Smith and Elizabeth Smyth. I also acknowledge the help I have received at both these institutions from the librarians. There are in addition many students and ex-students who, through attendance at my courses or the production of dissertations, added to my knowledge about teachers' work. Beyond those two workplace cultures, a long list of colleagues and supporters qualify for thanks, among them Michael Apple, Sari Knopp Biklen, Gill Blunden, Avtar Brah, Mary Lou Finley, Mary Fuller, Barbara Grant, Chris Husbands, Catherine Marshall, Sue Middleton, Sheila Miles, Virginia Olesen, Sheila Riddell, Caroline St John Brooks, David Warren Piper, Gaby Weiner, Johanna Wyn and Beth Young. More indirectly, I would like to acknowledge Jennifer Nias and Peter Woods for their scholarship on teachers, which has always been inspirational for me.

Certain brave individuals have read and commented on chapters for me, and I owe a tremendous debt to Michael Connelly, Miriam David, Kari Dehli, Andy Hargreaves, Gill Helsby, Geoff Millerson, Marilyn Osborn and Andrew Pollard for their generosity in this regard. Andy Hargreaves is the editor for the series in which this book is published and the person who persuaded me to sign the contract. He told me that this would be the most important book I would ever write – a statement guaranteed to slow me down for years, as I worried about how to live up to such a grand prediction. One of my other colleagues says that at our age, we do not have mentors, so I guess Andy cannot be a mentor if that is true; but he has come as close as anyone, and I truly appreciate all his efforts.

OISE/UT students Lisa Richards and Amy Sullivan deserve a particular thank-you for helping to get the bibliography in order and for merging chapter files into one big book. Lisa also transcribed some of my interviews and worked on the author index, as did Olga Williams. Beth McAuley used her exemplary skills to produce an exceptional subject index. I would also like to thank Ruth McCurry, Anthony Haynes, Helena Power and other colleagues at Cassell for working with me to turn the manuscript into a published work.

Finally, there is the list of publishers to thank for permission to adapt portions of articles and chapters previously published and blend them into this work. Acknowledgements are due to:

Blackwell Publishers, Oxford, for Sandra Acker (1990), Managing the Drama, *Sociological Review*, 38(2), 247–71; and Sandra Acker (1992), Creating Careers: Women Teachers at Work, *Curriculum Inquiry*, 22(2), 141–63.

State University of New York Press, Albany, New York, for Sandra Acker (1995), The Head Teacher as Career Broker: Stories from an English Primary School. In D. Dunlap and P. Schmuck (eds), *Women Leading in Education*, 49–70.

American Educational Research Association, Washington, DC, for Sandra Acker (1995–6), Gender and Teachers' Work. In M. Apple (ed.), *Review of Research in Education*, 21, 99–162.

Carfax Publishing Company, PO Box 25, Abingdon, Oxfordshire OX14 3UE, for Sandra Acker (1990), Teachers' Culture in an English Primary School: Continuity and Change, *British Journal of Sociology of Education*, 11, 257–73; and Sandra Acker (1995), Carry on Caring: the Work of Women Teachers, *British Journal of Sociology of Education*, 16, 21–36.

Cassell Publishers, London, for Sandra Acker (1997), Primary Teachers' Work: the Response to Educational Reform. In G. Helsby and G. McCulloch (eds) *Teachers and the National Curriculum*, 34–51.

This book is dedicated to my father, Charles Acker

PART ONE

SETTING THE SCENE

Chapter 1

Introduction

It is a hectic day in the office. The swimming gala occupied the morning and now there is a lot happening. The phone rings with a request for children's pictures to hang in a hospital. Liz Clarke, the head teacher, fills in an application for one of the teachers to go on a course and then picks up the phone to try to arrange supply cover for another teacher. Someone comes in to say the staffroom kettle is not working. Liz drafts the announcement for a 'celebration of culture' day that is to go home to parents after school. The phone rings again; it is Mrs Jakes from the local education authority who points out that a letter is not sufficient notification of a continuation of a teacher's fixed-term contract; a form is necessary. Liz firmly stamps a form with a blank stamp, and we both dissolve in laughter. The phone rings twice again; Dorothy, the secretary, comments 'Oh how do we get anything done!' Dennis Bryan, the deputy head, looks in and announces that the consortium supplies have arrived. Helen Davies, a long-serving teacher, comes in to say that a problem with the dinner ladies has arisen: one is said to be 'force-feeding' a child. While she and Liz discuss what to do, the phone rings again and Helen answers. The ice rink wants to know if Nancy Green's class is coming. Liz rushes out to check with Nancy. Meanwhile, Helen is looking, unsuccessfully, for the consortium catalogue in the file drawer. Dennis must have it, she says. 'Never a dull moment, is there', she remarks. (12 July 1988)[1]

The one thing with a school like this is that you're never bored, there's never a dull moment. There is always going to be something happening which is going to change how you expected the week to be, the term to run – which I don't mind, I like that. (Dennis Bryan, Interview)

Whatever primary [elementary][2] school teaching is, it is certainly not dull. Jennifer Nias (1989, p. 195) claims that primary teaching is 'living with paradox'. My study convinced me that she is correct. Primary teaching is incredibly difficult work, and its physical, intellectual and emotional challenges are generally unrecognized and unrewarded. Like mothering, caring for young children in schools is regularly regarded as a natural sphere for women, making monetary incentives or public tributes unnecessary. Teachers try to accomplish miracles when even ordinary accomplishments are thwarted by a shortage of time, space and resources, let alone children's social and educational problems with roots in structures far outside teacher control. Teachers feel underappreciated by the population at large, but also by the parents and even by the children. They are an easy target for politicians' wishful if not manipulative thinking, placing them in the firing line for society's ills, and creating the myth that the nation's prosperity can be regained simply by imposing reforms of the school curriculum, finance and teaching method.

At the same time, primary schools can be places of laughter and warmth, of caring and charm. The magic moments when a 5-year-old suddenly understands that letters represent sounds, the unguarded demonstrations of a child's affection for the teacher, the emotional attachment between teacher and class, the sense that one is doing a job that counts give teachers a sense of purpose to sustain them. In some schools, especially those where leadership is supportive and facilitating, the teachers become a collaborative and caring work group. Humour, kindness and shared tribulations bind them together.

There is a persistent notion that life in school is mostly spent in classrooms, bounded sites in which teachers teach and children learn. This is why so much emphasis is placed on reforming curriculum or pedagogy. Yet this model is oversimplified in all respects. In school, children are learning what is right and wrong, how to relate to peers, how to please or aggravate adults, what behaviour is encouraged, tolerated or proscribed. None of these understandings is straightforward, either, as they are mainly negotiated bargains that can be renegotiated as circumstances and players change. Cognitive learning is similarly complex – writing, for example, requires learning how to hold a pencil, how to make marks on a page, how to draw meaning from the marks.

For the teacher, the class is a diversity of abilities, temperaments, relationships and individual needs, with a tendency to become more than the sum of these parts: to have collective moods that can be well or badly behaved, calm or restless. Moods fluctuate predictably according to time of day, day of week, and weather, and unpredictably as well. Interruptions and changes of plan are endemic. Choices are made minute by minute: working with one child means others go unnoticed; responding to a child's question or unanticipated learning opportunity may delay other plans.

The day itself is divided into chunks, punctuated by assembly, playtimes and midday meals in a manner that varies slightly from school to school. Timetables for swimming, games, skating, language groups, music lessons, television programmes and so forth make each day in a week different from the others. These schedules are further interrupted by practices for school productions, visits by the dentist, trips to interesting places and *ad hoc* events.

While children clearly do more than sit in the classroom and 'learn', teachers are involved in even more differentiated activities. They participate in a host of meetings, formal and informal, brief and lengthy. They mark papers, keep records, and plan lessons before and after school, during breaks and at home. They attend courses, meet parents, decorate walls, assess learning materials, photocopy worksheets, sew costumes, organize school events, run assemblies, order supplies and peruse government documents. Intricate relationships among the teachers and between the head teacher [principal] and the staff are, like the teacher–pupil relationships, negotiated and renegotiated. Together, they construct a workplace culture, a sense of what they are, what they stand for as a community. It is this ecology that in 1990s Britain, and at other times in other lands, has been so disrupted by government mandates.

The school, as Waller (1932/1965) noted long ago, is a small society, with many of its rituals and folkways hidden from easy view. But it is not a society in isolation, as Waller also realized, for its boundaries are in daily negotiation with stakeholders such as the parents, the community, the church, other schools, the local educational bureaucracy and the political establishment. Teachers' career pursuits may eventually take them out of the institution altogether, to be replaced by new inductees into the culture. From a distance, national, state, or provincial politicians proclaim their priorities and enshrine them in statutory orders, supported by a mountain of documents on good practice in an ideal world.

The study that follows looks at this small society in one primary school in England. It is, above all, a study of teachers' workplace culture. My hope is that readers – including teachers, teachers in training, educational researchers, teacher educators and others who have an interest in educational processes – will grasp something of both the public and the hidden nature of teachers' work by reading this book. Work, culture and gender are themes that weave through all the chapters and will be expanded upon in Chapter 2. Other themes that will be taken up in appropriate places include context, collegiality, caring, careers and change.

THE SITE

From April 1987 to December 1990, I conducted the major part of the ethnographic research on which this book is based. Most of this book is about Hillview Primary School, with a small amount of supplementary

Table 1: Regular School Staff – Hillview Primary School (1987–88)

Name	Status	Year taught	Age of children
Liz Clarke	Head teacher FT		
Dennis Bryan	Deputy head FT	Older Juniors (Yr 6)	11
Debbie Stevens[†]	Teacher FT	Middle Juniors (Yr 4/5)	9–10
Sheila Jones	Teacher PT	Middle Juniors (Yr 5)	10
Rosalind Phillips	Teacher PT	Middle Juniors (Yr 4)	9
Kristin King	Teacher PT	Middle Juniors (Yrs 4/5)	9–10
Nancy Green	Teacher FT	Younger Juniors (Yr 3)	8
Helen Davies[‡]	Teacher FT	Older Infants (Yr 2)	7
Betty Chaplin	Teacher FT	Younger Infants (Yr 1)	6
Marjorie Howard	Teacher FT	Reception	4–5
Dorothy Lowe	Secretary & general assistant FT		
Beryl Tucker	General assistant PT		
John Rogers	Caretaker		

FT = full-time; PT = part-time
† Coordinator of special needs
‡ Head of infant division

material on Rosemont Junior School. The two schools are located in Wesley, a middle-sized city in southwest England. All names of schools, towns and individuals are pseudonyms.

Hillview serves the entire primary age range from four to eleven and contains about 200 children. There are seven classes: three infant classes and four junior classes.[3] The exact number of teachers fluctuated slightly during my research but the usual complement was a head teacher, a deputy head teacher, and eight others, three of whom were part-time. In order to help readers remember who does what among the cast of characters in this book, Table 1 presents a list of the teaching staff in the school, as well as the head teacher and deputy head teacher, and the main ancillary staff – the general assistants (one of whom was mainly occupied as school secretary) and the caretaker [janitor]. For the teachers I have indicated their class responsibilities in the 1987–88 school year, when my observations were most intensive.

There were also many other adults in the school with some regularity, including lunch-time staff, music teachers, remedial specialists, an educational psychologist, a nurse, supply teachers and parents. Chapter 8 expands on this point. The teachers and others listed in Table 1 are the main actors in this book, however. I do not wish to describe their personal characteristics in too much detail, given promises of anonymity, but a few words are helpful in conjuring up an image of the staff. As can be seen from the table, the teachers are all women except for Dennis, the deputy head and class teacher of the oldest children in the school. All but one were currently married, one was divorced. All but two had children. All the teachers and staff listed in the table were white, except Dennis who was black. All were born in Britain, though some came from outside England, namely Wales. There was something of an age divide within the teaching staff, with Dennis, Debbie, Rosalind, Sheila, Kristin and Nancy in their late 20s or 30s, while Liz, Helen, Betty and Marjorie were in their 40s or 50s.

Although Hillview is a centre city school, it is not in the heart of the inner city, not in a slum or 'ghetto', nor even in a clearly demarcated residential area. It is not far, however, from the city's shopping centre, the entertainment area, several hospitals, a university, and residential areas of varying socioeconomic levels. Through its long history, it has catered for a range of communities, as housing came and went through various urban renewal efforts and population movements. Hillview's children are very mixed in social class and ethnic terms. Some come from working-class white areas; some from upwardly mobile minority ethnic groups located several miles from the school; others from 'counter-cultural' families attracted by Hillview's tolerance of diversity. Others are middle-class children whose parents want them to experience a cross-section of society. Teachers spoke of the school as 'lively', 'busy' and 'energetic'. The teachers had to be very flexible and tolerant of ambiguity and disruption of plans. It was frequently suggested to me that instead of an ethnography I should write a soap opera or a novel.

In April 1988 I began a more limited programme of comparative observations and interviews in a second school, Rosemont Junior School. Although less than two miles from Hillview, it contrasts dramatically on many fronts. Rosemont is larger (around 360 children, in 12 classes); it is attended exclusively by 7- to 11-year-olds; it is newer and better resourced and enjoys a campus-like setting of green playing fields. The children come almost entirely from middle-class, often affluent, families, and all but a handful are white, as are all the 13 teachers (ten women, three men) and the head teacher (a man).

Regrettably, Rosemont is not discussed except in passing in this book. There are several reasons for this decision. I did not have as detailed a picture of Rosemont nor as deep an involvement as I had at Hillview. Thus I would have been able to incorporate Rosemont fully into some, but not all, of the chapters in this volume. Eventually I decided that not only would it be tedious to make sure I wrote about Rosemont whenever possible but that it might also lead to a suspicion that I was comparing the schools in a judgemental way, although that would not have been my intention. Anyone who objected on methodological grounds to my relying on a single case study for data would hardly be reassured by my adding just one more. And the book would have been twice as long! Nevertheless, my involvement with Rosemont helped me decide what aspects of Hillview as a workplace for teachers were likely to be significant and I enjoyed and learned from my association with Rosemont and its staff.

My research techniques were the usual ethnographic ones: participant observation, collection of documents and interviews. I estimated that by the end of the 1988–89 school year, I had spent over 1000 hours at Hillview and about 200 at Rosemont. After that point, I stopped keeping a careful log of visits, so it is more difficult to estimate hours spent in 1989–90 or the autumn of 1990. These estimates do not include telephone conversations, social occasions and interviews outside school. More detail of my methods and the various dilemmas that arose during the research can be found in the Appendix. People in both schools were extremely generous, helpful and kind to me. After December 1990, when I moved to Canada, I kept in touch with some of the teachers by occasional letter and telephone call. One person from each school came to see me in Canada while on holiday. I returned to England for visits in 1991 (twice), 1993, 1996 and 1997, and saw Hillview staff on each occasion.

GETTING THERE

When I began this project, I was an academic in a university school of education in England, although I grew up in the USA. Embarking on a study of teachers seemed a natural consequence of my personal experiences and my intellectual interests. Both my parents had been teachers. My mother taught until I (their eldest child) was born, while my father had a career as an art teacher in the Detroit schools. Like my parents, I went to Wayne State University as an undergraduate and ended up in teacher education, acquiring a certificate for secondary school teaching in mathematics. In my last term as an undergraduate, I did some substitute [supply] teaching to add to my teaching practice experience. Although I thought I would enjoy being a teacher, I decided to continue my own education first, initially aiming at a master's degree. By now I knew what I wanted to study: not mathematics but the sociology of education. In the later stages of my undergraduate degree, an introductory sociology course and a school and society course, both taught by brilliant teachers who could not have anticipated their joint impact on my future, caught and held my imagination.[4]

I went to the University of Chicago for my graduate work in education. Several experiences in Chicago may have helped me find my way to doing research on teachers many years later. Dan Lortie was a member of my thesis committee at the time he was writing *Schoolteacher* (1975). Teaching as a career was a subtopic in the main sociology of education lecture course given by Charles Bidwell, my thesis supervisor. And I learned about the 'Chicago School' traditions of first-hand research and ethnographic methods from a year-long qualitative methods course in the sociology department taught by Gerald Suttles. Although I did not use the method for my thesis (quantitative approaches being more respectable at the time), almost 20 years later, supported by a change in fashion toward qualitative research, I remembered enough to venture into ethnography once again.

After a brief period teaching sociology at DePaul University in Chicago, I moved to England and became a member of academic staff [faculty] at the University of Bristol, first in sociology and then in education. Although my own background was in secondary school teaching, in the 1980s I became more interested in primary teaching. As our daughter made her way through primary school, I felt more than once as if I were going to school all over again. I tended to avoid much in the way of helping in the school or participating in the PTA, as my life seemed crowded enough. Like many other parents, I would visit the school for routine meetings with teachers, for concerts and other public events, or if a problem arose. I remember going indignantly a few times to see the head teacher, once over an incident where a new boy in the class kicked my daughter, and another time in feminist mode to point out that the boys occupied most of the playground space while the girls were exiled to the periphery. Generally, our daughter was happy at school, although she seemed to underachieve there, compared to her more obvious displays of talents at home, a situation we found puzzling. I had good relations with the school but little sense of what went on inside its walls.

One more series of events pushed me in the direction of the eventual study. In the early 1980s, I wrote a critique of the way in which gender was conceptualized in the literature on teachers (Acker, 1983). A few years later, probably because of this particular publication, I was asked to write a chapter for a book on primary school teachers (Delamont, 1987). I agreed, and found myself immersed in a wealth of fascinating literature. The sociological study of teachers was gathering momentum around the late 1970s to mid-1980s in Britain and elsewhere. Collectively, this body of literature was moving away from the commonsense idea that the teacher was simply the instrument of children's learning. Instead, teaching was of interest as a career, as an occupation and as an activity conducted with colleagues in a workplace.

During my reading for that chapter (Acker, 1987), I repeatedly came across the argument that teachers were isolated from each other by their classroom focus and physical location, as well as by an ideological preference for independence rather than collegiality (Acker, 1991). To support this claim, British writers frequently imported American arguments, without making much effort to look for possible differences caused by the different national contexts and educational systems. (The importing was largely one-way, as American work rarely took into account British research.)

My developing interest in teaching as work led me to pose certain questions that became the basis for my own subsequent research. At the most general level, I wanted to ask something like 'what is teaching in primary school really like for the teachers?' Later I began to rephrase the area of my interest as 'primary school teachers' workplace culture', a phrase that seemed to describe well what I wanted to study. Although I was not at that point intending to do research on women, from time to time I also wondered what the women's world of the primary school might tell us about gendered workplaces.

In a brief conversation in a school playground with Liz Clarke, the head teacher of Hillview Primary School, I shared some of these thoughts. She commented, 'You should shadow a teacher'. The idea stayed with me, and finally, in the spring of 1987, I acted upon it. I was nervous about embarking on a fully-fledged research project, and not yet completely committed to doing research in the primary school, but I was ready to put my foot in the water. Looking back, I see with some amusement that my letter in 1987 to Mrs Clarke suggesting I do some 'limited research' with a 'fairly low-key approach' at Hillview School was dated April 1, perhaps a subconscious testimony to my ambivalence.

Following up my letter, I met with Liz Clarke for a few hours. Mrs Clarke was welcoming and positive, but also raised potential problems, including teachers' reluctance to have an adult in the classroom who might be evaluating them rather than helping. To avoid this difficulty, I would need to see an experienced, confident teacher. We agreed I would start by visiting the school on a date three weeks hence, and Mrs Clarke wrote it in her appointment book.

FIRST DAYS IN THE FIELD

My 'official' entry into the school was rather anticlimactic, considering I had spent a sleepless night in anticipation. Given the hesitation teachers might have towards an observer in the classroom, I had thought that perhaps my status as a university education lecturer would be intimidating. I soon learned that my arrival had little significance to anyone apart from myself. Here is an extract from my field notes from that day:

> I arrived at 9.05. Whirlwinds of children rushed past me. Mr Benton [the then deputy head teacher] was in the office. Mrs Lowe [the secretary] came out of the office and was moving

towards the staffroom; she said she thought Mrs Clarke would
be down shortly. . . . Mr Benton suggested I go up to the
staffroom to look for Mrs Clarke, which I did. Mrs Lowe was
there and said she'd find her for me. [Then] Liz came out of
another room . . . clearly she'd more or less forgotten I was
coming. (18 May 1987)

I ended up in the classroom of Marjorie Howard, the reception [kindergar-
ten] teacher. Mrs Howard's classroom was a good, if unplanned, choice. It
was what I later learned was 'language morning' where the younger
children were grouped and redistributed among several teachers who could
work with those at equivalent reading level regardless of formal class
assignment. Initially, children milled around, some playing word lotto
games with the teacher or a young woman aged 17 or 18 whose function I
did not yet know, others playing in a small outdoor playground reached by
a door from the classroom. Another teacher came in and exchanged a few
words with Marjorie. There did not seem to be any heating on, and with
the outside door open, I shivered despite being warmly dressed. Then
Marjorie gathered the children together and they sat on the carpet close to
her chair. 'Good morning, everyone', she greeted them. 'Good morning, Mrs
Howard', they chanted. She then called the register, using first names only.
Even this exchange contained praise and attention to individuals, mixed
with reprimands. There was considerable noise outside the classroom. The
children were then divided up according to what seemed to be reading level
and regrouped in the three classrooms nearby, and possibly elsewhere. A
small group remained with Mrs Howard. She put a blackboard up on a
table, and the children again sat down on the carpet. Games were played
involving the letters 'L' and 'N'. Marjorie did everything in very dramatic
fashion (for example, putting the children whose names began with 'N' into
a big box doubling as an imaginary witch's cauldron) and there was a lot of
laughter. The activity ran overtime and the educational television programme usually watched at 10 a.m. was missed. Children drew pictures
based on 'N' or 'L'. One little girl, Angela, copied the words from the
blackboard on to a piece of paper. Mrs Howard was pleased, explaining to
me how hard it is to get children to that stage.

On the way to assembly, we chatted. Marjorie said she had originally
taught in a comprehensive [secondary] school. She said she wondered if she
could keep going until retirement, as the work takes so much energy. She
added, referring to Angela's accomplishment: 'It's got its magic moments.'
After the assembly, the children went out to play, while the teachers not
on playground duty congregated in the staffroom for coffee. Marjorie left
before the end of break to set up some tapes in the classroom (that in the
event did not work). People were discussing what they had done on the
weekend or conversing about work. I was vaguely introduced as 'studying

stress among teachers', to some laughter. I met a new teacher, Debbie Stevens, who had just joined the school. Debbie had taught in London in an inner-city school but then moved to a local suburb when her husband obtained a job in Wesley. Debbie was to become a key teacher in my study.

Back in the classroom, the children were divided between Marjorie and the young woman, Marilyn, who I learned was on a 'youth training scheme', gaining work experience. Marjorie sat on the floor with her group to do a game with vowels. The children were involved in the game and she praised them liberally. The word 'boll' (as in cotton boll) came up and she explained what it was. My notes say:

> I am impressed at the way she can pounce on anything that comes up, explain and use it in a 'learning way', while being dramatic and witty for the kids. Reprimands are woven in, control seems fairly firm though noise levels, in and outside the classroom, seem high to me.

This account of morning activity proved to be reasonably typical. Like many school researchers, I initially found the physical milieu startling. There was noise; there was movement; there was routine (assembly, playtime, coffee); there were quick changes of plan (the missed television programme, tapes that failed to work); there was camaraderie among teachers; there was physical discomfort (cold temperatures, sitting on the floor or on tiny chairs). What captivated me most was Mrs Howard's intensity and dramatic performances. Was this what teaching in the primary school required? I wanted to see and know more.

From my hesitant steps into Hillview in the spring of 1987, the research grew and grew. By the end of the first term, I had several ideas of possible themes to pursue further. One was what I dubbed 'traffic', the continuous flow of adults through the school, which was so intrusive at times that the teachers might have welcomed a little of the isolation written about in the literature. Other early themes were 'hard work' and 'flexibility'. These observations were confirming my initial suspicion that what was going on in the school would not conform to many of the stereotypes about teachers and their work found both in educational literature and among the public at large. By the end of the term, I had decided to continue with the research, if the school were willing. Another theme had also captured my interest: change.

The theme of 'change' is now rather predictable, several years after the Education Reform Act of 1988 and its consequences (see Chapter 11). Yet in 1987, before even the red booklet setting forth the first public plans for such an Act had appeared, 'change' struck me as endemic in school life, paradoxically a constant (Nias, Southworth and Yeomans, 1989). It came from all directions – from the individual teacher, from colleagues, from the head teacher, from the local education authority [school district], and from the central government and its agencies. I saw it as encompassing what was self-generated and what was imposed, what was enthusiastically welcomed or bitterly resisted. During that first term, I had noticed day-to-day (or even hour-to-hour) examples of change: for example, a teacher deciding to move the tables in her room into a different configuration. A specific change, perhaps better described as an innovation, loomed on the horizon, lobbied for by the head teacher. This was what came to be called 'the Middle Junior Unit', or 'the Unit', a school-based attempt at innovation in the 1987–88 school year that involved nearly 60 children, integrating those formerly regarded as suitable for the separate special needs class into the ordinary classrooms and featuring four teachers, three of whom were part-time, working as a team. The middle junior children were approximately 8 to 10 years of age. They were divided into two registration groups according to age.

As the idea of a Unit was being discussed in the spring of 1987, I realized that it would provide a focus for my subsequent observations, and that Mrs Clarke would probably be pleased to have me record its development. Indeed, she thought that such a focus would be a good idea, and (luckily) that I should not 'evaluate' it, but that I could 'monitor' it. Between us, we raised the possibility with the teachers concerned who were already in the school (one had not yet been hired) and got their consent, although it was made clear that I would not intrude if a teacher did not want me there, and that the first days of the school year would probably not be the best time for me to observe. Before the new school year began, I interviewed on tape the head teacher and three of the teachers about their expectations for the Unit.

Being 'attached' to the Unit worked well for me, as I had a home of sorts, and a defined group of teachers to work with: Debbie Stevens, Sheila Jones, Rosalind Phillips and Kristin King (see Table 1). During 1987–88, I spent several days a week in the Unit, with brief periods observing the other two teachers of other junior classes (Dennis Bryan and Nancy Green) and three week-long blocks with the head teacher. I also attended and participated in other activities such as the school fair, concerts, curriculum meetings, staff parties and so forth. I interviewed each of the Unit teachers and the head teacher at three points in the year, and the other two junior teachers once each. In April 1988, I began to attend the weekly staff meetings. In the same month I began observations at Rosemont, usually visiting that school one day per week. I shadowed[5] three Rosemont teachers and the head teacher in that spring, following up each set of observations with a taped interview.

During the first term of the 1988–89 school year, I came into Hillview one or two days a week, now usually observing what had become the 'Older Junior Unit' with two full-time teachers, Debbie and Dennis. Again, I interviewed the Unit teachers several times. From January, I spent more time with the three teachers of the infant classes, Helen Davies, Betty Chaplin and Marjorie Howard, following my usual pattern of shadowing and interviewing. I continued to attend staff meetings. At Rosemont, I shadowed and interviewed another five teachers and shadowed the head teacher for a week, following this oberservation by an interview. I occasionally sat in on staff meetings. I went to school events and maintained informal social contacts.

In the autumn of 1990, my involvement was tapering off, as I made preparations to leave the country. Most of my notes from that term are from staff meetings at Hillview. During return visits to England in 1991 and 1993, I was able to question teachers and head teachers about the unfolding effects of the National Curriculum and new testing requirements and to spend some time with Betty Chaplin at Hillview in the spring of 1993 after the first Key Stage 1 assessments (age 7). She gave me a detailed account of what had happened in her class during the assessment period. I also saw teachers in 1996 and 1997, but not on school premises.

Overall, I spent many hours in the schools and with the teachers over the three and a half years (eight school terms) of my main study, as well as keeping in contact for eight more years. Clearly, an unusual feature of the research was its extended duration. One consequence was that I was able to see change as it happened, so to speak. I did not start the research in order to look at the effects of the introduction of the National Curriculum and other government reforms, but I was able to watch what happened in the early stages (Chapter 11). I was also able to see the careers of the teachers develop and note how often career plans were altered and altered again (Chapters 10 and 12).

OVERVIEW OF THE BOOK

The chapters in this book approach teachers' work in varied ways. Chapter 1 introduces the volume, gives some of my own background, and takes the reader with me into my first days in the field at Hillview. Chapter 2 considers some of the relevant literature on teachers, highlighting three themes of work, culture and gender. Chapter 3 expands on the description of Hillview given in chapter 1 with the aim of conveying the immediate context in which the teachers' workplace culture develops. This context consists of the characteristics of the children who attend the school, the physical setting, the resources available and the school ethos.

Chapters 4 and 5 describe the work of teaching, in and out of the classroom, and dispel some of the widespread myths and assumptions about that work. Chapter 6 focuses on the complementary work of the head teacher, who, while the teachers are in the classrooms, 'manages the drama' and communicates with the community outside the school. Chapter 7 is concerned with relationships among the adults in the school, the bedrock of the teachers' workplace culture. The impact of gender shows up here, as I question whether this particular culture should be seen as a 'woman's culture' and why 'caring' is such a predominant motif in this school.

The next two chapters show that just as the isolation of individual teachers has been exaggerated, so too has been the separation of the school from its surroundings, both its literal surroundings and in the sense of its location in time, in history. Chapter 8 considers who crosses the permeable boundaries of the school and how the school is situated *vis-à-vis* 'other schools'. Hillview's notion of what it stands for is constructed in relation to what is known about these other places. Chapter 9 concentrates on the most prominent boundary-crossers, the parents. Chapters 10 to 12 continue the consideration of the school as located in a wider community by looking at issues of careers and change. Chapter 10 describes the fluctuations in teachers' careers and the influence of factors in the workplace, including head teacher sponsorship. Chapter 11 features the impact on Hillview of the late 1980s education reform legislation. Again, the Hillview teachers' workplace culture plays a role, by mediating the impact of the legislation while at the same time responding to it.

Chapter 12 concludes the volume by sketching what happened to Hillview and its teachers in the 1990s, considering what policy 'lessons' we can learn from the story of Hillview, and commenting on the effects of time and place on educational research. A methodological appendix discusses the various decisions I made in the course of the study and some of the issues and dilemmas that arose.

NOTES

1. I have observed several conventions quoting from my field notes or interviews. They have been lightly edited for readability, to insert pseudonyms, and delete or alter identifying or irrelevant information. Ellipses indicate where anything more than a few words has been deleted. I use quotation marks only when I am reasonably certain that I have recorded a quotation verbatim. For ease of readability, I rarely insert a date or the phrase 'field notes'. If there is no reference to an interview, the reader should assume that the quotation is from my field notes.

2. In an attempt to make this study clearer to readers in North America, I have added the North American near-equivalent term in square brackets when I judge it to be helpful after the first and sometimes second use of a phrase that is specific to British usage or education systems influenced by British traditions. For example, in this chapter I use primary [elementary] and head teacher [principal]. On occasion I do the reverse, i.e. give the British version in brackets, where the context makes that choice more sensible.

3. I am using the terminology in place during the research. 'Primary' refers to the range of age 4 or 5 (depending on the local government's policy on age of admission)

to 11. Schools with any combination of these age groups are called 'primary schools'. Children spend their first years in the 'infants' (age 4 to 7) or in an 'infant school' and then move on to the 'juniors' or a 'junior school' (age 7 to 11). Current terminology is: Reception, Year 1, Year 2 (Key Stage One); followed by Year 3, Year 4, Year 5 and Year 6 (Key Stage Two).

4. A belated thank-you to Professors Mary Lorenz Dietz and Richard Wisniewski, respectively.

5. 'Shadow' was not my chosen term, but the one that the teachers liked. It seemed more comfortable to talk about 'being shadowed' than 'being observed' and there could be some joking around 'where's my shadow?'

Chapter 2

Studying Teachers

APPROACHES TO RESEARCH ON TEACHERS

In this chapter I situate my research in some of the literature on teachers. I draw on the theoretical approach called symbolic interactionism, especially as it has influenced British sociology of education. I then focus on my three major themes: work, culture and gender.

There is a huge amount of literature on 'teachers'.[1] Different disciplines and subdisciplines claim 'teachers' as their own. Thus, for an educational psychologist, the focus could be on the extent to which different teaching methods produce measurable learning outcomes. For an educational management specialist, the interest might be in the types of leadership in schools that contribute to efficient and effective organizations. The historian might want to know how conceptions of childhood have changed over time. Many other questions can be asked about curriculum, assessment, pedagogy or organization of a school, or about the educational policies that influence what goes on there.

Teachers appear as actors in all of these scenarios. Frequently, though, they are actors in a rather limited sense. They are the means to an end: effective schooling, children's learning, smooth-running institutions and so forth. In a reaction against the teachers-as-means approach, some literature of recent times has attempted to recover or sponsor the 'teacher's voice' (Goodson, 1991). Another approach that gives the teacher some potential agency is one from critical education theory or critical pedagogy. Here, the analysis starts from the constraining structures within which teachers and others must operate, but adds an enduring optimism that once teachers understand the oppressive conditions, they can be empowered to fight against them. (See Gore, 1993, and Weiler, 1988, for summaries and critiques of these views.)

My approach is predominantly sociological. In this era of postmodern critique, it is increasingly difficult to specify just what that might mean, but I see it as delimiting the field of interest so that questions about the influence of social context on teachers' actions become paramount. I allow 'context' to be a very wide term, however, encompassing current and past influences at the societal level (including politics, economics, demographics and ideologies); influences at the institutional level; and influences at the biographical and interpersonal level. The focus here is most obviously at the institutional level, i.e. what goes on in the school itself, but school processes are not detached from wider social change or from teachers' individual lives and careers. Although I am acutely aware of teachers' voices, and indeed seek to highlight them in my study, I try to avoid privileging them as any unique source of 'truth' (A. Hargreaves, 1996). Taking a sociological perspective allows me to downplay certain questions outside its scope, however interesting, such as the nature of the act of teaching, or the concept of teacher thinking, or the pedagogical influences on what children learn. I also try to avoid the evaluative tone so strong in much educational research: I hope to understand why certain features of the school work in the way they do, rather than identify good teaching, excellent leadership or effective schools.

Within sociology, I am drawn to what are sometimes called 'interpretive approaches': schools of thought that emphasize the importance of under-standing the interpretations that individuals place upon the world around them. One of these schools of thought, the symbolic interactionist approach, has been popular in the study of teachers, especially in British sociology of education.[2] Symbolic interactionists try to find out how people understand and interpret their own, and others', actions and reactions in everyday life. Paul Atkinson (1983) summarizes well the approach of those influenced by this particular tradition when he says that these researchers 'have studied how members of occupations operate pragmatically and survive amid conflicting pressures in the everyday performance of their work' (p. 227).

My attraction to symbolic interactionism is in part that I like its concepts – concepts such as teacher selves, identities, commitments, cultures, subcultures, careers and strategies. The focus is on the collective and negotiated nature of perspectives developed by actors as they live through shared situations. The concepts of symbolic interactionism strike me as flexible and malleable, and I like working with them as a potter would work with clay. Like clay, a symbolic interactionist approach is satisfyingly earthy, grounded in everyday life. Symbolic interactionism has frequently been criticized for overemphasizing individual interpretations while neglecting power, context, conflict and change, but on the whole the studies of teachers' work seem to have been aware of these influences. For example, Ball and Goodson (1985, p. 2) stress the importance of political, social and economic contexts of teachers' work.

To symbolic interactionism, I add a feminist perspective, which tells me that the role of gender in shaping teachers' work needs more attention than symbolic interactionists (among others) have typically given to it (Acker, 1995/6; Grumet, 1988). Although I do not consider myself a poststructural-ist or postmodernist, it would be difficult not to take into account that we live in, or are fast heading into, a 'postmodern society' (A. Hargreaves, 1994; Tierney and Rhoads, 1993), where many of the previous certainties have been rendered uncertain, including our confidence that we can find explanations for social happenings that transcend the individual instance. A poststructuralist will tell us we should no longer generalize confidently about, say, the 'teacher's role' or its part in producing social harmony or (alternatively) supporting capitalism. Teachers, like everyone else, are constituted (and can position themselves) as subjects in discourse. What this means is that the very term 'teacher' could signify various things according to the particular reading or perspective. For example, Valerie Walkerdine's (1981) description of a nursery school class where the 4-year-old boys participated in a gleeful dialogue of obscenity and anti-female sentiment turns on its head the more commonsense notion of the teacher as a powerful figure.

In its search for generalities about teaching and the teaching occupation, the literature on teachers has been guilty of creating a category of 'teacher' that does no justice to the diversity contained within the term. Perhaps this tendency explains why the gender divisions within teaching have frequently been ignored in accounts of 'the teacher'. And across gender cut multiple other identities and affiliations. With these points in mind, let us turn to the three main (and interrelated) themes in this study: work, culture and gender.

TEACHING AS WORK

As Connell (1985, p. 69) bluntly puts it, 'Teachers are workers, teaching is work, and the school is a workplace.' It would not be necessary to emphasize the obvious, were it not for the pervasive conceptions of teaching as a calling, and of teachers as adults who do what they do mostly because they care so deeply about children. The association of such images with *women* is important in shaping the occupational culture and the approaches of scholars. Thus an emphasis on teaching as 'work' serves not only to highlight the tension between 'work' and 'profession', but also speaks to a difference between work and non-work, the latter associated with the notion of women doing 'natural', quasi-maternal 'caring'. It also alerts us to the possibility that teachers – like other workers – can be exploited and that their work can be altered or their workload increased without their consent.

Apple's (1986, 1993) studies of teaching as work raise concerns about exploitation. He argues that tendencies towards 'technical control procedures' have entered the curriculum in American schools, and that teachers are deskilled by the impact of management systems, prespecified definitions of teaching competency and student response, 'teacher-proof' curriculum packages, and pre-test and post-test mandates (Apple, 1986, p. 32). Apple is particularly clear in his description of *intensification*, a phenomenon said to accompany deskilling. Intensification is the pressure to do more work in the same amount of time formerly allowed; it extracts more labour, thereby reducing costs and increasing productivity (Densmore, 1987, p. 148). Apple suggests that intensification for teachers results in cutting corners, destroying sociability and leisure, and displacing goals from providing quality service to 'getting done' (Apple, 1986, p. 44).

The spread of right-wing ideologies within a number of countries in recent years, together with widespread economic recession, seem to have created conditions whereby schools come under increasing pressures to produce measurable results via tight controls over teachers' work, though we should keep in mind that control over teachers is not a new idea (Lawn, 1996). In England and Wales in the late 1980s, central government policy went from one extreme (a hallowed tradition of the teacher's classroom autonomy; a belief in partnership among government, unions and teachers) to the other (extensive legislation designed to reshape school finance and governance and prescribe curriculum and assessment). Teachers had to bear the weight of excessive demands for record-keeping and cope with rapidly changing policy decisions as well as the deskilling tendencies inherent in a prescribed curriculum. Monitoring of teacher and school performance was stepped up in the 1990s, with a programme of school inspections and publication of 'league tables' of test results.

Some writers believe that teachers' striving for professionalism reduces their ability to recognize exploitation (Apple, 1986, p. 46; Densmore, 1987, p. 149). Questions also arise about the relationship of professionalism, intensification and deskilling to 'women's work'. For example, Apple (1986) claims that as a consequence of their protracted struggle to achieve professionalism, women teachers may misrecognize exploitation. On the other hand, there is an argument that such teachers display considerable skill in responding to government reforms, and that they are able to distinguish 'good' from 'bad' aspects of legislation and act accordingly (Acker, 1990b; Osborn and Black, 1994, 1996). Mac an Ghaill (1992, p. 194) believes that the torrent of reforms has made teachers more, not less, aware of work processes and conditions.

Other scholars have pointed to changes in patterns of production characteristic of postmodern times. Flexible work technologies depart from the 'Fordist' clear divisions of labour; tasks become variable and overlapping, while rewards are less predictable and less regulated by contract (A. Hargreaves, 1994, p. 49). Markets are globalized and deregulated. With such changes come requirements for workers with new skills and schools are, as usual, charged with producing them: 'qualities like adaptability, responsibility, flexibility and capacity to work with others' (A. Hargreaves, 1994, p. 50; see also Helsby, 1999).

The question for our purposes is whether teachers experience similar changes in their own work. There are certainly some trends in that direction. In the name of 'workplace flexibility' (Lawn, 1996, p. 113), teachers seem to be experiencing greater career uncertainty, with universalistic reward systems being supplanted or at least supplemented by flexible salary schemes, individual incentives or discretionary allowances directed at rewarding enterprise or recruiting elusive specialists in scarce subjects. Colleagues whose claims are based on loyalty and seniority may lose out in this 'marketplace'. Schools in Britain and elsewhere have been forced to compete with one another to attract students (Gewirtz, Ball and Bowe, 1995; Menter, Muschamp, Nicholls, Ozga and Pollard, 1997), and traditional forms of educational governance and finance have been displaced by a variety of alternatives including devolved budgets and charter school operations.

Nevertheless we cannot easily see teachers' work as simply mirroring these trends. As Lawn (1996, p. 117) remarks: 'Schools appear to have elements of the old and the new'. While hitherto secondary schools have displayed many features of modernist organizations (a division of labour, hierarchical management), primary schools – at least the smaller ones – have at times shown almost a pre-modern preference for strong collegiality and overlapping tasks (Nias, Southworth and Yeomans 1989; see Chapter 7), resembling Durkheim's (1893/1964) concept of mechanical solidarity (cohesion based on strong cultures founded on similarities rather than interdependence). Nor have recent reforms (Chapter 11) been entirely in the direction of workforce flexibility; the rise of specialized subject responsibilities in British primary schools (Webb and Vulliamy, 1996), for example, would seem to be more in line with modernist divisions of labour, perhaps supporting Hargreaves' (1994) argument that what we see in schools are 'postmodern paradoxes': attempts at modernist solutions for postmodern situations.

THE CULTURE(S) OF TEACHING

There are a number of enduring cultural images of teachers at work. One is classroom based, where teaching is an activity conducted by one person, often a female, with 20 or 30 young students. Children draw this scenario complete with blackboard, pointer, a dress on the teacher and an apple on her desk (S. Weber and Mitchell, 1995). Another increasingly common scenario, fed by films, novels and autobiographies, is the hero-teacher, usually male, who finds the magical strategies that will enable him to 'get through' to the resistant students, often underprivileged by class or ethnicity, who succeed under his tutelage (Biklen, 1995). The accent on individualism distracts not only from the idea that teaching is work, but from the understanding that the teacher is one of many. If we wish fully to understand teaching, we need to go outside the classroom. What teachers do is shaped by many contextual features, including the labour market for teachers, traditions and demographic factors (Acker, 1995/6; Evetts, 1989; Reynolds, 1990). One persistent influence might be called the occupational culture of teaching.

Occupational culture

Here we can hark back to Waller's (1932/1965) discussion of 'what teaching does to teachers' for an early exploration of the occupational culture of teaching. Waller argued that the further the teacher stepped into the role, the more distorted his or her personality became, given the unremitting pressures to be a figure of unquestioned authority. More recently, Lortie (1975), using questionnaire and interview data, carefully built a case that teachers respond to the structure of the occupation with a culture that contains themes of conservatism, individualism and presentism. David Hargreaves (1980) singled out concerns with status, with competence, and with relationships as enduring features of teacher culture.

Behind such claims is an assumption that cultures are predictable outgrowths of structures: either features of the occupation, as historically developed, and/or of the essential nature of the work of teaching (Feiman-Nemser and Floden, 1986). For example, Lortie (1975) showed that in the USA, as schooling began to be provided on a large scale, the one-room schoolhouse gave way to a series of adjacent rooms to which children could be allocated by age. Continued growth and the desire of school managers to expand or contract provision quickly reinforced the use of this cellular or 'egg crate' model. A consequence was physical and task separation among teachers, leading to a prominent feature of the occupational culture, teacher independence and individuality (but see Acker, 1991; A. Hargreaves, 1994). Other deductions are made from the nature of teacher work. We see that classrooms are busy places where teachers must respond immediately to a variety of demands from diverse children (Feiman-Nemser and Floden, 1986; Jackson, 1968). The associated need for order and predictability is thought to support a preference for the status quo and suspicion of innovations that would disrupt it (Doyle and Ponder, 1977).

These approaches have been tremendously productive in leading to research on aspects of teacher work such as collegiality and innovation (e.g. Lieberman, 1990; Little and McLaughlin, 1993). Yet there are pitfalls in trying to jump from structure to culture. One is the difficulty of demonstrating the connection empirically. Another is the problem of generalizing about a mass occupation with many dividing lines (Grossman and Stodolsky, 1994; Lacey, 1977). Siskin (1991, 1994) finds, for example, that many secondary school teachers do not experience isolation, but are deeply entrenched in subject department subcultures. Moreover, aspects of teaching in one society may not duplicate those in another (L. Davies, 1990; Dove, 1986), and even in the same society, persons from different gender, religious and ethnic groups may hold quite different ideas about teaching (Casey, 1993). Dealing with change is also problematic. The work of teaching is vulnerable to restructuring, subject to new political and economic forces, and affected by postmodernity (A. Hargreaves, 1994; Lawn, 1996; Menter *et al.*, 1997). Finally, some of these approaches tend to overstress the constraints of structures and cultures, and underemphasize the creativity and agency of individual teachers. The movement to recover 'the teacher's voice' and hear the stories teachers tell (Butt, Raymond, McCue and Yamagishi, 1992; Connelly and Clandinin, 1990) is an attempt to correct this bias.

Workplace culture

However, if we move too quickly from overgeneralized accounts of teacher culture to overindividualized teacher narratives we may lose sight of another form of teacher culture – the culture of the workplace. This level is the one of greatest interest in this volume. The 'meaningful system of beliefs and practices' which is culture (Lubeck, 1985, p. 14) varies from school to school. The specific variation developed in an institution – what I call workplace culture – has also been referred to as organizational culture (Nias *et al.*, 1989), institutional bias (Pollard, 1985) or professional community (Bascia, 1994; Little, 1992). Teachers in a given school need to acquire a set of specific understandings about what is required of them, not only in terms of skills or techniques but also values, attitudes and beliefs, in order to be a competent member of an ongoing social group. Culture provides a kind of stability, a set of guidelines in uncertain circumstances, although it is far from static. Symbolic interaction studies, as noted earlier, focus on the perspectives developed by actors in shared situations. As the situations change, so will the culture; but at the same time, the culture shapes the interpretations of the situations.

Teacher workplace cultures influence the process of implementation and the extent to which teachers define innovations as deskilling or professionalizing their work. The cultures also help members make decisions about career moves, as individuals exchange experiences and perceptions about what is possible and desirable. They contribute to ideas about what to expect and require from children and from their parents. They contribute to teachers' enthusiasm or distaste for collaboration. They can be close and warm (Acker, 1990b); divided and competitive (Ball, 1987; A. Hargreaves and Macmillan, 1995; Siskin, 1991); intense and personalized (Talbert, 1993); communal and religious (Bryk, Lee and Holland, 1993; Peshkin, 1986); or disempowered and resentful (Fine, 1991; Metz, 1989).

No doubt these workplace cultures can take a myriad of other forms. The variation is both fascinating and puzzling.

What factors shape the workplace culture of a school? Occupational culture has an impact. For example, primary school teachers in England share certain ideas about how children should be treated and childhood understood (Alexander, 1984). The head teacher's or principal's philosophy is frequently mentioned in the literature as a critical source of variation. Other variables such as the size of school, the age range, the type of children and community served, the physical setting and resources available to the school all play a part (Davis, 1992). Although it is possible to find out quite a lot about the ethos and public image of a school in a brief time (Lightfoot, 1983a), the teachers' workplace culture in a school is often hidden from casual investigators. Only a few studies have taken us very far inside the shared teachers' world in the primary school through ethnographic research, a method that involves lengthy immersion in a culture.[3] Examples are Biklen (1995), King (1978), McPherson (1972), Nias *et al.* (1989), Pollard (1985), L. Smith and Keith (1971). More common are studies that rely on interview data with some supplementary observations (e.g. A. Hargreaves, 1994; Pollard *et al.*, 1994; Vincent, 1996; Woods *et al.*, 1997). A major contribution of ethnographic studies is their ability to challenge or contradict widespread assumptions in the literature on teaching. For example, in the primary schools they studied, Nias and her colleagues (1989) discovered cultures of collaboration rather than individuality and isolation.

TEACHING AND GENDER

I have already made a few references to the gendered nature of teaching work. Gender, in sociological writing, is understood as a cultural rather than biological category, indeed one that shapes our notions of biology. It refers to culturally specific and changeable definitions of 'masculine' and 'feminine'. Applying gender analysis to teachers' work would mean calling attention to both the obvious and subtle ways in which cultural beliefs about women and men influence the nature of what teachers do. It is curious how often gender has been ignored, or trivialized, in the study of teachers, considering teaching is one of the few occupations with a relatively equal balance of women and men in its labour force. (See Acker, 1995/6, for a discussion and critique of literature on gender and teachers' work.)

In recent years there have been an increasing number of studies of 'teaching as women's work'. Highlighting the experiences of women started to fill the great gaps left in conventional scholarship and sometimes made accepted generalizations newly suspect. For example, we now have extensive historical studies of the experiences of women teachers in various contexts (Markowitz, 1993; Prentice and Theobald, 1991). We know a lot more about careers and leadership styles of women school administrators than we did in the past (Evetts, 1990; Goldring and Chen, 1993; Hall, 1996; Shakeshaft, 1989).

Putting women at the centre has begun to redress an unjust imbalance as well as in some cases suggesting a rethink of concepts (such as career or leadership) developed out of men's rather than women's typical experiences (Biklen, 1995; Grant, 1989; Reynolds, 1995). But there are several difficulties. One is the neglect of men's experiences. Another is the separation of feminist research on women teachers from mainstream research on teachers' work. A third stems from the increasing recognition that women are not all alike, but vary according to race, ethnicity, sexuality, marital status, age, dis/ability, and in many other ways. Studies of women teachers have expanded to focus on feminist teachers (Coulter, 1995; Middleton, 1989; Weiler, 1988) and lesbian teachers (Griffin, 1991; Squirrell, 1989a,b) and to examine the interactions of gender, race and ethnicity in women teachers' experiences (Bangar and McDermott, 1989; Casey, 1993; Delpit, 1993; Foster, 1993a,b). These studies are certainly welcome; the difficulty lies in the extent to which we can make meaningful generalizations about women teachers, when they are so diverse. Work on women in teaching, like feminist studies generally, must struggle with these challenges.

CONCLUSION

In this chapter, I have argued that teaching, whatever its associations with caring and commitment, must nevertheless be seen as 'work'. This work takes place in the context of certain features of the occupation that predispose teachers to share particular values and ideologies, the 'occupational culture' of teaching. Moreover, in the course of working in the same setting and sharing the same material and other conditions of work, perspectives develop that are best described as a 'workplace culture', one that differs from school to school. Teachers should also be seen as members of an occupation that presents its members with different career chances according to gender and is influenced by social understandings of what women's work should be like. All three of these themes are evident throughout the remaining chapters. In the following chapter, I focus on four key aspects of the workplace at Hillview: the children, the physical setting, the resources and the school ethos.

NOTES

1. See Acker, 1995/96, for a more detailed account of different approaches to the study of teachers.

2. Representative monographs, texts or collections from British sociology of education that tell us something about teachers' work and owe something to symbolic interactionism include Ball (1987), Ball and Goodson (1985), Broadfoot and Osborn (1993), Burgess (1983), Delamont (1983, 1984), Denscombe (1985), A. Hargreaves and Woods (1984), D. Hargreaves (1972), Lacey (1977), Nias (1989), Nias, Southworth and Yeomans (1989), Pollard (1985), Pollard, Broadfoot, Croll, Osborn and Abbott (1994), Sikes, Measor and Woods (1985), Woods (1979, 1980, 1983, 1990), Woods and Jeffrey (1996), Woods, Jeffrey, Troman and Boyle (1997).

3. There are, of course, other intensive studies that focus on the teacher in the classroom (L. Smith and Geoffrey, 1968; Clandinin, 1986), on the work of the head teacher or principal (Hall, 1996; Southworth, 1995; Wolcott, 1973), or on the children's social world (Pollard, 1985, 1996).

Chapter 3

The Workplace

In Chapter 1, I brought the reader into Hillview along with me, as I described my first days in the school and my early impressions. That chapter also gave a basic picture of the size, location and population of the school. Here, in Chapter 3, I elaborate on aspects of the school's immediate context that powerfully influence what it is like to be a teacher in this school. I describe the characteristics of the children, the physical setting, the resources available and the school ethos.

In this work setting, the teachers do a great variety of things, including constructing relationships with each other and the children, activities about which more is revealed in later chapters. The relationships should not be thought of as simply a direct consequence of the setting, as there is a dialectical relationship between structure and action. Thus, as described below, Marjorie Howard at Hillview changes her setting by washing the windows of her classroom and planting flowers outside the head teacher's office. Yet the power to alter the work context is seriously limited. Marx wrote: 'Men make their own history, but they do not make it just as they please' (quoted in McLellan, 1980, p. 137). We could say the same for these teachers, women and men alike.

THE CLIENTELE

Without a ready-made catchment area, the school attracted a mixture of children. This mixture could change, and did, even during my research. Generally, Hillview was a popular school, considered to do reasonably well academically and oversubscribed for its size and permitted numbers. Although an open enrolment system was not yet in place, the head teacher could (and was supposed to) admit children if there were spaces in the relevant age group (see Chapter 9). Children came to Hillview from areas of council [public] housing and from middle-class private housing, producing a social class mix. Some travelled to the school from a mile or two away, either in search of a better quality school or because they lived on a houseboat on the waterfront or living quarters above a shop or pub and did not have a more obvious local option. A few families in difficulties who were housed by the social services in local bed-and-breakfast accommodation also attended the school, usually temporarily. The school's reputation as being 'good with difficult children' meant that the local authority's educational psychologist often tried to place such children at Hillview, hoping they would fare better there than at their previous school.

Around one-third of the children could be labelled 'ethnic minority', but there was great diversity among them. According to the head teacher, a number of Wesley's black families saw Hillview as providing better schooling, and perhaps greater upward mobility for their children, than was available from their local alternatives. Mixed-race families came to the school in search of an environment where their children would be happier than in an 'all black' or 'all white' school. Other families, mostly white, sometimes headed by single parents, were thought of as 'countercultural', attracted by the school's tolerance for diversity and eccentricity. Mrs Clarke told me that some of these families saw Hillview as the last stop before heading to alternative schools such as the progressive private schools based on the ideas of Rudolf Steiner (the 'Waldorf Schools') or into home schooling. This group gave the school a reputation as 'the hippie school' or 'the weirdo school' or the school with 'alternative parents'.

In an interview in 1988, Liz Clarke described the parents to me at length:

> They're thinking people, who've got very definite views about society, and children, and bringing them up, and a lot of them go along with the feeling that, you know, being happy is the most important thing in school . . . They're centre city people, they're not quiet, ordinary people who are prepared to live out their lives in their little semi with their garden and their car. Whatever range of life they come from, they tend to be somewhat deviant people really . . . I should think they are almost entirely anti-Thatcher, radical people . . . I can't think of anyone at all who would be really pro-government.

> I mean it is not a middle-class school. It does not have middle-class values. It has some middle-class children there, but they are deviant middle-classes . . . If they are doctors, they're working in the centre of the city so that they are committed to disadvantaged people. If they are solicitors, it's the same thing. Or else they're foreigners who've come to work in the centre. . . . I mean, some of them move away and move off to [the suburbs], sometimes they do . . . But it's vibrant and exciting and interesting [at Hillview].

[Then] there is a goodly number of people who are not very educated themselves and who are . . . a nice kind of family to have because they believe in education. They believe that what you are doing is good for their children and you know, they're really pleased to see their child learning to read and write better than they can . . . This year, now, I've got a plethora of poly lecturers[1] and PhDs but I've also got people who are not very educated and . . . like to see their children developing skills and are very proud of what their children do. So that's a nice mixture, really.

Dennis, the deputy head teacher, said about the parents:

They're just so mixed, it's untrue really. I think that's the only thing that's really struck me, the fact that you can have somebody who's a lecturer at a poly, for example, and you've got somebody who's on a boat, and yet they've all got such definite ideas about education – what they see is right and what isn't right.

'Vibrant', 'exciting' and 'interesting' did not produce children who were tractable for teachers. In response to an interview question asking them to describe the children in the school, some teachers replied 'very affectionate' or 'lively'. However, others were more critical:

I suppose selfish, self-centred, very confident in themselves and with adults, children who wouldn't suffer fools lightly if you couldn't teach. They're very quick to suss people out. They're quite demanding kids really. They've always got an opinion about most things. And whatever you do, you've got to have a good reason for asking them to do it. Keeps you on your toes, really. (Dennis)

I'm surprised they don't have more responsibility . . . for their own things, putting them away. If you let them, they'd stand up and leave everything about them. It's quite surprising. They drop, discard things. I've noticed that throughout the school. Coats are everywhere. They are quite a happy lot . . . I'm struck by the way they don't realize how precious the materials are. (Kristin)

Most classes held at least one really 'difficult' child. Chapter 4 describes an extreme case, 'Peter'. Children who posed major problems became the stuff of folklore in the staffroom. Marjorie talked about Ian, now in one of the upper year groups:

When he first came to school he turned his milk upside down and calmly poured it on the carpet. When I said 'stop', he said 'how much will you pay me?' He went under the table and threw everything everywhere. I remember when he destroyed Laurie Smith's model and the look of pure pleasure on his face. With Ian, I had to get the mother sorted out first. She was in tears all the time. I had her in to help and encouraged her to be firm at home or there was nothing I could do.

Generally, teachers saw the 'vibrant' mix as a challenge. Despite exasperation and exhaustion, they were proud to be 'making a difference'. They believed that not all teachers would like, or could cope with, a school like Hillview. Marjorie reflected the mixed feelings of many. Speaking of another teacher, she said:

But to her it is just a job . . . and, really, where a few years ago I'd have automatically thought she was wrong, because I was dedicated . . . I'd do it for nothing – in the end . . . it is a job . . . Saying that, of course, it's hard to switch off . . . although you know it, you can't actually do it . . . I don't know if I want to go for a quiet life now . . . I think I would rather go somewhere where the kids are in desperate need . . . I think I would rather do that than know that I'd settled into a backwater, just for a quiet five years. I couldn't come to terms with that, really, I would rather burn out, almost.

When asked in interview how they would describe the school to a friend looking for a job, the usual answer began: 'It would depend on the friend'. Marjorie again:

Well, I'd tell him it's interesting and to go for it because it's always different, never boring . . . as long as they've got their own inner discipline to sort themselves out . . . But if you can sort yourself out on that discipline side, then if you enjoy teaching in an imaginative way and wanting to do your own thing and perhaps even break the rules and change the timetables and, you know, you just don't want to be so regulated . . . I like it here. I sort of recommend it to anyone, only because I happen to like it that way.

Betty Chaplin said:

I don't think a lot of people would find it an easy school to get on with. I mean, I suppose when I think of my friends, they are all very middle-class people who think in middle-class ways . . . [It would have to be someone] with the right sense of humour. If you didn't, some days you'd just go home and, you know, curl up in a corner and wish to die because sometimes, there's quite a lot of hassles . . . They're not always easy children to work with and I think you've got to have a certain amount of inner reserve to keep going in certain cases.

Others were more upbeat in their descriptions:

I would say that this is a very friendly school. I think it's a very nice atmosphere being at this school. The children are very, very lively – you've got to be prepared for them because they are extremely lively. That's what they are. We do try to make them independent. (Helen)

PHYSICAL SURROUNDINGS

Hillview consisted of two buildings, close together: one a structure, nearly 100 years old, of three storeys with a great deal of charm but badly in need of decoration, and the other a two-storey, two-classroom modern wing of the church hall. The 'new building' was also used for activities in the hall, including assemblies, lunches and physical education for the younger children.

Kristin King's first impression of the school was: 'What an amazing place to have a school! It was dwarfed by the buildings around it.' The school, tucked behind the church, could be reached by walking through one of several narrow lanes leading from main streets, or by driving around narrow alleyways, making a sharp right turn, and continuing down a short slope between the two buildings into the school parking bay and playground. Usually a chain was put across the slope as a safety precaution. The visitor could pull into the tiny car park wedged between the school and the older children's play area, although chances of finding a space would be slim. Marjorie Howard joked that to get a job at the school, a teacher would first have to pass a parking test. On more than one occasion a bump or scrape was the result of the manoeuvres required.

Proceeding through the school gate, under a stone arch, and walking a few steps brings the visitor to the front door of the school and into the small foyer. Often flowers would be on a narrow table pushed up against a wall which would contain a display of some sort. The opposite wall held notices and parents' advertisements. When the infant classes got a shared computer, it was squeezed into this area as well. On the right of the foyer was a small cloakroom, mainly for ancillary staff and the head teacher and secretary, and then the school office, which miraculously (given its size) contained the head teacher, the secretary, a large storage cupboard [closet], the telephone, the photocopier, a few chairs for visitors, some bookcases and files, children's artwork and photographs, and lots of green plants.

Three classrooms opened from the foyer as well, and there was a stairway to the upper floors. Behind one of the classrooms and accessible from another was the 'activities area', a large, multipurpose room for art and other work. Children's toilets and another small room, the 'kiln room' or 'pottery room', were part of this complex and there was an area for the caretaker's things. Small play areas outdoors were also reached from the activities area and from one of the classrooms.

Upstairs there was a narrow hallway, and an open library area. As well as bookshelves, the library area included several tables, chairs, floor cushions and a mural featuring a black mermaid that had been painted by a parent working with children. After a small lavatory for teachers, a door to the outside led to the playground used by the younger children, surrounded by a brick wall and containing a small amount of equipment and a building with outdoor toilets. A dragon design made with colourful blocks was placed on the wall during my time at the school, as was additional equipment in the other playground. Steps at the side led down to the slope where cars and walkers entered the school area.

Inside the school, another flight of stairs led, first, up to the teachers' staffroom. Here, teachers gathered before school, during morning playtime, after lunch, and after school when there was a staff meeting. Various items were stored here and the room contained a sink, refrigerator and coffee- and tea-making facilities, as well as chairs, old sofas and a coffee table. Like all the rooms at Hillview in the old building, the staffroom was both cramped and cosy. A few steps away were more classroom areas: two rooms adjoining without a door, with a third room around a corner. The wide corridor outside these rooms had multiple uses: a television made it the 'TV room' for classes brought upstairs, and cupboards held supplies for music and other materials. Opening on to the TV room opposite one of the classrooms was another storage cupboard and a room known as the 'cookery room' which also had multiple purposes, e.g. the site for the visiting nurse, a meeting-place for helpers in the school on a training scheme, an area for remedial help. The staffroom was also used for remedial help on occasion, and the secretary would work there on an ancient portable typewriter if privacy in the office were required.

Teachers liked the charm of Hillview's building and the village-in-the-city setting. But they invariably added a comment on the run-down quality of the school:

> The setting is very nice. But it's tacky, tatty – a shame. The cleaning isn't very good and it always looks a bit grubby. The whole place gets in a mess. (Sheila)

> I think the place could be much enhanced by a completely new paint job, really. I think that people try very hard to make it

look attractive but things fall off the wall, the paint is peeling, you can't really disguise that. (Rosalind)

Dennis's response shows his mixed feelings of pride and distress:

I think the upkeep of the building is disgusting . . . I think the upkeep of this building is diabolical. I think something ought to be done about it radically and all I can see happening is teachers getting desperate enough to do it themselves and I refuse to do it myself really . . . A friend came down . . . and she asked to be shown around the school, so I took her around. And at the end, I was quite proud that I worked at the school – I said a whole bunch of things. She said, 'Oh look at this! Isn't it horrible, isn't it horrible.' And I thought that yes, it is really and made excuses . . . I mean, the building is great. It's really interesting. I mean there are not many schools like it where you can go in all these little corners . . . I think the building is really nice.

Helen made a similar point:

It's got character. Every classroom is different. There are schools that you go into where once you've been into one, you've been into them all.

More cynically, Debbie suggested that the teachers had to think about the building's charm in order to keep working there:

Well the buildings are just grotty, aren't they? What other word could you use – disgusting? There's a character about them but you've got to say that, because if you don't feel something about it, you are just going to make your life misery working here all the time. You know, if you don't look at the crumbling walls and things, I suppose it's got its little character, the little village school, but the trouble is there are two hundred children in there. It's really not a village school, is it?

In the quotation above, Dennis referred to teachers carrying out their own maintenance work. Generally the position held by teachers was that they should not have to do this work because it was the responsibility of the local education authority (LEA); resisting it made a political point. In efforts to save money, the LEA, like others in the country, had radically cut down on the maintenance of school buildings. But Marjorie felt it was up to her to improve her surroundings if she could. Like Debbie, she said that the building was:

really grotty for the children . . . I hate it. This is one reason why I go out of my way when I can to wash the walls and to

> clean the windows, even though it gives me a lot of scorn from
> Mrs C . . . She told off very strictly that this wasn't my job. Then
> I thought,'Whose job is it anyhow?' Nobody will do it . . . But I
> only do it when I can't bear it, when I can't see out of my room
> anymore. You know, and I clean the sink in the staffroom and
> again that's no one's job and things like that. And I just look
> down at all the bulbs I planted, sort of outside Liz's office, you
> know, and the pansies and the ivy and all that – just to try to
> tart it up – not only for the kids but for me as well.

Certain opportunities, and many logistical problems, were created by the structure and setting of the school. A great advantage was the relative ease of accessing sites in the city. Classes could walk to the skating rink or to the museum or library. Yet there was restricted playing space around the school, a typical feature of inner-city schools in Britain (Mortimore, Sammons, Stoll, Lewis and Ecob, 1988, p. 9). Consequently, complicated arrangements had to be made for children to get to 'games' at a playing field several miles from the school. Coaches could not come right up to the school, and the children walked down a lane and waited on a busy street. On some occasions, the coach did not show up, and someone would have to trek back to the school so a phone call could be made. (Near the end of my research, Debbie had acquired through her own resources a cellular phone, which made such arrangements much easier.)

Noise carried from one room to the next, especially upstairs where the classroom and 'TV room' areas might be used simultaneously for different activities. More problematic was finding enough space for activities such as the language morning described in Chapter 1. Small groups would spread out all over the terrain – including the open library area, the staffroom, the cookery room, the parish lounge and even the church crypt. Violin lessons usually took place in the room in the new building called the parish lounge, as did some small group work. While the sound was well contained, the room was often too cold and the visiting music teacher risked missing an announcement or a cup of tea because no one remembered she was there.

Decisions had to be made about the allocation of building space. For example, which two classes should be housed in the modern building? The children there had more room, but the teachers would be isolated from colleagues or from help in an emergency. (Phones were installed in some of the rooms near the end of my research. There was no intercom.) Some teachers liked the separation and relative quiet; most did not:

> This is something which I have noticed when I came over here
> [new building], it's very isolated over here. I'm used to somebody
> being next door; there's always somebody around. Whereas here,
> unless they're coming into the classroom, they've lost their way.
> (Nancy)

The 'infants' (5- to 7-year-olds) were taught in the three classrooms and the activity area on the ground floor in the old building, Some remodelling had been done to accommodate this arrangement. The three classrooms, especially Helen Davies's, were rather small for the number of children occupying them (sometimes more than 30).

Betty Chaplin made reference to the control problems caused by the physical setting:

> Our lack of space is really our biggest constraint. It creates a lot
> of problems. Because the children are on top of each other, and
> it doesn't take much in some situations for what is probably
> trivia to blow up into something more important . . . Helen's
> room is probably the worst of the lot. I mean she's got such a lot
> of children and such a small space . . . In September, when these
> children are smaller, it's not such a problem, but you see, now
> [in July], if all my children are in, I can't sit them all on a seat, I
> haven't got a chair for them all, for one thing. They sit on the
> carpet, and they're all squashed, and it doesn't take much [to
> start a fight] . . . I can't organize this room as a [fully-fledged]
> infant classroom. I don't know what the answer is, really,
> because every time you have an idea, you've got to think 'have I
> got the space to do it' and very often the answer's 'no'. I mean,
> we should have a computer in here. And where could I put it?
> (She laughs.)

The three infant teachers, Marjorie, Betty and Helen, worked together and coordinated many of their activities. They were grateful for the shared space the activities area provided and the general assistant, Beryl, who was based there. The children did not spend all their time in the classrooms, of course. They had to be taken upstairs for television programmes or to the library; across the way to the hall for assembly and lunch; sometimes to the church for a rehearsal. They spent time in the 'infant playground' or in small play spaces outside the activities area or the reception classroom. I recall watching the 5-year-olds being 'taught' how to go as a group (with the teacher) down the stone steps from the infant playground and across the small road to the hall and back again. In an interview in July, Betty commented on the inadequacy of the playground: 'It's very hot on the infant playground. There are no real facilities for them to get drinks. And there's nowhere for them to sit. Now, it would be nice on a hot day to let them sit in the shade and do things.'

The teachers had no place for their coats or personal belongings. A coat might be put over the back of the desk chair, or hung on a cleverly arranged hook in a narrow cupboard. Privacy was at a minimum. I could rarely find a suitable place in the school for an interview. Those in the staffroom were likely to be interrupted two or three times; those in classrooms at lunch-times generally had the background of children playing noisily in the playground and running through the classroom itself to get a coat or put away a lunch box. The same constraints obtained at my other research school, Rosemont. It is rare for a school-based tape to be free of background noise, either from children or cleaners or even thumps on the ceiling from the class above.

RESOURCES

While there might be mixed feelings about the buildings, the paucity of resources in Hillview was bemoaned by all. The kindest remarks I have recorded in my interviews or field notes are Nancy's comment, 'Well I think there's still plenty of room for improvement' and Betty's 'improving, gradually'. Others include 'very poor', 'poorly resourced', 'appalling' and 'absolutely diabolical'.

No one was ever sure quite why the school was so poorly equipped. It was thought that decisions made in the past had been bad ones; or teachers had perhaps moved on, taking equipment with them; or the practice of teachers ordering supplies individually made tracking difficult. Persistent comparisons, to Hillview's detriment, were made with other schools, either those where teachers had worked in the past or others they visited (see also Chapter 8):

> When you go round and look at other schools, and you come back, you think, 'why haven't we got all this'. Because usually you start off with the equivalent amount of money. And I don't know why, why it should be, because I'm sure the money is used wisely . . . [Other schools] must get far more support from parents . . . [A school she had visited] raised something like £1400, just on a sponsored walk, so they bought an extra computer and they spent £500 on musical instruments. And the construction toys in that school were incredible. I mean, not just one box of whatever, but box after box with a variety of different things, which really we're not able to offer here. (Nancy Green)

The chronic shortage of pencils was almost a joke. When I helped in classrooms, children frequently wandered around looking for a pencil.

> Ian says he doesn't have a pencil. Mrs Clarke asks Sheila Jones what he should do. 'I tell them to look,' she says, 'they always find one. If I give them one it gets lost.' Mrs Clarke says 'Look in the office if you don't find one. You children must eat them for breakfast.'

> Lawrence comes up to me, says he had two pencils in his drawer, they're gone now. Debbie gives him another one. Nina comes up and shows me her pencil, in her drawer, has been split. Says she has another four, takes them home with her, because they get pinched [stolen].

In a staff meeting discussion of resources, it was decided that certain equipment, including pencils, should be on each teacher's desk, and it should be clear to children where to get them.

> Helen Davies comments that it is bad practice to give a child a pencil as soon as they lose them. They disappear at a fantastic rate. There is a heated discussion about pencils. We have no pencils, say Sheila and Debbie. Someone says they break them, chew them, lose them. There is a discussion of various places to get cheap pencils. Nancy saw some on holiday. People ask which shop they were in, wonder if they could get someone to bring some.

There were many complaints of insufficient equipment for teaching certain subject areas. In the pottery room were stored gallons of poster paint left over from some ordering decision of the distant past. I chatted to Kristin King while she worked very concentratedly in the pottery room with a small group of children making clay houses. She pointed out that the aprons were too small for the big children. The poster paint from the past was the wrong type. The clay was the wrong kind, too. But she was pleased to be doing pottery in a primary school: 'very unusual', she noted.

Similar problems were encountered with equipment for physical education (PE), science, mathematics and reading. Mathematics provides an interesting example. Although the mathematics scheme in use in the school had great drawbacks, the fact it had been ordered for hundreds of pounds (shortly before Liz Clarke arrived at the school) almost dictated its continued use. There were consequences of using this scheme. Usually, children worked through it individually, asking for help from the teacher where necessary. The advantage of such an arrangement would be that no piece of equipment – say scissors – would be needed by 30 children at once. Typically the school purchased partial sets of items, to save money. The disadvantage was that children were constantly looking for equipment whenever they came to a lesson that required it; those who had less initiative, or could not locate the equipment, might simply skip that topic. Often, when I helped children with mathematics, I faced the same challenge:

> Some of the boys are doing maths. I help. We have to hunt for scales and weights to do some of the problems, also squared paper. Rosalind finds it for me in the big cupboard.

> Harvey couldn't do the work because he needed a balance.
> Sheila told him to skip it for now. He needed gummed paper; we
> got some from Mrs Lowe. He enjoys doing it. The next page also
> needs complicated equipment.

This process that Kristin called a 'scramble – must be here somewhere' was
responsible for some of the 'traffic' in the classrooms. One morning, Rosalind Phillips counted the interruptions:

> Rosalind has J3 this morning. She's trying to do some 'base
> time' maths sheets. She's counting the interruptions; we get to
> 23 by 10.15. Some are about tomorrow's red nose day [a charity
> event], most are children from J4 walking through looking or
> asking for paper, rubbers [erasers], staplers, pencil sharpeners.

Rosalind was particularly disturbed about the lack of computers in the
school. There were two: one for the infants and the other for the juniors. As
noted earlier, the infant classrooms shared one computer that was positioned so that it could be reached from all three classrooms, but in a noisy
area. The junior teachers had to share one computer among four classes
and two buildings, and generally rotated it so that each class had it for six
or seven weeks at a time. Rosalind believed this limited access was
insufficient, especially when so many children had special needs and could
have benefited from computer activities. She thought that the school should
have three or even four computers. She pushed the head teacher to phone
the computer advisor for the district. 'I saw a film about the use of LOGO,
how it was used in some other schools and what the children knew – I felt
like resigning. I thought maybe the parents could contribute, but they've
already bought one.' She was upset to see the infant computer 'sitting idle
in the hallway. So much comes from it; it motivates children; it is a lifeline
for some children.'

On some occasions, advisors from the local education authority came to
a staff meeting to give some input about their specialization. These visits
had a disturbing edge for the teachers. Although they were happy to learn
about whatever the topic was, they could also see how difficult it would be
to put new ideas into practice. During one inservice training day, an advisor
and a local head teacher spoke with the teachers, talking about ways to
organize the classroom for the 'negotiated curriculum' where children had
maximum choice of activities. My notes say 'No one said straight out, but it
was clear that there was an awareness that all these good ideas could come
to nought without the resources.' The advisor offered to help with small
items like a pinboard. Later on, when the school was gearing up for the
technology requirements of the new National Curriculum, the visiting
specialist remarked 'You're in desperate need of equipment.'

The shortcomings of the buildings interacted with the shortage of resources. Remodelling the infant classroom area to make three classrooms where once there were two did not increase the resources:

> In some ways this room is very badly resourced as an infant classroom. Because we created three infant classes out of two when this was all reorganized, a lot of the stuff was split between us . . . If this is a true infant classroom, I should have sand, and water, all the time! And things like that. There's no way . . . I think I'm short of construction equipment for these children. We've built up a lot of other things (games), but . . . they need a space to do it, and it's not easy when you've got all your children [in class], or even three-fourths of your children. The activities area is our biggest advantage. It's an essential.
> (Betty Chaplin)

In the upstairs classrooms of the old building, much energy was spent in figuring out ways to cover up the peeling paint and provide cheerful spaces for displaying children's work. For example, in planning their 'Older Junior Unit' for the following year, Dennis and Debbie gave a lot of thought to the walls in the classroom area that had been used by Debbie and others for the middle juniors. Debbie remarked: 'Look at the flaky wall. Can we do anything? Sand it down? Cover it up for display? I always used to pride myself on my display. Here I feel ashamed, have to apologize.' They went on to discuss the possibilities of cork tiling or backing paper, and how to attach things because 'Blu-tack won't stay'. As the new autumn term opened, I noted that blue paper covered that display area, with a small section of yellow where the blue ran out. Dennis had put up an attractive display about design and technology on the backing paper. Later that day, Dennis told the children (the oldest ones, around age 11) that 'Mrs Stevens and I have worked very hard to get everything ready'. A child, Charles, commented about the blue and yellow on the wall: 'Not too good'. Dennis explained frankly that it covered up the peeling paint and plaster.

There were several ways to obtain resources. Most of the funding came from 'capitation', i.e. an amount of money corresponding to numbers in the school, supplemented by allowances based on certain characteristics of the school (e.g. for a split site). LEA advisors could add small amounts of money and a certain amount of effort was spent in lobbying these individuals. (This system predated the 'local management of schools' (LMS) where the LEA played a much reduced role.) Fundraising or donations could increase the school's working capital. When a local business asked about using the teachers' car park, the head teacher negotiated the use of two spaces in return for a sum. Each year the school fair brought in money and the Parent–Teacher Association (PTA) might find additional sources. Donations came occasionally; the widow of a local author donated some children's books, and several boxes of fabric appeared that were made into costumes.

There were hidden subsidies. Children might bring their own materials such as pencils or calculators to school. (This practice was relatively rare at Hillview but common at Rosemont.) Teachers might use some of their own money. Nancy said 'I know at home and in my cupboard I've got stacks of things which I bought personally when I had [taught] infant children.' Rosalind brought items from home or borrowed them from another school she worked in. Teachers also quietly subsidized the school by their labour: for example by making costumes for a play, or refreshments for a school event.

However raised, the funds never seemed to meet the need. The lack of resources was distressing for the teachers. When she looked for reasons that the Middle Junior Unit had not been as successful as it might have been, Liz Clarke noted: '[Another reason is] resources, lack of resources, not enough of the right kind of books, you know, the minute you want them. I mean, that frustrates you as a teacher. That demotivates you.' Yet, looked at now, from a distance, I also notice that the teachers were remarkably tolerant of a situation where others might have made even more of a concerted protest. Although the teachers certainly complained, they seemed to accept that the money was simply not there, and that it was up to them to work around it. Perhaps they were aware that provision is poor in many British primary schools: Wragg (1993) reported teachers using phrases like 'diabolical', 'barely adequate' and 'the Cinderella of the education system' to express their 'concern and shame over the working environment' (p. 41). As I commented in my field notes: 'It all seems a struggle, rather like a poor family trying to make ends meet, beg and borrow things, enormous efforts to keep a minimum level of what's needed.'

Work around it they did. What my notes also show is that faced with building limitations or resource deprivation, the teachers became 'resource/ ful'. Over time, the situation improved as they revamped the ordering system, made named individuals responsible for ordering in particular subject areas, began to keep inventories of equipment, cleared out cupboards and reorganized storage. The infants got a television and video, which cut down on the traffic outside the upstairs classrooms. Discussions of how to do these things often took place at staff meetings, so that the whole school could be involved and ideas could be shared. Other staff meetings were devoted to hearing and prioritizing the various needs.

They also coped by using humour (see also Chapter 7). For example, when two children spilled some paint on the floor, a nearby teacher said dryly 'there goes the year's supply'. On another occasion, a staff meeting where resources were discussed as well as charity efforts for the needy turned into an ironic discussion of where Father Christmas comes from (Norway? Finland? A local department store?) and where the teachers could write to him for charity for the school. Another initially serious discussion of resource needs eventually turned into mock requests for dried flowers in vases, Laura Ashley wallpaper and Austrian blinds on the windows.

Games for the juniors provides an example of a situation that taxed teachers and created resourcefulness. The effort of moving four classes of children by coach to playing fields, having them change, play and change back again, and dealing with the various organizational and control problems was great. There were always complicated discussions about which teachers and which helpers (e.g. a student teacher) could take which group. My notes from a staff meeting show Liz's concern that people were not getting satisfaction (both teachers and children) and that children were not getting experience of all the different skills. There followed a discussion of whether the play surface could be used for a netball activity. Liz reported on her efforts to get some equipment from the LEA advisor: 'We're in a queue'. Use of a local sports centre was suggested by someone; the apparatus there might be a good alternative.

This kind of open discussion was common and led to changes. Sessions at the local sports centre were scheduled. Similarly, swimming was reorganized to take place at a nearby hospital pool and a different public pool, after the previous one proved increasingly unsuitable (a tramp washed his clothes in the pool; some possibly racist remarks were made by pool staff). For every adjustment, there was a readjustment; for example, one of the teachers did not have the qualifications to be allowed to teach at the hospital pool.

HILLVIEW'S ETHOS

What teachers could do was shaped by the characteristics of the children in their care and by their physical surroundings and the resources available. A less tangible but no less influential context for their work was provided by the prevailing school ethos. By ethos I am thinking of the school's guiding beliefs as a community rather than what I have called the teachers' workplace culture, although they are interdependent. Loosely speaking, the Hillview ethos could be called 'child-centred', along with that of many other primary schools in the country. There are a number of discussions in the literature of what 'child-centred' and related concepts such as 'progressive', 'open', or 'developmental' education mean to teachers, many of them rather critical of such views as ideology or an expression of values rather than the outcome of sound theory (Alexander, 1984; King, 1978; Sussmann, 1977). One definition says that child-centred education is 'a phrase which became prominent in the 1960s to describe methods of teaching based on the interests of the child and individual stages of development ... it claims support in the work of Piaget and employs discovery approaches to learning' (Campbell, 1988, p. 90). In recent years, typical primary pedagogy based on

41

this ideology has been attacked by politicians and some educators and efforts have been made to change it. The implications for the teacher of being expected to show unlimited caring for children have also been cast as problematic in feminist writing, a point taken up in Chapter 7.

Child-centredness at Hillview was diffused throughout all activities of the school, which is why I regard it as a component of school ethos. In keeping with many other schools, Hillview had a commitment to help each child reach his or her potential, both academic and social. Other aspects of Hillview's ethos might not be as widely shared. Hillview made an effort to raise the self-esteem of each child; to provide an educational experience free from bullying and prejudice and to teach the child not to be a bully or prejudiced person; to instill tolerance and to welcome difference; to celebrate individual and collective successes and efforts; to develop qualities of kindness and compassion. By and large competition among individuals was avoided. Widespread participation was encouraged in all activities, as was allegiance to the school as a whole. Individuality, initiative and independence were encouraged within limits. Being 'sensible' was a virtue. In King's (1978) study of three infant schools, he too found the 'silly versus sensible' dichotomy prominent in teachers' admonitions to children.

Examples from field notes can provide a more vivid picture of the school ethos than a summary. In Britain, school assemblies are key points for the transmission of basic values (Burgess, 1983; King, 1983; Pollard, 1985; Woods, 1987, 1990). On most days at Hillview, the entire school met together for assembly for about 20 minutes during mid-morning. The children sat in rows on the floor in the hall, the large open room in the new building. The younger children sat in front. The teachers, helpers and visitors were in rows of chairs along the sides. The two teachers who were on playground duty that day did not stay, so that they could have a coffee and put the kettle on for the others, as playtime for the children and a break for the teachers followed assembly. The head, deputy head, or one of the teachers took the lead role. Ostensibly religious observances (required by law), these are in practice multipurpose occasions, mixing moral tales, songs, rehearsals, silent prayers, class performances, listening to music, group discussions and tellings-off. They are a celebration of the collectivity and an occasion where 'what we stand for' can be articulated. Sometimes a lecture made the point:

> Mrs Clarke speaks reprovingly, loudly. 'There have been several situations in the last few weeks where children have been unkind or unpleasant to each other . . . This is Christmas-time when a baby was born to bring love into the world. It is not about presents but about being kind and loving. No more teasing [gives an example of an incident]. That is bullying, unkindness, and it's going to stop, Hillview School. We pride

ourselves we are reasonable people to each other. Being reasonable is not teasing people because they look different from you or speak in a different voice.'

At other times, the atmosphere is warm and close:

Assembly is very moving. Mrs Clarke plays a tape of Jacqueline du Pré playing Fauré's *Elégie* as the children come in, then talks quite a lot about her [the cellist who had died the day before, after a long battle with multiple sclerosis]. Then she shows the card put together for David Marlowe [the vicar of the church associated with the school, who had suffered a stroke] and plays the tape made by some of the girls for him. The children sing along with the tape; there is a very close feeling.

On another occasion:

Helen Davies gets everyone singing: 'Sing, sing a song . . .' She has the older children standing. It is a touching sight.

Sometimes the assembly took the form of 'school meeting', where an important issue (often connected with behaviour) was discussed with the children. At one such meeting, children suggested words to describe the school including, to Liz's delight, 'respect' and 'responsibility'. Liz was open and honest with the children and tried not to talk down to them. In a conversation, she told me that she tackled 'the worship problem' head-on in an assembly. She explained to the children that it is a problem: not everyone has a religion or has the same religion but we have to do an 'act of worship', the legislators say. The Hillview solution was to have 'a prayer or a shared thought'.

At one school meeting, Liz explained the school's new anti-racism policy:

'I want to talk to you about something important . . . We at Hillview are especially lucky because lots of people are different from each other. For example a Sikh boy has a topknot, an adult man a turban. You are used to this sort of thing . . . We have obvious differences. Let me show you. You stand up, Sarah and Kenneth. There's an immediate difference – who knows?' Hands are raised. The child called on says, 'Sarah is wearing a dress.' She calls on two South Asian brothers to stand up: 'What's different?' They have different jackets, are different ages. Then Kevin and Sam. Lots of hands: 'One's black and one's white.' 'A harder difference now': She calls on Noelle, who is black, and a younger black girl to stand. Denise (also black) says: 'One is lighter than the other.' I think Liz had meant something about how they were dressed. Liz goes on to read the anti-racist statement, simplifying a bit, saying that differences don't matter, they are not to treat people differently because they are a boy or girl, or because of colour. Are there two messages here? – emphasizing differences, then saying they don't matter.

Teachers reinforced messages about 'difference' in their classrooms. An African girl in Helen's class came to school with her hair in tightly braided plaits. Helen asked her who did it (her aunt). She commented: 'It's nice we are different; if we were exactly the same it would be boring.' The class (of 7-year-olds) began a discussion of whether there should be differences between boys' and girls' hairstyles, interrupted by the bell for assembly. A few days later, Helen continued with the same theme:

> 'It's nice to have differences; it would be a boring world if we were all the same. It doesn't matter what colour skin someone has, whether they're short, tall, old or young.' Olive says 'If we're walking on the street and see someone who doesn't look nice, my mother says don't judge them.' 'What's in their heart and head is important', says Helen. 'If someone came into my house dressed nicely but stole all my money . . .' Victor contributes: 'Someone next door has a motorbike and looks like a noisy person but is really kind, plays records and tapes for me.'

Assemblies were not the only occasion for communal participation. At the end of each term there was usually a production of some sort, such as a Christmas concert in December. Rehearsals for concerts, plays, assemblies and similar school productions took many hours. 'Days of rehearsal for two and a half minutes' [performance]', Rosalind commented glumly about one such case. Rehearsals could be rather tense and present problems of coordination and control, but sometimes the communal spirit came through. One day I came into the hall where the older two class groups were with several of the teachers:

> The children are either sitting around the edges or on the stage. They are rehearsing the 'Alternative Pied Piper', with guitars, etc., and a 1960s theme. The children wrote the songs. Helen and Dennis are rehearsing them. Rosalind is sorting out costumes for the 'townspeople'. There is a lot of camaraderie and laughter and bustle. I feel happy and relaxed – and think this is hardly a school.

Hillview's commitment to maximum participation generally meant these productions had 'casts of thousands', in Marjorie's words. The 'Alternative Pied Piper' was planned in detail in a staff meeting about five weeks before the event. Teachers discussed which children would be in it, what role each class would play, what was wanted from the teachers, how much class time and assembly time would be needed. Other topics included schedules for rehearsal and singing, building the sets, the type of costumes required. The basic storyline was repeated, although it was to be worked on by the older children. Whole classes would be 'rats', 'townspeople' and 'children', so that all could participate.

The head teacher put a high value on relationships in the school: 'I do know all the parents and that is as important to me as knowing all the children . . . I know a new face in school immediately. I know who everyone belongs to.' What 'the school' believed in was constantly being repaired, reconstructed, underlined and explained to children and visitors by Mrs Clarke, as shown in several of the extracts above. My field notes record a long conversation Liz had with parents of a child likely to start school at Hillview in 1989. As well as stressing the school's ability to teach skills and help children gain confidence in their learning, she told them:

> We work as a team here . . . with a united view of children.
> What's most important is helping children develop good
> relationships with each other . . . Our mixed character and being
> interested in everything is something parents have to take on
> board . . . The children get used to the whole of society.

Shortly after they left, a child was sent in for fighting on the playground: 'What is the most important thing at Hillview?' she asked him gently but seriously. 'Work?' he guessed. 'No, that's the second most important.' 'Teachers?' 'No, children are more important than teachers . . . being friends with other children is most important.' Later that morning there was a meeting with the 'dinner ladies' [lunch-time staff], at which Mrs Clarke spoke again about the importance of good relationships and setting a model for the children. She read to them the new anti-racism and anti-sexism policies, too.

Like many other primary schools in England prior to the Education Reform Act (Mortimore *et al.*, 1988), Hillview rarely tested children and almost never assigned homework. Although teachers spoke of marking children's work, this term meant checking and commenting, not giving letter or percentage grades. Reading ages were tested once a year at Hillview, and during my research a schoolwide tables test each spring was introduced. A letter to parents explained the process. Each teacher gave this test to her children, its content and delivery depending on the age of the children and style of the teacher. It was stressed that children were not competing against each other, but 'against themselves'. One of the parents, a polytechnic lecturer, wrote a note to the head teacher complaining that her 10-year-old was being put under too much pressure because of the testing. Later, in 1989 as the assessment requirements of the new reform legislation were being discussed at a staff meeting, Liz remarked: 'Our parents are very frightened by assessment. They are worried it will be a demotivator if the child does not do well.'

Demotivation was a concern in another staff meeting, when Liz stated that she was concerned with the effects of the mathematics scheme on the children. Those who did not make progress through the books were demotivated, while it worked as an incentive to children who achieve. She suggested different ways of using the scheme: 'The book shouldn't be the starting point.' Other teachers offered ideas.

Dennis redesigned the school sports day. Although the point was not made explicitly, the new version de-emphasized individual winning and gave children a chance to participate in enjoyable games instead. Similarly, at a school assembly, Mrs Clarke was effusive:

> 'This has been a wonderful weekend in terms of school', she says. She talks about the cricket match on Friday against [a boys' private school] where Hillview 'came second' against a side which had every advantage including a professional coach. They were very intimidating. 'I am very proud to be a head teacher of a group of children who could perform so well and behave as well as you did on Friday. It doesn't matter that you didn't win.'

She went on to praise the group who participated in English folk-dancing on Sunday:

> Other children looked at their teachers before they did anything, but always the ones in blue and red [Hillview's] were ready. They did something really good for us, just as the boys did on Friday.

Clandinin and Connelly and their colleagues (1995) suggest caution when embracing concepts such as ethos. They write about school stories, and especially those that have become 'sacred stories', where personal reservations or departures from what everyone else appears to believe (or from prevailing mandates, policies and prescriptions) are kept under cover. At Hillview there was a sense in which the ethos I have described was a sacred story. Teachers had some reservations, though I did not sense that these ran deeply enough to be considered resistance. Sometimes teachers dreamed of an orderly school, obedient children and old-fashioned teaching methods. Yet by and large they were convinced that the good of the children demanded otherwise, whatever the cost to their peace of mind. Thinking about one's own good is often considered selfish in the world of elementary school teachers (Clandinin and Connelly, 1995, pp. 95–6), a feature not unrelated to gendered expectations placed on women (see Chapter 7). Any teacher reservations also stemmed from the dilemmas and contradictions that are key features of primary school teaching (Berlak and Berlak, 1981;

Nias, 1989), especially when the dilemmas and contradictions seemed to be intensified by the school ethos.

For example, teachers could not celebrate the individual without remembering the needs of the collectivity. If meeting Peter's needs took most of the teacher's attention, how much was left for the other children? One of Mrs Clarke's accomplishments was the abolition of the 'special class' and integration of those children into the mainstream, where they were no longer so stigmatized. But in every class there were a few children who caused major behaviour problems and a few who were well below the average accomplishments of the others. Teachers were painfully aware of how little attention certain children received compared with what they needed; no form of classroom organization could fully deal with the huge ability range in each class. Special needs provision was very limited. The needs of quiet, undemanding children in the middle ranges of ability could also be overlooked.

How could children's eccentricities be tolerated if they clashed with sensible behaviour? Children were encouraged to show initiative, choose and organize their own activities as they got older, but were also to stay within prescribed limits and rules. Alexander (1995, p. 205) reminds us that choice can be illusory. How was a child (or a teacher, for that matter) to know where the line should be drawn? When did the good of the children clash with the good of the teachers?

It was difficult for a teacher to be absent, because supply [substitute] teachers found it very difficult unless they knew 'our kind of kids'. Debbie told me over the phone about a hard day she'd had. 'The children were terrible, really awful. We think we can't be ill, we can't go anywhere . . . How can we get a supply teacher?' At the same time, the teachers seemed rather proud of the children's spunk, their toughness. After a lively rehearsal by the third and fourth year juniors for the Harvest Assembly, Liz Clarke, pleased with their efforts, told the children that a recent visitor had made a comment about another school where the children were 'so listless'. 'Some of the older children will know what that means. Well, you, children, are the opposite of listless!' The children's assertiveness might be amusing. When the teachers from the Middle Junior Unit asked Leonie to finish what she was doing at the sink so they could start their meeting after school, she responded: 'Can't you go in the other room for your meeting?'

There were other contradictions. Despite the rhetoric and many actual examples of caring about children, no one seemed to notice that the children went out to play with wet hair directly after swimming. A rehearsal in the church brought out my maternal side:

> The church is cold, the rehearsal long . . . the teachers seem a
> little tense. Helen shouts at the children at the end . . . I put my

warm scarf around Tina, who looks cold. I notice other children who aren't very warmly dressed, perhaps because they are in costumes. Then I put my scarf around Nell for playing outside as she is shivering and says she doesn't feel very well.

Lectures to the children at school meeting about their behaviour were sometimes met with glazed eyes and obvious ennui. After one such meeting I mentioned to Liz Clarke how strange it seemed that the 'lecture' in assembly seemed to be on another plane of reality from the children's actual behaviour. 'But we can't *not* do it', she said. 'Then we reinforce it with individuals.'

The strictures against racism and bullying worked well. One child came in protesting: 'He called me a racist remark!' All such situations were taken very seriously. Yet, at least in the junior classes I watched, where children mostly chose to sit with friends, these groupings were usually demarcated by gender, race and (as far as I could tell) social class. Few efforts were made to encourage the children to work or play across these lines. Again, perhaps there was a conflict between two abstract principles: choice for the child and encouragement of tolerance. Were differences good, or didn't they matter?

Teachers had to work around such dilemmas rather than resolve them (Lampert, 1985). That they did so well could be seen in the generally positive atmosphere: one of the conditions for an effective school (Mortimore *et al.*, 1988). The next chapter looks more closely at teachers' work in their classrooms.

NOTE

1. 'Poly[technic] lecturers' appear in several of the quotations in this chapter. At the time, Britain had both universities and polytechnics; currently the former polytechnics are also called universities. In Britain, 'lecturer' is the generic name for a teacher in post-secondary education. A 'poly lecturer' in the context of descriptions of Hillview parents seems to signify a well-educated and assertive character.

PART TWO

DOING THE WORK

Chapter 4

The Teacher and the Class

MYTHS AND STEREOTYPES

Sara Delamont (1987) opens her collection on primary school teaching with a chapter on myths and realities. She comments:

> The biggest problem facing the primary teacher . . . is that what they actually do in real classrooms is totally obscured by myths and prejudices held by parents, adults who are not parents, governors, journalists, and even other primary teachers . . . There is a powerful rhetoric of abuse levelled at primary teachers, which has little relation to facts or evidence, and is remarkably resistant to rational argument. (p. 4)

In Britain, the abusive rhetoric was to escalate in the early 1990s, as the Conservative government made efforts to move teachers away from 'progressive' ideas towards greater structure, standardization and accountability in the classroom (see Chapter 11). Delamont argued, as have others (e.g. Galton, Simon and Croll, 1980), that the progressive classroom was itself something of a myth. With discipline problems and the difficulty of implementing the progressive ideal, the appearance of informality prevailed while interaction patterns were traditional and teacher-directed.

Other stereotypes and myths about teachers, especially primary teachers, abound. Ironically, some stem from the efforts by researchers to capture the essential nature of teaching as an occupation or activity. Teachers are said to be: 1) isolated in cellular, closed, 'egg-box' classrooms; 2) individualistic and resistant to collaboration with colleagues; 3) conservative and uninterested in innovation that would disturb the classroom order; 4) unintellectual and narrow or at best intuitive; 5) (for women) uncommitted to a career and exclusively classroom focused; 6) (for men) uncommitted to the classroom and exclusively career focused (see, for example, Doyle and Ponder, 1977; Dreeben, 1970; D. Hargreaves, 1980; Jackson, 1968; Lanier and Little, 1986; Leggatt, 1970; Lortie, 1973, 1975; Waller, 1932/1965). Latter-day stereotypes might be the teacher who has been deskilled or proletarianized by the forces of late capitalism and the various forms of state intervention into teachers' work (Apple, 1986; Densmore, 1987; Ozga and Lawn, 1988), or the teacher so mesmerized by progressive ideologies that her class consists of little but play and discovery activities (Alexander, Rose and Woodhead, 1992). But in the past decade or so, the stereotypes have been challenged by studies which present a more favourable and sympathetic portrait of teachers, especially at primary or elementary level (for example, Cortazzi, 1991; A. Hargreaves, 1994; Nias *et al.*, 1989; Woods, 1995).

My view is that any search for the nature of teaching is bound to be troubled by at least two considerations: 1) social change; 2) diversity among teachers and settings (see also Chapter 2). The effects of social change are easy to see – with hindsight. The studies of the 1960s and 1970s, for example, reflecting commonsense assumptions of the time, tended to take for granted that the domestic commitments of women teachers would not allow them to take their paid jobs seriously. Diversity presents a particularly thorny problem for efforts to generalize, one that has hardly been tackled (Acker, 1995/6; Feuerverger, 1997; Young, 1995). Teachers come from many backgrounds, work in many different types of school or out-of-school settings, teach contrasting subjects, hold various types of contracts, enjoy greater or lesser status and operate within different political and economic constraints. Ethnographic case studies, especially those extending over a significant amount of time, offer a chance to understand the effects of context and the material and cultural setting of small numbers of teachers. Yet such studies are relatively rare, owing to their labour-intensive nature, difficulties of access, long timespan, and perhaps researchers' doubts that significant insights can stem from small-scale studies.

My case studies of Hillview and Rosemont suggest to me that almost all the teacher stereotypes are (as is their nature) oversimplified. I found evidence of intelligent and committed teachers (including women with family responsibilities); collegial and caring ways of working; and sensitive and strategic responses to innovations. Chapter 3 sketched in the parameters within which the work of teaching was conducted. Chapters 4 and 5 look more closely at what that work is. I hope to show that primary school teaching is difficult work; that it requires versatility and openness, planning but flexibility; that it extends well beyond the classroom and even beyond the school.

CLASSROOM SNAPSHOTS

I start with four extracts from field notes, taken in classrooms of the Middle Junior Unit. As explained in Chapter 1, there were two groups, known by the initials of the surnames of the two teachers who had the main responsibility for each group. The younger group (second-year juniors, aged 8 to 9) was called SP after Debbie Stevens and Rosalind Phillips; the older group (third-year juniors, aged 9 to 10) was called SJ after Debbie Stevens and Sheila Jones. Debbie was the full-time teacher who divided her time between the two groups; Rosalind and Sheila were part-time teachers who worked mostly with one group or the other. Another part-time teacher, Kristin King, spread her hours across both groups as well as some of the other classes. The classes occupied the upper floor of the old building described in Chapter 3: three classrooms, two of which were adjoining without a door, all with easy access to a corridor known as the TV lounge or TV room and to the 'cookery room'.

Snapshot no. 1

Debbie talks to SP as a group. She sits on the children's table. 'In some maths books', she says, 'children are skipping all around. You need to write the date and underline with a ruler. Do you know why? It's so the teacher can see how much work you've done. With four teachers, each needs to know you did work with her. Write the [maths] book you're on and the page and a title. At the end of the page turn over and carry on on the next page. If you skip around we can't see how you've improved.' This is all done in a friendly way with some jokes. Then Debbie gives out some work on tens and units. 'This is to sort out who knows what', she says. She gives different work to different groups. 'If it's easy, OK I'll know you know. If not, don't worry, I'll come round and explain it from the beginning' . . . [Later] Debbie sorts books into three groups, at various levels of understanding . . . It seems extraordinary (to me) to look at the maths books and see some children write down the problem number, some don't; some move all over the page, others squeeze into a little bit. There were five problems across on this worksheet. Many put four problems across, then no. 5 on the next line. It's surprising how hard it seems to be. (13 October 1987)

Snapshot no. 2

Rosalind Phillips gets the children's attention in SP. She tells them to put their pens and pencils down; it will only be for a few minutes; she's going to explain what we will be doing; they should face her. 'There are a lot of us in the room today', she says, 'only Delia is away, so we need to be careful. Someone in the class has told me there are lots of coats and bags flung down. I'd like to think it isn't anybody in here – you could go and hang them up before I look. If it is from next door, I could tell Mrs Stevens so she could talk to her class' . . . She continues: 'We're doing something new today. The words on the board are called a letter string. What do they have in common? [They all have 'ar' in them.] Feel your chins, say "ahr".' There are ten words written on the board. Rosalind says, 'When I've finished talking, this is what you're going to do.' She tells them to take their handwriting books, fold a page in half and write each word. 'Look at the word, then cover it up, write it again. You see it in your memory. If you forget, it doesn't matter, go back to it again.' She says we are going to do this each Monday and explains that they should aim to do better each week, saying this is not a test but competing against yourself. On the board it says 'LOOK, COVER, WRITE, CHECK'. Rosalind has a book on her desk that explains this method and has been on a course where the idea was suggested. Before they start, she reminds them again about the fallen coats, and about twelve children go out to hang up the coats. (Later they are on the floor again; the games bags are too heavy for the pegs.) The children begin the work; most have not understood exactly what to do. Most are copying LOOK, COVER, WRITE, CHECK instead of the spelling words into their first column; others are writing across, or on more than one column. We move around and help. (11 March 1988)

Snapshot no. 3

I come into Sheila Jones's room at 1.30 p.m. The children in SJ are reading. I go round the middle table hearing the boys read . . . Things on the board are about the life-cycle of the butterfly. Sheila gets their attention and says she wants them to do pencil drawings of nature: butterflies, or snails or similar. There are some books of pictures. The drawings can go into their folders either under nature or animals. When Sheila is giving instructions about drawing butterflies, she shows how it's not just the usual form but they need to note that there are three parts of the body; the wings come out of the main section . . . Some children go on to the computer with Rosalind. Rosalind helps Ronald . . . and integrates him with the group. A few children are painting. Tim is finishing off a beautiful painting of a wildflower . . . A small group is drawing and painting driftwood. (17 March 1988)

Snapshot no. 4

At 9.00 a.m. I go to SJ. Sheila is there. Children are reading, or moving around talking . . . At 9.30, Sheila says, 'Could you close your reading books . . . turn your chairs right round.' She gets the children to talk about what they did during the holiday. Discussion seems quite amiable and participatory. 'I am going to do what I often ask you to do', she says, 'write about your holiday. If you don't want to, write about something else.' She says to Patrick, a new child in class, 'As I don't know anything about you, if you want to write about yourself, who you live with, etc., you could do that.' (I notice later he writes about his holiday.) To the class: 'If you don't want to write about your holiday, I'll leave the choice up to you. It will go into your folder, so make it neat, you won't copy it again. I expect most of you will write with full stops and capitals . . . I don't expect reams but I will not accept just a few lines from most of you. Most of you are capable of writing a side or two. I don't want any poems today; write a story if not about a holiday.' There are various questions from the children, asking if they can write a story or a diary. Yes, Sheila says, or a letter. 'Right . . . pencils. Mrs Clarke has given us some because she felt sorry for you' (said with a smile). 'You are all entitled to one until half-term. Some are not very good quality, so if yours keeps breaking I'll see what I can do. I'll collect them in and put names on them later. If you prefer, you can use one from home; that's OK.' (She passes them out.) 'Put your name, and the date, and a title – if you can't think of a title add it later.' In response to a query, she says, 'You can write anything at all, it doesn't have to be about your holiday.' (Choruses of 'Ohhh'; they've finally caught on.) The date and 'My Easter holiday' are on the board.

The children work quietly. Sheila talks to some of them. Even when the children are absolutely quiet, the noise outside from the programme and children in the TV room is very intrusive. Sheila ends up at her desk. I help some children and some come to her for spellings or ideas. They are still working when it is time for assembly. [After assembly and playtime] the children carry on, or go on to the mathematics scheme. There is a queue at Sheila's desk. Some are there with questions about maths, others to show her their stories or accounts of holidays. She talks with them about what they've done. She asks for a few who haven't come up of their own accord. Mrs Clarke comes through at 11.30, on 'tour' with a prospective parent.

[Later] at 2.15 or so, I discover Sheila's class has gone outdoors. They have clipboards and paper and their pencils and are sketching school or other scenes. The sun is coming and going and it is very pleasant. Some children are worried about making mistakes, not having rubbers [erasers]. Some are very sketchy, others take enormous trouble over details. There is great variation in the product, not entirely correlated with effort. Sheila is also doing a sketch. The children spread out into groups and pairs. Jason and Patrick (the new child) are together; I hear Jason explaining who all the children in Mr Bryan's class are to Patrick when that class comes outside to play cricket. Some of the children watch the game. Many of them go back into the school with Sheila, but about eight stay out, some drawing, some watching, some doing both. (12 April 1988)

We can notice a number of things from these field note extracts. They are all normal, uneventful days in the life of Hillview. During the day, a class changes activities from time to time, and may be engaged in more than one activity at a time, as in Snapshot 3. Typically, the teacher explains what work is wanted, the children ask questions and then work as individuals while the teacher (and the researcher!) move around helping children. A list of activities is often on the blackboard. The teacher may also sit at the desk and children come to her. The children sit at tables and often talk to each other while working. As others have noted, there is a lot going on at one time in the typical primary school classroom (Jackson, 1968; Wragg, 1993). Making this point, Andy Hargreaves (1994) calls the elementary school teacher's world (meaning the classroom) 'profoundly polychronic' (p. 104).

The tone of the instructions is usually relaxed and often reassuring. Note that in Snapshot 1, Debbie explains that the children are not to worry if they can not do the problems because the purpose is for the teachers to know how much the children know; if they don't understand it, it will be explained. In the second snapshot, Rosalind says 'If you forget, it doesn't matter, go back to it again' and explains they are not being tested. Sometimes, the interaction contains joking remarks or banter and there is a camaraderie between teacher and class. In an account of 'first encounters' in the school year, Wragg (1993, p. 48) notes that the tone of voice used by primary teachers was firm but gentle, with little or no use of the public shaming, dominance or aggression observed in secondary school lessons.

The snapshot extracts show that the process of giving and following directions is not always straightforward. Apart from the work itself, there are a number of conventions to be followed, such as writing one's name on the page, dating or titling the work, using a particular notebook, deciding how many items to put on a page, and so forth. The teachers try to make these understandings explicit. Along with expressions of the school ethos and the teacher's values (e.g. the reassurances that work is not competitive or a test; the encouragement to hang up coats and bags), these messages become part of what children learn in school.

In general, the children were cooperative and there was a buzz of activity. In every group, there were always some children who put in little effort or did not do the work at all. Some children were frequently in this mode, others from time to time. The large ability span in each group was one reason for this situation. In SP, for example, in addition to Peter (see below), two other boys could not do the regular work at all; one of these children was tiny and could have been taken for a 5-year-old. Four or five others were seriously below average in their ability to read or do other schoolwork. There were also children at the top end of the ability spectrum. Alexander (1995) notes that with a large group of children:

> [T]he achievement of a lasting communal or group balance between skills and challenges is virtually impossible; there will always be some who are bored because they are marking time and others who are anxious or alienated because they are struggling to keep up. (p. 163)

In the face of this dilemma, one strategy teachers use is to present material to the class and then have the children work individually while the teacher moves round adapting the task as necessary or giving further explanation (Gipps, 1994, p. 35). Hillview teachers tended to plan activities where children could work as individuals. Sometimes the teacher could work more closely with a small group while others kept busy. There were limits to this strategy. Kristin King commented to me: 'People like Leonie need so much help it's impossible to keep them all going at once.' Children with very short attention spans would lose interest quickly, especially when the work seemed hard or did not appeal for some other reason. And, like adults, children had moods and off-days.

For such reasons, it was understood that some negotiation around 'doing work' was possible. In Snapshot 4, we see that the children are given alternatives when Sheila reiterates that if they don't want to write about their Easter holidays, they can write something else; and that they can write a story, diary or letter as well as straight description. When the children go outside to sketch, there are no restrictions on what they can draw, and those who wish to stay out longer, or watch the cricket game, are not stopped. On another occasion, SJ did handwriting, copying a poem from the blackboard:

> Sheila says to Dale: 'Dale, come and do your handwriting now.'
> 'I don't want to do handwriting.' 'Well, it's got to be done this morning.' A few minutes later, Dale proposes 'Miss, can I do my maths instead?' 'Well, if you work hard.' I think Sheila is implying he could do the handwriting afterwards.

Negotiation did not necessarily mean a victory for the child. In class SP, Billy, Perry and Leila wanted to do a play. Rosalind discouraged them, saying there was not enough space, they were in the room designated for quiet work, other spaces were already being used, and they should work on something related to the zoo project now. The teachers tried to emphasize that 'manners' were not negotiable: Rosalind told SP 'I'm not going to read while people are talking because that is extreme bad manners', and a few months later Debbie said to the same group 'There is no excuse for bad behaviour and bad manners. It's all right to have jokes now and then, but you have got to know where the limit is.'

THE CLASS TEACHER SYSTEM

Several consequences flow from what has been dubbed the class teacher system: 'one teacher for all or most of the child's schooling for a period of one year and often for longer' (Alexander, 1984). At the start of my study, primary school teachers in the local education authority (LEA) of my research and in much of England had no 'non-contact' [preparation] time apart from breaks and lunch-times. Any subject specialist teaching had to be devised within the constraints of the class teacher system. If teachers had responsibilities for particular subjects or other activities (visits; special needs; display), this meant they would keep on top of developments in the subject, order and catalogue school equipment, advise other teachers, and so forth. No teacher in my study exclusively taught art, music, drama or games. Every full-time teacher, including the deputy head, had a class responsibility. Individual teachers, especially part-timers, might be deployed or released to work with small groups or other classes in these and other specialist areas, though: for example, Kristin King for pottery; Rosalind Phillips for drama and special needs; Debbie Stevens for special needs. The class teacher system has a basic assumption that all teachers can and will cover the entire curriculum.

It was obvious that some teachers had special talents or interests, or conversely were less confident in certain areas. For example, not all teachers could read music. Areas of the curriculum might also be covered by regular watching of educational television programmes with follow-up classroom activities. The middle junior classes watched programmes on science and on music as well as another programme for the younger group that reinforced reading and language use. Music was also handled in other ways, such as singing in assembly or in concerts led by Helen Davies, recorder lessons by Betty Chaplin, and guitar and violin lessons for selected children by teachers who came into the school once a week.

Generally, there was a mixture of subject-based and integrated teaching. Mathematics was the subject most likely to be taught in isolation, and room was made for it virtually every day. Reading and English language activities were also clearly identifiable. History and geography tended to be merged into project work, which could also include elements of art, language and science. Although there were LEA guidelines and school policies on some curriculum areas, most of the responsibility rested with individual teachers. Time at staff meetings would be spent in discussing continuity and progression and teachers would consult with others taking different age groups, in efforts to avoid repetition (e.g. of units on the Vikings). Staff meetings would also be devoted to particular topics such as handwriting. A mathematics scheme in use throughout the school allowed individual children to progress (or not) without necessary reference to a class standard.

My sense was that each teacher went through an informal process of diagnosing her children's understanding, and designed activities accordingly. For example, a teacher might realize that many of the children could not tell the time and then find or invent activities to fill in this gap. Teachers also got ideas through reading magazines on children's education, through educational television programmes, and through inservice training courses. Each teacher had a repertoire of ideas and activities, which extended as the years went on. For many this repertoire took concrete form as a box or other collection of activities, handouts, articles and other materials. Even supply teachers had portable versions of such boxes. It was said that when American teachers visited, they always asked 'where's the textbook', to the amusement of the staff.

While highly creative, this improvised curriculum could also be haphazard. The educational rationale for the introduction of the National Curriculum as part of the government's reform package of 1988 was the argument that it would be better to standardize the curriculum and give guidelines as to what children should be expected to accomplish at different stages. Researchers have found that many primary school teachers have praised, or at least accepted, the merits of this structured approach, although it has been said to replace spontaneity and individual creativity with prescription; intensify teachers' work and increase their workload; and be more difficult to implement in schools with special needs children or inner-city type problems (Campbell and Neill, 1994; Pollard et al., 1994; Woods, 1995).

The class teacher system is also sometimes regarded as responsible for the mother-like intense attachments and dedication primary school teachers show for their classes (McPherson, 1972; Kidder, 1989). Teachers spend long hours with 'their' children, often in relative isolation from other adults, in their classroom equivalents of mothers' kitchens (Grumet, 1988, p. 85), in 'enforced intimacy' (Beynon and Atkinson, 1984, p. 256). McPherson (1972) explains:

> Associating with a group of children continually and with her peers only occasionally, identifying her interest more and more with these

children and standing with them against the world, she began to think and act as her pupils did ... So Mrs Gregory fought for a playground field as if she were ten, not fifty-five. Mrs Cornhouse and Miss Tuttle regaled the other teachers with first graders' jokes. (p. 119)

We can also see parallels to what Griffith and D.E. Smith (1991) call the 'mothering discourse', the expectation that mothers (teachers) will love, care and sacrifice the self. Chapter 7 will explore this imagery and its consequences in more detail. Hillview teachers identified with their classes. Liz Clarke explained to me that for a teacher, having 'her own class' is the special characteristic of primary teaching, in contrast to secondary teaching. There were regular references to 'your children' and 'my children', meaning the children in a particular teacher's class.

Teachers valued their relationships with children. They felt guilty when they found a child difficult to like or when things went wrong. Rosalind Phillips worried about her feelings towards one of the children: 'I know it's wrong to dislike a child but I feel very negative about him – he's deceitful.' Marjorie Howard talked about her problems with a child in her class: 'I lost my temper with Ned, I was shouting and shouting ... then lay awake thinking it must be my handling of him, how can I do it differently?'

Although the bonding of teacher and class was clearly evident, the Hillview teachers did not experience the extreme isolation from other adults that McPherson and others see as responsible for the phenomenon. Perhaps the amount of time Hillview's teachers and children experienced together, and the sense of responsibility teachers carried for their class, were sufficient for identification without the extra burden of isolation. When something went wrong with the bonding, it was distressing for individual teachers and for their colleagues. The next section shows how fragile the negotiated order might be.

THE FRAGILE ORDER

The snapshots presented earlier in this chapter were all successful examples of what, following a common approach within symbolic interactionist sociology of education, could be termed a negotiated order or truce or working consensus (Delamont, 1983; Denscombe, 1985; Pollard, 1985; Woods, 1983, 1990). These writers see teachers as developing strategies and making implicit bargains so that the teachers' decisions and desires are given legitimacy and priority and social life in the school and classroom can proceed routinely. Some writers suggest that such bargains can result in downgrading teachers' expectations, especially when teachers are trying to motivate pupils by encouraging them to choose what they will learn

(Alexander, 1995). Pupils, too, have strategies (Pollard, 1985) and they try to avoid high-risk situations such as being questioned publicly or asked to do difficult work (Gipps, 1994). Teachers learn through experience how to act like a teacher, developing skills such as 'omniscience' and 'orchestration' (Woods, 1990). King (1978) describes ways in which successful infant teachers stood, spoke, looked round the class. He also notes their 'professional equanimity' – staying remarkably calm – in the face of things going wrong (pp. 71–2). His description parallels what I saw at Hillview.

By and large, Hillview teachers and children cooperated and activity took place. Yet the order could be easily disrupted. On occasions when I was left in charge of a class for ten or fifteen minutes due to some emergency, I could feel the discipline rapidly disintegrating (see the Appendix for further discussion of such events). The presence of a supply teacher, a teacher who was on a short-term contract or a student teacher could produce problems, although this consequence was by no means inevitable. Here are some notes from a middle junior session taught by Della Monk, a regular supply teacher in the school:

> Della is trying to get the middle group settled . . . There is an animated class discussion based on a science programme. But Dale and Ian are on their own agenda, blowing pencils across the table, putting their feet up, pushing the table away. Work starts. Dale and Martha have a dispute over a ruler. Della tries to sort it out, gives it to Martha to use. A few minutes later, when Della has her back turned working with another group, Dale grabs back the ruler. It breaks. Then he grabs Martha's pencil case to get something of hers to break. Martha looks at me for help so I get Della who sorts it out. Later Dale is putting plasticine on someone's chair, I notice.

Disruptive or disturbed children in a class create difficulties for experienced teachers, too (Abbott, 1996). Dale was one such child in SJ. The following extract shows the uneasy atmosphere that could arise:

> In SJ, I spent quite a lot of the time with a group of girls who were sitting on the far side, near the art area, mostly doing maths. I also helped Tamsin in the other room. I spoke to a couple of kids from Rosalind's class who were painting pictures of the knight from *Dark Towers* (television programme). Dale hovered all the time. He didn't seem to know what he was supposed to be doing but he wandered around annoying people. Most were ignoring him. He played with a plastic figure around the ceramic pots as if the figure were climbing. He seemed unable to settle and Debbie appeared to be ignoring him, was busy with others in the other room . . . At one point he threw a

pillow but it didn't go near anyone. I put it back. A couple of times I reprimanded him mildly and once gestured to Debbie who came over and settled him down at a table. Even when the girls were working pretty well, there was a lot of chat.

The impact of a child I call Peter on the ecology of SP was an extreme example of challenging the negotiated order. Peter was first mentioned in December 1987, when it was rumoured that a 9-year-old child with a fearsome reputation might be transferred to Hillview. 'He's rude, obnoxious and violent', a teacher had heard. 'His mother was crying in the staffroom, saying he needs psychiatric help. Charlotte [the educational psychologist] recommended us.' At the end of January my notes say:

> Teachers are agitated because the troubled boy may now be coming here. Liz has apparently told the teachers she can't say no. No one seems to know why. 'We are the social work school for the area', one teacher comments rather bitterly.

Peter indeed proved to be seriously disruptive and very disturbed, lacking in self-esteem, unable to work without one-to-one attention. My notes for a period of several months are full of 'Peter'. The teachers were distressed; the educational psychologist in and out; staffroom discussion featured his exploits for days on end. The head or secretary sometimes took him into the office for a spell when teachers could no longer cope. Liz Clarke had to engage in a considerable amount of careful talking over the two terms, with Peter's mother, the support services, the teachers, Peter himself and the other children. Professional equanimity was certainly at risk.

The following field notes show the problems of moving outside the school (in this case for swimming) with Peter, and the involvement of teachers beyond the classroom teacher.

> I go along on the bus at 9.15 with Debbie Stevens to swimming with SP . . . Mrs Green's group [first year juniors] arrives at 10.00. A problem arises when it is discovered Peter hasn't got changed. Nancy Green said to him (not without humour) she'd have to get him changed on the poolside if he didn't move. He went on and on about what crap these changing rooms are, and when Nancy made her 'threat' he said if she did he'd kill her. Debbie tells him they're not responsible for the changing rooms, that's the County Council. He talks about writing to Mrs Thatcher. She says she hopes he will so he can do some writing. Nancy brings SP back on the coach and Debbie brings Nancy's group back. On the coach ride back, Debbie records the incident in her notebook [a record is being kept of what happens with Peter].
> Back in the classroom for the last hour of the morning.

Debbie looks around, quietly calls up eight or so children, one at a time, saying will you please come to my desk. The class gets very quiet, wonder what's going on. She takes them out into the TV room. She is giving them each a spoken part, connected with a radio programme, to rehearse. It's quiet in the classroom but Peter starts up a bit – mackerel mouth, wimp this and that. Billy says shut up; he's obviously trying to concentrate. Cripple guts, Peter says. Darren goes by and gets pushed; a few minutes later he pushes Peter. I can feel the temperature rising and signal to Debbie who comes back in . . .

I come back to SP around 2 p.m . . . I hear Peter saying to Debbie that he can't draw people. She suggests he draw matchstick people. He says to me that what he doesn't like about Mrs Stevens is she doesn't know what people can and can't do; she wants them to do things they can't. He goes up several times and looks at the board with the instructions for the activity, but then puts big crosses all over his page saying 'I won't do it'. He starts to say things about Debbie. She is at her desk trying to hear people read. Annie is standing, waiting to read to Debbie. Peter says something with 'bloody' loudly. She can't ignore it and tells him not to swear. He gets angry and starts to say she is stupid. She takes him out of the class, saying 'come outside with me'. So I find myself left with the rest of the class, who have been taking it all in, for about fifteen minutes. I hear Annie read. Peter and Debbie come back and Peter plays with Lego.

I chat briefly with Mrs Clarke, who is very serious. She is trying to arrange for someone to come in to work with Peter for five hours a week. It upsets her to see teachers under this pressure. 'He'll be with us at least until the end of the term, probably until the summer', she says.

When I go back upstairs, Debbie tells me that Peter hit Billy, and Billy was crying, though he wouldn't say what happened, and others, like Robert, at the table, their eyes were filling. She wrote a note to Mrs Clarke, and was writing everything into her book. It seems he called her a witch, said he hated her, hated the school, thought he was worthless, never going to have a job, hated Mrs Thatcher and the government . . . I feel very upset – upset because Debbie was under such pressure and because this child has had such a terrible time in his life.

Peter failed to honour all the tacit conventions of teacher–pupil inter-action. He went beyond what even the naughtiest child had dreamt of in terms of abuse to the teachers and often total refusal to do any work. The other children in class SP, at first fascinated and rather admiring at his daring, had to come to terms with him as an exception, and with the double standards his behaviour required the teachers openly to operate. Other children were supposed to put down pencils and listen if a teacher wanted to talk to the whole class – while Peter carried on drawing or playing with construction toys. A few days after his arrival, Debbie Stevens spoke seriously to the class in his absence about how they should behave to help Peter learn 'our ways'. They seemed to understand. About a month later the head teacher had a similar talk with the whole school. As we have seen in descriptions of school ethos and classroom snapshots, the standard Peter was unable to comply with was not unduly authoritarian or rigid. As shown above, Peter's presence did disturb the other children; however, it was also thought that they learned a lesson about supporting and caring for others, and that the group itself developed more of a bond through the experience. It was harder to see what the gains were for the teachers.

Peter's story was resolved, as far as the school was concerned, by his pending transfer to a small special boarding school. Some success could also be claimed for the school in the other children's reactions and the fact that what seemed the right provision for Peter had been found, which Liz believed would never have happened if he had stayed in his previous primary school.[1]

CONCLUSION

As Abbott (1996, p. 118) points out, there is no simple formula that solves teachers' classroom dilemmas; 'something' too often intervenes between planning and execution that thwarts teachers' hopes for effective teaching and learning (p. 102). Negotiating and maintaining a working consensus with a group that may contain over 30 children is a major occupational challenge. The teacher is concerned that the children learn skills, content knowledge, problem-solving, values and routine practices that ensure some predictability and order. Her task is made more difficult by factors such as cramped classrooms, insufficient resources, and a large ability range within a classroom group. Typically, she is trying to plan around individual needs as well as classroom order. In the pre-National Curriculum era, she was also responsible (together with colleagues) for creating the curriculum. With the class teacher system she needs to be at least minimally competent across the subject spectrum, although help from others mitigates somewhat the effects of these expectations. The classroom order can be fragile. The appearance of Peter in Hillview's Middle Junior Unit made more transparent than usual teachers' efforts to negotiate, both with Peter and with the rest of his class.

Our abiding cultural image is of the teacher in her classroom, not on playground duty or drinking coffee in the staffroom or on the coach to games. In this chapter, I have deliberately stayed mostly within the classroom boundaries. But important as this venue is, it does not tell the whole story of being a teacher. The next chapter goes beyond the classroom walls in order to flesh out our portrait of teachers' work.

NOTE

1. It should be noted that Peter's story, like other elements of this book, appears from the perspective of the teacher, as interpreted by the researcher. A view from Peter's perspective, or within a disability framework, might read very differently.

Chapter 5

Beyond the Classroom

Although the classroom snapshots in Chapter 4 were typical of middle junior classrooms at Hillview, the picture is limited in several important ways. There are variations from classroom to classroom according to the age of children and the teaching style. Teachers move between groups, or groups are divided up. What goes on in and out of the classroom changes according to day of the week or time of year. Daily activity extends beyond the classroom walls and sometimes outside the school. The teachers' day starts before 9 a.m. and continues well past 3.30 p.m.

AGE VARIATIONS

Looking back at the snapshots of classes SJ and SP in Chapter 4, it may be evident that SJ is an older group than SP, and better versed in the practices of writing on the correct page and so forth; yet even they found it hard to follow Sheila's directions about writing about their holidays. If we were to look at the younger classes, we would see still more effort is necessary to instruct the children on these conventions. We would also see more play, more movement, and quiet periods where the children sit on the floor in a carpeted area in the classroom, perhaps listening to a story. In Chapter 1, we viewed Marjorie Howard's dramatic and playful style of interaction with the reception class. Another technique sometimes used, especially with younger children, was 'choosing', when a number of different activities are set up and children move around among them. Rosalind Phillips also used this approach with SP. Conversely, for the older children, there is less need for repeating instructions and more self-direction and self-pacing. Thus the children in Dennis Bryan's class typically had a series of assignments, some short and some that would take a number of days to complete. They had some control over the order in which they worked on these projects or tasks.

The interviews made it clear that those who taught younger children tended to leave more room for changes of plan. Helen Davies, for example, who taught 7-year-olds, would be more likely to plan from day to day than a week at a time: 'The night before, I will work out which group needs [what] . . . so I will prepare sheets for that group. The groups vary . . . they will vary according to who needs what particular instruction.' Helen added that she might change the plan according to events that arise: 'Like this morning, if I had been in here, there was snow and ice and things, so that would have been something that the children would have brought with them into their day and I would have been going with that.' Similarly, Marjorie stated: 'I have a sort of structure to the day, because the kids know where they are and I know where I am, but at the same time, I can adapt it and change it around if I want to, or I'll change it within the pattern.' Marjorie, like other teachers, made a plan at home for what she expected to happen. She explained that with reception, you never knew who was going to be in and who was not. She would make a weekly plan but with general topics like 'counting to 4' or 'the sound of "p"'. Then she would write out details for one day at a time. Each night she would make a note of who had been absent that day, so that she could do the work with them at another time. My field notes include an example of how Marjorie would take advantage of a serendipitous opportunity with her 5-year-olds:

> Mrs Howard seems pleased to see me and starts to explain what they've been doing. The school had a delivery of builders' sand, 10 bags. She put them into different arrangements of 10 ones, 2 fives, 5 twos, and the children counted. She used 's's' and 'sh's', e.g. 'shape of shells in the sand'. She showed them the effect of water, i.e. erosion. They noticed there were two kinds of sand, washed and unwashed; it had little shells in it, etc. They compared the two kinds, looked at light and dark, decided on the colour, looked under the magnifying glass. It was science, geography, maths, language, she said. Marjorie is excited. I asked if the lesson was planned. 'I knew we were going to get the delivery and thought about it, but didn't know exactly when it was coming.'

DIVIDE AND EXCHANGE

Other variations involved teachers collaborating in various ways. In Chapter 1, I mentioned the language morning where once a week, infant children and younger juniors were divided up according to level of progress and placed with a teacher or helper in small groups. The Middle Junior Unit, from which the classroom snapshots in Chapter 5 were taken, displayed an alternative pattern. One full-time teacher and three part-time teachers were assigned to about 50 children (a number that grew nearer 60 over the year).

Quite quickly, a conventional pattern of two classrooms reasserted itself. The children were divided according to age into two registration groups, each with a classroom. The full-time teacher, Debbie Stevens, spent half her time with each group. Sheila Jones worked almost entirely with the older group and Rosalind Phillips with the younger group. The third part-time teacher, Kristin King, could be deployed more flexibly, for example taking out smaller groups for pottery. Occasionally both registration groups would be together for an activity, although classroom size limited the potential for such work. For a time, the teachers tried an operation similar to language morning, whereby children were for several sessions in the week divided into three groups according to general progress and levels of achievement. One teacher worked with each group. This strategy was reasonably successful for the high achievers and the teacher who worked with them (Sheila Jones), as the children could be stretched and challenged by the activities she designed, and for the low achievers who got a certain amount of individual attention and carefully chosen material from Debbie Stevens. But it was not successful for the large middle group, for several reasons, among them the illness of Kristin King and her replacement for a term by a supply teacher, Della Monk. Art, games and science were also handled with children in groups and several teachers involved beyond those in the Unit.

Moving teachers around for these purposes was contingent on alternative ways to handle their own classes, for example the head teacher taking the groups on a regular basis for a story or other input, or classes going to the swimming pool or skating rink without one of their regular teachers. These exchanges were common. The school made whatever use it could of parents, other volunteers, persons assigned to the school as part of a youth training scheme or nursery nurse training, part-time teachers, student teachers, and occasional extra help from the local education authority for children with special needs.

THE WEEK AND THE YEAR

Teaching has a public image as work with short hours and long holidays. We might surmise that with the publicity surrounding teachers' responses to the National Curriculum and other imposed reforms in Britain, this image has faded. Researchers have known for some time about its inaccuracy. Hilsum and Cane (1971) studied 129 junior school teachers' use of time in one English county through systematic classroom observation and teacher diaries. Adding together time spent in teaching sessions and in professional work during breaks, lunch-times, and after school hours, they calculated that the average working day was 8¼ hours; the week, 41¼ hours (p. 89). They noted that just under 60 per cent of that time was spent in direct class contact, about 15 per cent in school doing other tasks, and 25 per cent outside school hours (p. 91). More recently, Campbell and Neill (1994) conducted studies with a total of 326 primary school teachers in order to see whether time demands had increased. Teachers filled in a pre-prepared record form. The 1991 figure for total hours worked per week was 53.6 hours, a substantial increase over the hours reported by Hilsum and Cane (Campbell and Neill, 1994, p. 44). When asked what they thought a reasonable work week would be, the teachers in the Campbell and Neill study gave an average of around 42 hours (p. 46). Campbell and Neill found that about 45 per cent of teachers' time was spent in direct pupil contact, a dramatic drop from the corresponding Hilsum and Cane percentage. Yet the absolute teaching time was similar; it was the time spent on activities such as preparation and professional development (including staff meetings) that had soared (Campbell and Neill, 1994, pp. 51–3).

Perhaps more interesting than the precise number of hours worked is the phenomenological side of time for teachers: what do they think about it, how do they control it, how does it contribute to their sense of self? Ball, Hull, Skelton and Tudor (1984) point out the importance of the 'social calendar of temporal arrangements – the school day, the school week and the school year' (p. 56) in forming the subjective meaning of teachers' work. 'Time' as a feature of school life in this sense has intrigued a few writers (Ball *et al.*, 1984; Clandinin and Connelly, 1986; Connelly and Clandinin, 1990, 1993; A. Hargreaves, 1994). Researchers' typical emphasis on classroom observation can obscure weekly or annual patterns and cycles. Connelly and Clandinin (1990) identify ten main school cycles observed in their research, which they name 'annual, holiday, monthly, weekly, six-day, duty, day, teacher, report, and within-class cycles' (p. 45).

When, in interview, I asked teachers to describe a typical day or a typical week, the first response was often laughter and a denial of the possibility of typicality: 'Well I would think at Hillview it's difficult to say anything about a typical week [laughter]' (Nancy Green). 'One week is never the same as the next – what is routine?' (Sheila Jones). Teachers would proceed to outline their week, day by day, often breaking into the account to add something that had been initially forgotten about a different day. These answers are lengthy and often confusing. I will give just one of the shorter examples from Nancy Green who taught a class of 8-year-olds (first-year juniors):

> Monday morning, normally, we join the infants and we have language morning, so, that's our start to the week. Children go off to various teachers and I get a few extra from Helen and on Monday afternoon we tend perhaps to do some sort of topic work or art craft work. Tuesday we split up because of swimming . . . What makes up Wednesday? Well I've got hall time on

Wednesday morning . . . sometimes it doesn't get used, but if I can I do. And I tend, because we've got some children who are particularly keen then to do things like their maths in a concentrated time, usually on a Wednesday morning we've actually done that, but this week is different yet again. . . . if it was a morning like today, which took 40 minutes to sort out what money had come in and well it's a Wednesday morning, it's a Wednesday morning with skating and things, and obviously two different lots of money for the fare coming in today, plus there are still some children who haven't paid for the zoo and all this sort of thing. Wednesday afternoon we usually watch *Zig Zag*, so that follows up with a topic activity and Thursday after play in the morning I've got another hall time. And so it goes through Friday. Friday, again, I think tends to be a mixture of the things that we haven't managed to get through in a week, because sometimes it can get to the end of the week, and you think 'aaahh' you haven't done any maths. We haven't really thought very much about perhaps a topic or language in some way, so Friday tends to be a catching up day, plus the fact that now, Friday afternoon we've got games and I find that quite a drastic end to the end of the week.

I asked whether there would be set times for subjects like mathematics or language:

Well, really apart from Monday morning and as I say, usually on a Wednesday morning, I wouldn't say there was definitely a specific time. It might be that those things were going on at the same time.

The teacher's week had to be planned within certain parameters that were schoolwide or depended on other teachers. Swimming, games, skating, language mornings took place on particular days. Teachers had access to the hall or to the television, or help from a general assistant or other adult according to a schedule. Assembly, playtime and lunch-time punctuated each day predictably. Superimposed across these routines might be rehearsals for a particular event, or visits outside school, or schoolwide projects. Certain daily tasks, such as taking the register and collecting money, had to be accomplished. Otherwise, teachers were free to organize their day as they saw fit. Often they used rules of thumb, such as the morning for harder work, the afternoon for topics; or early in the week for concentrated work, later for catching up or art. Although there was some timetabling by subject, for example 'language morning', times that each class could use the hall for PE or drama, and schedules for skating, swimming and games (which required going outside the school), there was no equivalent to

Connelly and Clandinin's (1990) 'six-day cycle' where the five-day week gives way to an artificial week with an even number of days, in order to have a sequencing of subject matter that gives a pre-planned amount of time to various subjects. Some of my local high schools have a 'Day 1, Day 2' timetable that accomplishes the same objective.

At Hillview, there were three terms in the school year. Each term was about fourteen weeks long and divided by a week's holiday called 'half-term'. The school year began in early September and did not finish until late July. Observations at the start of the autumn term show more efforts to establish rules and set up the negotiated order. The first weeks were stressful times for the teachers. 'Beginning of term madness', Debbie Stevens dubbed the first few weeks of the year. 'I hate the beginning of term', Helen Davies remarked, 'all new children.' Researchers are often kept away at this time of year (Wragg, 1993, p. 37). It was not until my second full year of observations that all teachers felt comfortable with my presence in those weeks.

> I ask Marjorie how the little ones are doing and unleash a torrent of troubles, though told with humour. One child has cried through assembly, saying 'I want my mummy and assembly's too long'. The children aren't used to control, she says. Three are very naughty – not their fault – and two are way ahead. 'I had to have two homemade sloe wines though I don't drink.'

A contrast was Debbie's experience at the beginning of September 1988. The Middle Junior Unit had become the Older Junior Unit, and Debbie benefited from having worked in the previous year with all but a few new children. My notes say, 'For Debbie, it's like being with old friends after the summer holiday.' Her relaxed style was evident in a class discussion, when she pointed out to the group (the former class SP) that they were lucky to have three new children in the class (including a brother and sister from another country who spoke little English), and then asked the other children each to say one sentence about Hillview to the new children. 'Only nice things', she said, then laughed – 'or justify it.'

At particular times of the year, all routines would take second place to seasonal events: celebrating harvest festival in September; rehearsing for a Christmas concert in December; participating in sports and swimming events in July. Towards the end of the school year, the pace of such events seemed to intensify, as activities such as the school fair, a musical event, sports day or the swimming gala went by in quick succession. Usually the school did a collective project based on an excursion, such as the trip to the zoo, in this term, with follow-up work in each class. Around this time, the children were restless, the weather was hot, and the teachers showed signs of fatigue. 'They've worn me down', said Helen Davies one day in July. 'I've never felt so tired as I have this year.'

Marjorie Howard found particularly disturbing a visit at the end of the school year of the new children who were to start school in her reception class the next September. They were so young (some not yet four), so undisciplined, that she felt herself going backwards in time, starting again some endless, repetitive task.

IN AND OUT OF THE CLASSROOM

Time in the classroom did not fill the entire school day. The school day began at 9.00 a.m. The morning was broken into two segments by the assembly at 10.15 a.m., followed by playtime and at the same time, the teachers' coffee break. Two teachers would be on playground duty during the break. The assembly and playtime together took up about 40 minutes, leaving another hour or so before dinner [lunch]. The teachers were not required to be on duty during the lunch period – this task fell to the 'dinner ladies' who came into school for a short time in the middle of the day for this work – but there was an understanding that if they chose to take lunch with the children (as several did, at least during the early part of my research), they could not avoid sharing some responsibility for supervision. The deputy head and head teacher were also on call during this period, which ran from 12.00 noon to 1.30 p.m. Children played in the playground for part of this time, supervised by dinner ladies. Rainy days meant the children had to stay in the classrooms. The afternoon session did not have a formal break time at Hillview, although many schools do schedule such a break (Mortimore *et al.*, 1988). School ended at 3.30 p.m.

Playground duty can be a fairly unpleasant activity for teachers. Hillview teachers tried to help each other by bringing out cups of coffee or treats, and sometimes replacing each other so that the teacher on duty could get warm when the days were cold. I found the 'infant playground' a rather disturbing place where the aggressive side of some children flourished, while others took evasive action:

> I stay with Debbie; she's on duty in the infants playground. It's freezing and starting to rain. We get brought coffee. Most of the children have coats on. Some have wellies [galoshes] and keep going in the puddles. Many without wellies also go in the puddles. It takes lots of energy to stop them and keep them away from the roped-off play equipment which seems to act like a magnet. Constantly children come up to say someone is hitting someone else or that something like chasing is going on in the toilets [an outdoor block]. Two shy girls stay close to me, Leila

from Mrs Chaplin and Polly, new in Mrs Davies's class. I ask Polly if she has new friends, she says no. A few others come over from time to time to cuddle up too. The noise and danger of the playground is too much for them perhaps. It's too much for me, anyway.

Playgrounds are thought to be places where child culture flourishes. Much of this world is outside the boundaries of the negotiated truce and teachers do not fully enter it (Best, 1983; B. Davies, 1982; Pollard, 1985; Sussmann, 1977). King (1978) comments that 'for some teachers playtime was an awful warning of what might happen if they did not exercise control in the classroom' (p. 23).

Moving out of the classroom was necessary for assembly, dinner-time and breaks, but also occurred for other reasons. Where space was available, small groups or individuals would move around to find a quiet nook or table. The middle juniors had easy access to the cookery room, the TV lounge and extra classroom space, so that children spread out when possible, although they were never far from the teacher. Small groups or individuals might be withdrawn for remedial help or pottery or violin lessons. Watching a television programme generally meant a move for the whole class. PE, drama or concert rehearsals required use of the hall, the church or outdoors. Swimming, skating and games were regular excursions outside school for juniors. Classes might take a walk, perhaps following a nature trail at a nearby park, or visiting a historical site in the city. Smaller groups might be involved in a rehearsal for a city-wide concert, a sports event, a visit to the secondary school and so forth. A more elaborate visit by coach to a site in another part of the city or in the country might be arranged from time to time. The curriculum was thought to consist of a range of experiences beyond simply subjects.

As indicated in Chapter 3, games, and to a lesser extent swimming, were stressful for the teachers. The juniors went once a week in coaches to a playing field about fifteen minutes' ride away. Organizational matters might go wrong, and frequently did, for example when a coach failed to turn up. Discipline was more difficult away from school. One Friday evening, Debbie Stevens told me over the telephone about her 'horrendous afternoon':

> Nancy and Rosalind and I are continuously talking about it. We had a supply teacher who hasn't been there before. The children were all over the place. We led them across the field to shout at them in private [another school was nearby]. They ran around wild. I was never embarrassed before, but today I was. Rosalind and I warmed up our two groups together, then split them. Two of us were facing the field. Peter [see Chapter 4] started shouting 'I don't want to do that fucking pissing warm-up'

behind us. We were looking at each other with glints in our eyes. We carried on as if he wasn't there. In the end we started, then played. When it was time to go in, he shouted again, waste of time, fucking warm-up. Then a woman came up. She lives in one of the select houses nearby. Could we ask the driver to park on the other side of the road, she said. We told her we can't even get the drivers to say hello . . . It's a good job we're all together, a good thing we have the same standards. We're all good teachers with the same standards, yet the children are so obnoxious. There was spitting on the coach. I was a shouting, nagging, old ratbag. We'll have to come back to Liz on Monday about it.

Even when the situation was not quite so fraught, moving out of school presented dilemmas. The walk to the skating rink, or another city site, posed problems of children's safety because of traffic and large numbers crossing busy streets. On one occasion, several children were inadvertently left in the city library. Routines needed to be devised to keep children safe. Such an issue would be discussed in staff meetings. On the other hand, going somewhere out of school could be fun for children and teachers alike. Two teachers, two parents and I went on a walk to a park with class SJ. I was in charge of a group of five boys. At the park:

They were clearly enjoying themselves just being out and about, and it was nice enough for me to enjoy that too. They loaded me up with coats, rolled down the hill, tried to climb up the walls. Harry insisted on walking along the back of a bench while the others held it.

More elaborate excursions needed detailed planning and help from other adults and could be very tiring. I went on two visits to the zoo, which helped me understand what was involved:

At first I was assigned to Helen but one of Marjorie's parents didn't come so I was moved. I had four 5-year-olds. I had to be vigilant all day because they easily went around the wrong corner, or stopped to get something out of their bags or wandered into the wrong school group. Sarah, slightly lame, lagged behind, more so when she got tired; Mia usually bounded ahead. Lola was colder, more reserved. Opal followed rules and stuck by me, for which I was grateful.

Mrs Howard did lots of performances and pointed out exciting things . . . But I'm sure she found it tiring, especially as the children got more tired. It's a very long day – leave school 9.35, coach back at 2.35. Mostly we [the class] stayed together, moving slowly around. Sarah wanted to go to the toilet. I walked some distance with her to get there. Meanwhile she'd decided she didn't have to go. When we got back she wanted to go again and so did Mia. I took them again.

BEHIND THE SCENES

Thus far I have argued that while a classroom focus is evident for teachers, the actual work went well beyond interacting within classroom walls. We can add further layers to our portrait by considering what the teachers did without the children present and extending our purview beyond the school day.

Teachers meet and talk

Cortazzi (1991, p. 8) suggests that researchers have underestimated the extent and importance of teacher-to-teacher talk. Throughout the day (and outside of it) Hillview teachers spoke to each other, comparing notes on particular children, planning shared activities, or just conversing more generally. The location of rooms made it easy for one teacher to have a quick word with another. The head teacher frequently looked in or brought round a message. During breaks almost all teachers were together in the staffroom, although they might use part of their lunch period to do prep-aration. Before 9.00 a.m., too, teachers usually gathered in the staffroom:

> I go up to the staffroom. It's St David's Day [the patron saint of Wales]. All the teachers are standing drinking the coffee, discussing leeks, daffodils, who should wear them – do you need to be Welsh?

> 8.50 a.m. I go up to the staffroom. People are having coffee, mostly standing, near the sink. It is as if they are gearing up, ready to take off.

Staff meetings took place one day per week, after school. The four teachers in the Middle Junior Unit had a short meeting on Thursday afternoons, until it became evident that there was not enough time to accomplish much. Planning took place in twos, over the phone, during breaks, and whenever time permitted. When I was away for a few weeks in September 1987, Debbie kept some notes for me that illustrate the extent of teachers talking together:

> 22 September 1987: Arrived at school. Kristin and I discussed fish! (for Harvest Assembly panic). Tried to sort out Special Needs Resources. Sheila and I have decided to meet tomorrow

lunch-time. I have to pass on lots of info re children from Friday and Monday. But there is not enough time . . . [at lunch-time]. Go to find Mrs Clarke to see about a new child from yesterday as she has found out more about him. We can't talk as there are too many people around. Discussion with Kristin re (1) approach to handwriting; (2) the move towards a more structured approach to education; (3) what specific skills need to be taught. Run back to staffroom – 1.20 bell, no time for drink. Take Middle Junior Unit for TV. Back to own classes for follow-up work. Sheila has photocopied worksheets, thankfully.

29 September 1987: This week is particularly pressured due to the Harvest Assembly. With us not being in on the same day and not seeing the children regularly we seem to be getting what we can done when we can . . . Meetings: all the time! Standing in rooms. On the phone Sunday evening. In playground. Lunch-time. Entrance hall. On stairs. Staffroom. Car park. Pub. Coach to sports field. Swimming pool between coaches!

When the Middle Junior Unit was replaced by an Older Junior Unit the following year, with two full-time teachers, Debbie Stevens and Dennis Bryan, planning was simplified. Debbie and Dennis lived near each other; they saw each other frequently outside school and their families socialized together.

The full staff met as a group not only weekly but on designated inservice training days. It was traditional to schedule one of those days just before the school year started, part of which was devoted to getting the classrooms in shape. I was surprised that teachers did so much of the physical work of moving furniture about:

This is the day before the children arrive, now officially a day teachers are supposed to be in school having meetings. The staff had meetings and lunch together. I arrived around 2.00, at the point the teachers were moving into their classrooms to sort things out. Sheila, Debbie and Kristin were there; Rosalind came later. They seemed glad I was there, as the main activity was moving chairs and tables and help was appreciated.

The rooms had all the furniture moved to the edges and the floors were polished. We put scuff marks on as we dragged heavy furniture. I asked Debbie whether all this manual work was allowed by the unions – teachers' or caretakers'. They didn't appear to expect much from the caretaker. She said everywhere she'd worked teachers always spent the day before term moving the furniture. Debbie and I organized the furniture in the alcove, and then it was realized that the other room, which would house the older kids, had the smaller chairs, so we all had to move all the big chairs and big tables out and the smaller ones in. Eventually the caretaker, after watching a bit, helped.

Debbie said lots of stuff was left by [a former teacher] and she'd never got round to going through some of it. Sheila was friendly, saying to me don't you wish you'd never started this. Rosalind was very concerned about the books . . . she did a quick sweep through. We cleared out some antiquated books that were in poor condition or in one case wouldn't muster up to equal opportunities scrutiny. I helped Debbie write names on two sets of labels, for coat hooks and lockers.

At these inservice training days, extended discussions could take place about schedules and events to come. For example, one such meeting before the summer term began in April 1988 included a series of brief discussions of forthcoming events.

April: visit of the LEA art advisor; a visitor from Capetown, South Africa, via the university; a performance by a woodwind ensemble for the juniors; assemblies and hymn practices; beginning of rehearsals for a city-wide concert production and the school's version later in the term.
May: visit by Chair of the school governors;[1] governors' meeting for parents; a curriculum evening about writing put on by teachers for parents; country dancing performance for some children.
June: school visits to the zoo, followed by projects; camp for some children and teachers; parent interviews (one-to-one discussions between parents and teachers).
July: sports day; swimming gala; school fair.

These events were discussed at this point in order for teachers to know their dates and for preliminary planning to take place, especially for activities coming up shortly. Some of the talk was about adjustments that needed to be made to normal timetables, e.g. whether or not the juniors could still go swimming on the day of the woodwind ensemble visit. As the term proceeded, staff meetings would include further consideration of each of these matters, filling in gaps and extending plans and sorting out alterations to normal routine. Clearly, teachers spent much time talking together – in and out of school hours – and an account of their work is not really complete without this dimension. More evidence of teacher collegiality can be found in Chapter 7.

The long day

Lightfoot (1983b, p. 242) comments on the presentist portrait of teachers that emerges from research: teachers are seen as having neither past nor future and without life beyond the classroom (see also Seddon, 1991, p. 47). It is indeed curious that despite the pervasive assumption in older literature that domestic responsibilities depress women's aspirations, and a more sensitive recent appreciation that women teachers' responses to innovations that call for extra work might be related to the extra burdens or responsibilities they already carry (Apple, 1993), there are hardly any studies that investigate exactly how teachers deal with the home and work interface.

There are a few exceptions. One is Spencer's (1986) intensive observations in the USA of eight women teachers at home, leisure and work, combined with 42 additional interviews. She concludes that few teachers could compartmentalize home and school. Nelson's (1992) historical study of teachers in rural Vermont from 1915 to 1950 also tells us about the interpenetration of domestic and working lives. She interviewed 40 retired teachers about their life stories. Their teaching, mostly in elementary schools, seemed to be a parallel to and extension of their domestic and child care activities. The structure, the skills and the outlook required were similar in each site. The 'two worlds slipped and slid into one another' (p. 31), as the women teachers brought their children into school or dashed out to check on their welfare, their own mothers or daughters assisted or substituted for them in the classroom, and their husbands helped run special events.

Clandinin and Connelly (1995) tell the story of Michael Connelly's mother, Marion, teaching in a one-room rural Alberta, Canada, grade 1–9 school in the 1920s. Like the teachers Nelson interviewed, Marion Connelly lived a close relationship between school and home:

> On many days, the personal landscape and the professional landscape seemed to be the same landscape. For example, school was occasionally held for blocks of time at the house when the weather made it difficult to heat the school or when Marion was hurt and could not walk or ride to school; the inspector responsible for her evaluations picked raspberries on summer weekends with the family on the ranch; and, in years when Marion did not teach, the teacher boarded at her house. In all three examples, the boundary lines in the matrix are blurred. (p. 30)

The convenience of the blurred boundaries was somewhat tempered by vulnerability through visibility, for teachers had to be moral exemplars in both their personal and professional lives. Gradually, such close scrutiny receded as schools became larger and more segmented and a bureaucratic hierarchy of control operated within schools and districts. The classroom survived as the 'secret place on the professional knowledge landscape' (p. 31), though less successfully secret in current times, subject to scrutiny by parents and to prescriptions and mandates from governments.

Generally it is thought that teachers' professional and personal lives no longer 'slip and slide' together (Nelson, 1992), but that may be partly because researchers have not looked closely enough at the interface. Teachers may also cover up their domestic demands as the discourse of professionalism seems to allow no competing commitments. Domestic and school lives cannot be totally segregated. Young's (1992) interviews with four Canadian women educational administrators, for example, are filled with descriptions of day care, crises, driving and domestic coping strategies. She is struck by their sheer 'busy-ness' and their abundant energy (p. 154). Teachers I studied also seemed to live their lives in a whirl of activity. Unlike Spencer's subjects, the teachers believed school influenced home life much more than the reverse (Acker, 1992). Work and worries from school intruded into non-school time. Nearly all the teachers said that they thought about school while at home, although only rarely did they think about home at school. If things were going wrong or they were in crisis situations they might be 'in tears at home', or 'doing action replays in my head'. Even in normal circumstances, as Hillview's Debbie Stevens put it, 'It's always there'.

Other school-related work went beyond teaching and extended into teachers' lives at home. Debbie Stevens made a video of children working on writing activities to show to parents and worked late into the night editing it. Betty Chaplin took home the tea towels from the staffroom to launder them. Marjorie Howard baked scones for refreshments at the school fair. Marjorie and Nancy Green sewed costumes for school productions. Costumes might be for sheep, monks, stars, rats or whatever characters a performance required, sometimes in mass versions, given Hillview's commitment to widespread participation (Chapter 3). Making costumes was hard work: Marjorie was said to be 'up all night sewing'. Even on holiday, teachers kept a lookout for materials they could use in the classroom, noted where cheap pencils might be bought, and picked up interesting stones or feathers.

Earlier in this chapter we saw that teachers regularly engaged in reviewing the day's teaching and planning for the next day at home in the evenings. Some put in time on the weekend, like Dennis, who came into Hillview every Sunday. Sometimes they had marking to do as well. As the National Curriculum and the testing arrangements began to operate, this out-of-school time commitment increased, reflecting the findings of Campbell and Neill's (1994) study.

Women teachers and the double shift

For women, in particular, school and domestic routines were intricately interconnected. It is important to note that the men teachers (in both Hillview and Rosemont) tended to be family-oriented and spoke of playing with and looking after their own children. But it was the women who worked a double shift, juggling domestic work and teaching commitments with the finely honed skills of circus performers.

As noted in Chapter 1, all but one of the Hillview teachers were married and the other teacher was divorced. All but two had children at home. Most of the women teachers were in relatively traditional domestic roles. They generally felt they had support from their husbands. Marjorie explained that when there were concerts or school events 'all our relatives come'. 'Fred will build anything I need for school. Mike the same for Helen', she added. A husband's support might be practical, financial, or moral, but it was less often domestic. Like many people, Debbie's husband did not appear to comprehend the difficulty of the teacher's job:

> I do think Jack underestimates how tiring teaching is. The zoo visits that we went on, I'd gone on two like you had, and I came home one night and it was about half past seven, eight o'clock, and Jack pulled up and I was just absolutely worn out. I mean I was lying on the settee and Jack said, 'What's there to eat', or something, and I said, 'I just can't move. I'm going to lie here and I'm going to go to bed in a minute.' And he said, 'But you've only been to the zoo for a couple of days.' I mean it's that sort of not understanding the real tiredness that you can get. I mean I'm sure he thinks it's an exaggeration when I see him and say, 'Oh, I just can't move to go up to bed, I'm that tired.'

In interviews, many teachers mentioned that they came in early in the morning, worked through much of their lunch-time and sometimes after school too. Some preferred this routine in order to keep some separation between work and home. Most, however, said they took schoolwork home, some every night. Leisure activities were minimized. When I asked Helen Davies what she did in her non-teaching time, she replied with a laugh: 'At home? The washing, and the ironing, and the cleaning, and the cooking'.

In the 1987–88 school year, five of the Hillview teachers had young children at home. Women teachers with small children had to be even more skilful at juggling, for they had a triple shift, namely, work, home and child care responsibilities. Some were also enrolled in courses to gain additional qualifications. Two of the teachers had live-in nannies; others worked part-time and made complicated arrangements with childminders, relatives, playgroups, nurseries, and eventually, when the children were old enough, schools. Teacher–mothers had to have plenty of stamina.

Debbie Stevens

Debbie Stevens is a case in point. When she began working at Hillview, at about the time I started my research, she had a child only a few months old. She had recently relocated from London, where she had taught in an inner-city school. She came to Wesley because her husband got a job there, and because it was a few hours' drive from the part of the country where she had grown up and her parents still lived. Her grandmother and her brother also lived within a short distance from Wesley. Debbie had found someone to look after her daughter, but the arrangement broke down some months later. Luckily, the young woman working in Mrs Howard's class on a youth training scheme agreed to work for Debbie privately as a nanny. Marilyn lived with Debbie's family during the week and went home to her own parents on weekends.

In the next few years, Debbie had two more children and two maternity leaves, as well as a sick leave after a miscarriage. During her maternity leaves, she continued to come into the school for staff meetings. She also took courses at the university and acquired an M.Ed. degree. Although I saw Debbie and her husband Jack at social occasions involving the school, and was at her house from time to time, I gained further insights into her domestic situation once I had left the city, when I returned for a visit in 1991. Staying with Debbie for nearly a week allowed me to witness her domestic routines in detail. At the time of the observations below, Debbie is about to turn 30, is acting deputy head at Hillview, and is pregnant with her third child.

> Debbie and Jack have arrived home from a weekend with her parents. The children are given their tea [supper]. Marilyn comes in with a cold, announces 'I'm dying' and goes to bed. Debbie takes her up a hot lemon drink. Alternative child care arrangements are going to be necessary. Debbie phones her nan [grandmother] and checks on her commitments over the next few days. She is free apart from an appointment with the hairdresser on Tuesday afternoon. Debbie discusses the situation with Jack, then phones back her nan and arranges she will come on the bus the next day. Marilyn will have to cope until she gets there at 11.00. Debbie will take Katy to nursery in her lunch-hour. Marilyn will find someone to collect her from nursery.
>
> Nan plays an important role in Debbie's life. Debbie drags a big bag of children's clothes up the stairs: 'Thank goodness for Nan', she says. Debbie's grandmother has ironed all the clothes. She seems to do much of the housework as well. Debbie tells me that her nan worked in a factory, is a 'workhorse'.

On the wall on the noticeboard in the kitchen is a list for
Marilyn of school events in the evenings. Everything costs
Debbie extra, she tells me. Monday is a governors' meeting.
Tuesday is an evening for parents and teachers in the park.
Debbie has arranged for Marilyn to come with the kids. (In the
end, it is cancelled due to rain. Debbie pays Marilyn despite the
cancellation.) Debbie is heavily pregnant yet makes few
concessions. Her feeling is that she needs to last out the term, I
think.

I got back on Monday night about 6.15. The children went to
bed around 6.30. Debbie made two sandwiches for herself and
ate them in the bath, then dressed and went to the governors'
meeting. She is the teacher governor. She came home again
around 10.00 p.m. She ate a bowl of porridge in bed, turned the
light out about 10.30. The morning routine is to wake up at 7.30
or even 7.40, and be out of the house by 8.00 and to school by
8.15. She doesn't have a coffee, just pops two pieces of toast in
the toaster, wraps them in a tissue and eats them in the car.
She jokes about being like John Cleese in the film *Clockwork*.
Once a week she clears all the tissues out of the car. She gets to
school early to sort things out for Liz Clarke, who drives in from
a town some distance from Wesley, and sometimes to talk to her
before school starts. Liz tells me that Debbie has a very difficult
class this term as well as the deputy headship.

On Friday, the plan is for Debbie to drive to her parents
again for the weekend. Marilyn is to bring Nan and the children
to Debbie after school, and Jack who is away in connection with
his work is to join them later that night. But Marilyn's car won't
work, so it is rearranged that Debbie will come home to pick up
everyone. She is hoping to leave at 3.50. In the event, Liz leaves
early and Debbie has to stay. An 'incident' has occurred on the
coaches back from games – a coach broke down in the middle of
heavy traffic and the children 'went mad' – and the teachers
who were with them came in to school upset and let off steam
for nearly an hour. Debbie phones home several times.
Eventually we get back and the family piles into the car for the
trip. (Week of 30 June 1991)

It may be evident in the notes that Debbie has almost the entire responsibility for domestic arrangements, although she plays a very full part in
school activities too. Her husband is fully occupied with his job and travels
a lot. She does not assume that he will share child care or housework. She
relies on her grandmother and her nanny instead. Domestic arrangements
as well as school activities are subject to sudden changes of plan. Debbie

needs to be very flexible and calm to deal with both the routine and the unexpected in her complicated schedule. Her situation is a far cry from the image of half-hearted work commitment of married women teachers that we find in the older literature on teachers.

CONCLUSION

Chapters 4 and 5 have been devoted to describing the work of the teachers at Hillview School. As the literature notes, the classroom focus for the teacher is very important. There is an intense interaction between teachers and class, one that has to be negotiated and renegotiated. But it is highly misleading to regard the teacher as simply a prisoner in a cellular classroom. In some schools, of course, the image is closer to reality than we find at Hillview. At Hillview, teachers have an extensive life as a collaborative community, with and without the children present. They manage a complicated week and year as well as day; they plan and replan their work.

Despite the amount of detail in this chapter, I have only been able to describe a portion of what the Hillview teachers did beyond classroom teaching. Teachers ran assemblies, kept records, put up displays, led singing, taught the recorder, organized country dancing, took children to sing in a home for the elderly, collected money, conferred with parents, met together, consulted educational psychologists and other specialists, purchased or collected supplies, presented curriculum evenings for parents, attended PTA activities, ran sports matches, reorganized the school library, took charge of the school fair and went on courses. Home time blurred into work time. For women, especially, fulfilling domestic and work responsibilities involved intricate planning and careful time management.

Up to this point, I have kept away from the question of leadership in the school. Superimposed over the teachers' activities is an equally complex task of managing the school. In the next chapter, I look at the work of the head teacher of Hillview.

NOTE

1. School governing bodies will be described in Chapter 8.

Chapter 6

Managing the Drama

> The teachers think something dramatic always happens
> whenever I'm away. In fact something is always happening, but
> my job is to manage the drama. (Liz Clarke, head teacher,
> Hillview Primary School)

I was rarely bored at Hillview. On the contrary, I found life there exciting
and dramatic, sometimes even exhilarating, especially on the days I was
the head teacher's 'shadow'. Then I felt as if I were in the control tower,
had the pulse of the school, helped to steer the ship. A day might turn into
a race against the clock, say, to get an important letter for parents written
and distributed to children by home time. We would find ourselves laughing
as we scrambled around, sometimes finding that haste made for waste. I
knew the viewpoint from the classroom was different. Teachers tended to
think that the hard work was at the chalk face, not in the school office. In
the previous two chapters I looked closely at the work of the Hillview
teachers. This chapter is about the work of the head teacher.

WHAT DO PRIMARY HEADS DO?

A number of empirical studies of the primary head teacher's role have tried
to develop categories by which a head's time can be classified (e.g. Clerkin,
1985; Harvey, 1986). There are now several important studies based on
intensive interviewing or participant observation in primary [elementary]
schools that give us a richer portrait (Hall, 1996; Hayes, 1994; Nias, 1987;
Southworth, 1995; Wolcott, 1973). The educational reforms in Britain in
the late 1980s focused researchers' interest on head teachers' responses to
those reforms and stimulated a number of publications that highlighted
the head teacher's changing role (Grace, 1995; Jones and Hayes, 1991;
Menter et al., 1997; Pollard et al., 1994; Webb and Vulliamy, 1996; Woods,
1995; Woods et al., 1997).

All the attempts to pin down head teachers' tasks seem to conclude
that the head teacher's day is fragmented and unpredictable. Holtom (1988,

p. 275) describes a 'confusion of activity with heads being pulled one way and another, unable to stick to planned activity without being distracted by interruptions'. One of the heads in her study comments that 'planning seems to be a useless exercise, because things don't go the way you planned' (p. 160). Hill (1989) refers to the 'daunting picture of the primary head's fragmented day with the brief, people-centred activities of an immediate short-term nature getting interrupted by unanticipated events and visitors' (p. 78). In his classic study of Ed Bell, an American principal, Wolcott (1973) reports similar pressures: 'The greatest part of a principal's time is spent in an almost endless series of encounters, from the moment he arrives at school until the moment he leaves' (p. 88). Hayes (1994), who studied a school much like Hillview, emphasized the persistent demands made on the head, in comparison to which 'plate spinning on a weekend variety show seemed relatively straightforward' (p. 70).

DOES GENDER MAKE A DIFFERENCE?

Feminist writing about educational administration in the 1970s and 1980s pointed to the under-representation of women in the management of education and identified barriers to their progress up the ranks. According to Sadker, Sadker and Klein (1991), some of the barriers identified in early studies began to disappear by the mid-1980s in the USA. Perhaps as a result, theorists shifted away from questions of equality (do women administrators have as many opportunities as men?) to those of difference (what is a female administrative style?). Feminist scholars attacked theories of administration that took insufficient account of women's experiences (Blackmore, 1989; Ferguson, 1984; Intriligator, 1983; Shakeshaft, 1989).

It is sometimes suggested that women's typical leadership styles are superior to those of men and better suited to running effective schools (Fullan, 1991, p. 165; Sadker *et al.*, 1991, p. 284). I tend to agree with Valerie Hall (1996) that such competitive comparisons are unhelpful. Instead we can usefully examine how both men's and women's ways of operating are influenced by prevailing conceptions of masculinity and femininity and by their experiences in a world where gender is a key organizing principle. We must be cautious in how we approach this task. Case studies where women head teachers emphasize caring and collaboration and men display dominance and power (Woods *et al.*, 1997; Southworth, 1995) simply do not allow us to conclude once and for all that these are 'natural' preferences according to gender. The situation may be more complex on closer examination. Southworth (1995), for example, states that the head teacher he studied, Ron Lacey, was 'powerful to the point of dominating the school' (p. 149), yet *simultaneously* 'kindly and caring' (p. 151). Hall (1996), too, showed that the women head teachers in her study could be 'both hard and soft, tough and loving, controlling and caring' (p. 135). There are studies of both women and men primary school head teachers trying to introduce (and sometimes force) collaboration into their schools, more likely as a response to educational policy developments than to any gendered preferences (Hayes, 1994; Woods *et al.*, 1997).

I shall return to the question of gendered headship styles at the end of the chapter. First, I want to describe what daily life at school is like for Liz Clarke. Smulyan (1996) makes a strong argument that we need more such case studies to move us away from the typical abstractions found in much of the literature. I describe the routines, events and stories that together constitute the work of Hillview's head teacher. I then turn to her interactions with teachers and the various ways she supports their work and careers, in the process deploying and developing teachers for what she believes is their good and the good of the school.

TYPICAL DAYS

An account from my field notes of the first part of a spring morning in 1988 may capture the dramatic and event-filled life of the head teacher at Hillview.

> When I arrive at 8.45, Liz Clarke is outside in the car park telling Kristin King, a part-time teacher and art specialist, about a course on art in the primary school the head had attended the previous evening. Just inside the school the other teachers are congregating around Nancy Green, a teacher who has been at the school for eleven years and has 'news': she has been successful the previous day at interview for a deputy headship in another school. There is intense interest in what the experience had been like and shared pleasure in her good fortune, mixed with regret at losing a colleague and concern for other staff who have not yet managed to achieve a similar goal. Into this discussion a child comes to say that Harry, a third-year junior boy, has been hurt on the playground. The story is that after some horseplay, involving a mock judo hold, he was on the ground saying he couldn't get up. There is some doubt about the veracity of the claim, but as a passing medic (who turns out to be a psychiatrist) said an ambulance should be called, this is what was done. Dorothy Lowe, the school secretary, waits with Harry and eventually accompanies him to hospital. For about ten minutes the office is empty, except for myself, and I answer the phone to a parent who says her children might, or might not, be in later as they'd been sick in the night, a message I pass

on to the appropriate teachers. The head, who has gone out to see if the ambulance had arrived, comes back in and phones Harry's mother, telling her what has happened.

Another parent has been standing outside the office waiting for the head's return. The school day has by now begun. She explains to Mrs Clarke that her son Malcolm, a second-year junior new to the school, says he is being bullied and won't get out of the car. Mrs Clarke goes upstairs to get the boy's teacher, Debbie Stevens, who heads out towards the car with the mother. Meanwhile, Daniel, a fourth-year junior boy, has also been waiting patiently to give Mrs Clarke a present from his parents to the school, a book. She asks him to ask Roger, a boy who had been playing with Harry, to come over to see her.

It is now 9.35 and the phone rings. It is a parent, very anxious to see the head. 'I'm teaching this afternoon', Mrs Clarke says, arranging to see her first thing tomorrow instead. Mrs Lowe has returned and tells Mrs Clarke that the father of a child in top infants has been in to complain that his son's mouth was hurt during play the previous day but the family not told. Liz goes into the classroom to have a look at the boy's mouth, which looks rather worse than it did originally. She checks the accident record and finds that in fact there was a report made out, but the teacher had failed to give it to the child to take home. She looks irritated and makes a note to phone the father. Then, as Roger has not yet appeared (Daniel having forgotten to give him the message), she goes over to the other building to the fourth-year classroom and speaks to him, trying to find out what happened with himself and Harry. She tells him to write it out.

In the office, Malcolm, his mother and Debbie Stevens are waiting for her return. The whole story gradually emerges and Liz spends considerable time talking it through with the boy and his mother and calling in the main culprit for a strong warning. She explains to the mother that this kind of lecture wouldn't work with the other boy said to be involved and that she'll have a word with him later. She promises that the case won't be left, that it will be mentioned in school meeting.

Some of the background is filled in after the parent leaves, taking the child with her for today. 'It's not school really', Liz says to Debbie and myself. 'The child knows everything's wrong, clings to mum.' Malcolm's brother is very ill and there are tensions between the parents. Harry, who turns out to be unhurt, is also upset because his mother has split up from her boyfriend, an event he has experienced several times already this year. 'How do we get plusages [extra staffing] for this?' Liz asks rhetorically.

Roger comes in with his account of the accident. Mrs Clarke goes upstairs to talk to Ian, a third-year junior, the boy who has been peripherally involved in the bullying. On her return to the office, Mrs Lowe tells her that Mrs Lester from the local education authority has phoned: 'Is your literacy and maths cards order on its way? Mrs Lester is anxious to know.' She also mentions three other letters that have to be dealt with. It is now 10.15 and time for assembly.

This account covers only one and a half hours and is dominated by unplanned events. There are only a few minutes spent on routine tasks and some are postponed until later. Behind the events, there are stories: the particular family circumstances and motivations of the children involved; Liz's support for Nancy Green's career.

ROUTINES, EVENTS AND STORIES

Such observations suggested to me that the head's work might be seen as encompassing routines, events and stories. Routine tasks are those that are predictable and repeated at regular intervals, although their exact content will vary. Events are relatively short but unplanned occurrences. Events might be the visible tip, or the start of a story. Stories carry on over time and can be complicated, with characters, action, episodes and (sometimes) resolutions. Some of them are so complex and lengthy that they might be termed sagas. Examples from each of these categories are given below.

Routines

Liz Clarke often worked standing up at her desk, especially when sorting and disposing of post, which she did at times through most days. She looked ready to take off – as indeed she might be called upon to do. Much of the rest of the time she was still on her feet. Each day brought some contact with parents, teachers and other staff. Messages were frequently received or something happened that required a child or teacher being told or asked something, and Liz generally took these messages to the classroom right away. This gave her a feel for what was going on in the school, an acceptable reason to see what teachers were doing.

Form-filling, which occupied a great deal of time for Liz and her secretary, might be considered a routine. At this time, the local education authorities (LEAs) had a more powerful role in overseeing British schools than they currently do. Whenever I was in the office, it was likely that someone would phone up from the LEA wanting their particular overdue form, or saying that the form sent in was the wrong colour or type, or that a letter wasn't sufficient because a form was also required. Forms had to be completed when any child or teacher started at or left the school, for supply teachers, for school dinners each week, for inservice training days, for teachers on courses, for accidents and for orders of all kinds.

Three or four days a week Liz ran the assembly or school meeting. Other routines, such as staff meetings and working with an infant language group, occurred once a week. Some routines came at longer intervals, often once a term. In a given term, Mrs Clarke would attend a meeting of each of several heads' groups, the school governors and the PTA. She would usually participate in a curriculum evening for parents and two or three case conferences on children.

At least once a year, Mrs Clarke tried to talk to each member of the teaching staff about their work and career plans. Near the end of the school year she prepared class lists for the following year and sorted out staffing allocations. Several times during the year she looked through results of the reading age tests given to the children. Twice a year parents came in with appointments to see teachers, some during the day, some in the evening. Liz might teach each class for a half-day to free the teacher for these appointments. She took a part in termly school productions involving music and drama and events such as sports day, school fair and swimming gala. Thinking about curriculum, staffing, and pupil progress in the school were also ongoing activities, although not so visible.

Events

The fragmented quality of the day to which other researchers allude is due to events. My typology is not meant to be rigid and some of the routines shade into events, where something assumed to be predictable takes on an unexpected form. For example, visits from prospective parents were frequent enough to qualify as routine, but as each parent is different, these discussions often held unanticipated features. Some of the events I witnessed were relatively mundane: a phone call asking for children's art work to be donated to a hospital, a drop-in visit by the vicar, a contact with Oxfam or the BBC. Others were more dramatic: someone drove into a teacher's car; there had been an attempted break-in during the night; a child was hurt; there was a fire in a nearby building and a bomb scare in another one. Teachers' illnesses were events. Arranging supply teacher cover would then be a task for either the head or the secretary, and sometimes the head taught a class at short notice.

Stories

Once stories are initiated (sometimes by 'events') they are 'on the agenda' and can be pursued by the head or any other character from time to time. There was great variety in the stories. Stories and events together gave the dramatic – almost soap opera – flavour to school life that I remarked upon earlier.

It should be noted that some stories were by their nature difficult for outsiders, including myself, to observe, or even identify, either because they involved thinking rather than doing, gradual implementation or modification rather than a clear-cut set of operations, or were confidential matters to the parties concerned. Some curriculum planning and innovation came into this category, as did counselling of teaching and ancillary staff.

Children's and parents' stories

In a sense each child had a story – one for which the school would quite likely never know the ending. 'We run on faith', Marjorie Howard commented in one staff meeting. Mrs Clarke spoke proudly of some of the children's stories: about those who came to us with a 'horrendous reputation', yet settled and thrived; about others who changed over their time in the school from being timid and fearful to confident and mature.

The problems of parents and their children provided the more poignant stories. The day before the children began school was an inservice training day for the teachers, mostly devoted to moving around furniture and sorting things out. I arrived in early afternoon. 'If you want to know what I did today', Mrs Clarke said, 'it was marriage guidance counselling.' 'With staff?' I asked. 'No, parents. They seemed to know the school was open and phoned and made appointments. I've heard a steady stream of problems all day. I haven't got to the post yet.' One of these cases continued over several weeks, as Liz helped a parent get legal advice, spoke to her for long periods of time, arranged a change of school for the children in case their father should snatch them. Months later this story surfaced again, Liz asking teachers in the staffroom what they remembered about the woman's relationship with her children, for evidence in a custody dispute. Maintaining relationships with parents was a major part of the head teacher's role and will be explored in detail in Chapter 9.

Equipment and services stories

Other stories came closer to farce than to tragedy. Trying to get equipment through the local education authority fitted well into this category, perhaps explaining why some head teachers were happy to replace this form of governance by one that allowed budget management at the local school level (Pollard *et al.*, 1994, p. 67).

The climbing frame for the infants' playground arrived, after long delays, with two left sides. Phoning around other schools produced one with two right sides and arrangements were made to borrow a van from a parent to pick it up. But this proved not to be the solution: 'Do you want the bad news?' Dorothy Lowe said. 'Their two bits of climbing frame are the same as our two bits.' Getting playground surfacing under the climbing frame was an even greater marathon, with parents' petitions and articles in the local paper. The school was short of play space, and in fact playground development was an old story. The head had kept a file of letters to and from agencies involved over four years, trying to get improvements.

Acquiring a television and video for the infants was another year-long effort. The problem was that the school could not simply go out and buy another television. The LEA needed to give permission (which it had done) and ordering and installation had to be done through LEA-approved firms. Mrs Clarke had made many phone calls, over months, to try to get this problem sorted out. When eventually the television and video arrived, they turned out not to be compatible with each other. Liz was on the phone soon after, trying to arrange for an approved firm to do the required alterations.

As I noted in earlier chapters, getting the juniors to games was a continuing problem. On the morning of the first day with games after the Easter break, Mrs Clarke phoned up Mr Bell, the named contact in the LEA over such matters, saying she wanted to double-check that the coaches would be there, given the trouble in the past. In the school meeting that day, the head made a big point to the children who had forgotten their kit or developed mysterious maladies that did not allow them to participate:

> Games is a privilege we have at this school; will you please take advantage of it. I mean it, children, or we'll be like all the other inner-city schools without playing fields who don't get any play.

I had decided to go along to games with the juniors for the first time on that day. This is what happened:

> All four junior classes troop down to the collection point. Not a coach in sight. It starts to rain. One of the older children is sent back to tell the office no coach had arrived and a few minutes later one of the teachers also goes back to check. The word is that the coach is on its way but after another ten coachless minutes in the rain we turn back instead. One of the coaches eventually turns up and takes some of the older children off, with Dennis Bryan, as there is a match on with another school. The other children stay at school and the teachers improvise an afternoon's work.

I speak with Liz the next school day. The coach was not there to get them home either, she tells me, and they didn't get back until 4.30. Dennis was exhausted. When he finally reached Mr Bell he said he'd passed along the request to Transport. My coming in reminds her she'd meant to pursue the matter further and she phones the Transport section herself. This is apparently unorthodox as all contact is supposed to go through channels. She points out that she had rung her correct contact, Mr Bell, to ensure that the coaches would come. It soon becomes clear that the correct contact had not in fact rung Transport. 'What does a head have to do?' she questions. She explains what problems the episode had caused, with 120 children waiting in the rain and traffic, children back late, nobody official around at 4.30 to sort out why the coaches weren't there to bring the children back. 'Can I have your personal assurance', she asks, 'that in future two coaches will be waiting at twenty past one and that they will wait at the field to return?'

Then Mrs Clarke phones Mr Bell. He admits – as he now has to – that he had not in fact phoned to check on the coaches, explaining he can't do everything and the sports transport people had the wrong times down. Mrs Clarke is full of magnificent anger, stressing the safety factor with 120 children on a busy inner-city street and pointing out that if anything happened the finger of blame would point at him. Her voice is strong and penetrating: 'Could you actually do it, not think it's something not important in your busy schedule . . . You're my point of contact. This is a quality of experience I'm not prepared to have for the children, or the teachers. So if you're asked, by an ignorant head, to check, will you please do it. It's not an idle request.'

Extended stories or 'sagas'

Some stories become very lengthy, with episodes over a term or more. They could perhaps be thought of as 'sagas'. An example might be the long account of trying to get the school playgrounds improved, resurfaced and extended, an effort on Liz Clarke's part that extended intermittently over the period of my research and beyond. Peter's story, which I related in Chapter 4, was another saga. A third example was the efforts by a group of parents to push the school to engage in more anti-racist efforts, and I take up this story in Chapter 9.

THE HEAD TEACHER AS CAREER BROKER

Liz Clarke saw encouragement and support for teachers as a major part of her role. Her efforts extended beyond advice and encouragement, however, to more subtle manoeuvres. Below I discuss the ways in which the head teacher influenced working experiences and career prospects for her staff.

Support

My field notes contain many expressions of encouragement and praise for the teachers from the head, often spoken at staff meetings. There were also tokens of gratitude such as chocolates or a bottle of sherry at the end of the term. Support was also evident for teachers' efforts to add to their qualifications or advance their careers. When teachers were about to be interviewed for posts elsewhere, the head teacher provided advice about interview technique. Liz suggested to one teacher that she write down the questions after an interview for a deputy headship, both for her own future use and to be shared with the other teachers. In two cases where teachers had unsuccessful interviews for positions in other schools, she arranged for county advisors to come in and 'debrief' the teacher concerned.

At Hillview, career advice carried extra weight because Liz could be a role model for the women teachers. Debbie Stevens commented, 'Liz is a woman, and I feel that if I wanted advice about career development I could get it from her.' Debbie, Rosalind Phillips and Dennis Bryan were all encouraged by Liz to enrol in an M.Ed. programme in management education [educational administration] at a nearby university. Later, Helen Davies began an advanced diploma course, Kristin King an M.Ed. programme, and Sheila Jones an extended course on school libraries. Marjorie Howard, Helen Davies and Liz herself had paid sabbatical terms to pursue areas of particular interest.

During the early part of my research, it was possible to receive 'day release' from the LEA to attend courses for master's degrees. The teacher would have a half-day off each week, usually for two years, with money provided to the school for a replacement. It was thought that management courses had the best prospects for such support. At the start of my study, Rosalind Phillips was working part-time in each of two schools. She worried about whether her part-time status would make her ineligible for day release. In a telephone conversation with me, she commented that Liz would support her, 'she's so good, she'd probably let me go even if I weren't released'. In an interview, she gave a fuller account of Liz's advice:

> She said to me all along that she didn't think I ought to do this
> two-school job for much longer for my own career prospects . . . I

had to put down my roots . . . She has mentioned it on a couple of occasions. She's never said what she thinks I ought to be doing, but she's always said she feels I ought to make a commitment. She has said that she didn't think I ought to pursue the special needs role any more.

She contrasted this kind of support from Mrs Clarke with its absence from the other head she worked for:

Tony Richards doesn't really go in for that kind of talk . . . in the very first place, he didn't think I'd even get my place on the M.Ed. degree because I was only part-time in his school. He's probably done the most to discourage me.

Mrs Clarke went beyond simply encouraging and supporting her teachers. She took care to hire teachers who would share her vision for the school, and put a great deal of energy and thought into their deployment within the school. When the time came for them to move on, she went to great lengths to help them. Many of her efforts took place behind the scenes. More discussion of teachers' careers and the head teacher's impact can be found in Chapter 10.

Selection

Head teachers I spoke with while doing my research explained that it took a long time to stamp one's own influence on a school staff; one estimated that it could be as much as ten years. Liz Clarke had been at Hillview for four years at the start of my study and was then just beginning to see hoped-for changes materialize. Such estimates are based on the time taken for teachers with divergent views or practices to leave the school for one reason or another, to be replaced with those more in the image of the new head. Another parallel process involved longer-serving teachers modifying their practices or views to be more in line with those of the head. These stories tended to have a ring of heroism about them: the new head 'turning round' the school, remaking it in his or her own image. Reflecting on this point, Liz said to me in an interview (somewhat tongue-in-cheek): 'I identified the true nature of the school and intensified it.'

The idea that a head could shape a school over time is predicated on a system that allows head teachers to have a major input into selection of teachers for their own school and where head teachers do not themselves have a fixed term in a school. Murnane, Singer, Willett, Kemple and Olsen (1991) describe several alternative practices in school districts in the USA. During the major part of my study, head teachers had considerable control over hiring; later on, government policies diluted this power as the school governing body came to hold formal responsibility. There were two particularly interesting features of Liz's hiring practices. The first was reliance upon personal networks to find appropriate individuals (see also Evetts, 1989, 1990, for a parallel finding). Vacant posts had to be advertised, at least in the LEA circulars, and often in national newspapers. In several cases, advertisements brought in teachers from outside the city, or whose past experience had been elsewhere although they were now living locally. In 1987, new appointments of Dennis Bryan, Debbie Stevens and Kristin King, all of whom had previously worked in other parts of the country, added a cosmopolitan touch to the school, complementing the depth of experience and local knowledge teachers already in the school possessed.

In addition to major appointments, there were part-time and temporary positions in the school that became vacant more frequently. Here the head had a large element of control over staffing. Many of the teachers working in such a capacity were known to Liz prior to appointment. Rosalind Phillips, when she was previously working in secondary education, had taught Liz's own children. Della Monk, a regular supply teacher in the school, lived in Liz's village and had taught at a school where Liz had worked in the past. A retired teacher who did volunteer teaching one day a week in the school had also taught with Liz in earlier days. Dennis Bryan's wife did some supply teaching for Hillview. Amanda Prentice, who joined the school in 1989 to replace Nancy Green, had taught at a nearby school and was a friend of Rosalind Phillips. Marjorie Howard, who was part-time at Hillview before Mrs Clarke arrived, had found her way to the school through having taught with a friend of the previous head teacher. In several cases when a vacancy occurred, efforts were made to give the edge to someone already connected with the school; for example, a job specification could be written to match the person's particular talents and experiences.

The second notable feature of Liz's hiring efforts was her support for teachers with young children. Debbie Stevens, Rosalind Phillips, Kristin King, Sheila Jones and Dennis Bryan all had small children. The other full-time teachers were either childless or had older children. Liz herself had three children, now grown up, and she could empathize with teacher parents. When scheduling parent interviews after school and in the evenings, Liz tried to adjust the timetable so that teachers with small children could go home in between if they wished. Debbie Stevens said in an interview 'I'd never worry [about the head teacher's reaction] if I had a problem at home, say if things got bad with Katy [her child].' On another occasion she repeated the point: 'I think she is very understanding of the family situation and doesn't expect anyone to be at school till 6.00 every night, doesn't judge people by the amount of hours they're up in the classroom.'

It seemed that such an outlook was relatively rare among head teachers. In an interview, Dennis Bryan commented that 'Liz cares about everything' and added that it makes things more difficult for her. In 'everything' he included 'teachers' children; their husbands'. Debbie reported that she and Dennis had discussed this way of working:

> Dennis made a remark the other day about how kind and considerate she was in taking into account everyone's timetabling problems, whereas his previous head, and mine, would have said you've got to do this, that's your hours. Whereas Liz thinks, oh, so-and-so can only get child arrangements then; that would interfere with so-and-so's other job elsewhere; this would interfere with another commitment. And we spoke to her about that then, and she said that was the way she liked to work, and it made her feel better; if she thought it was harming the children in any way, then she would change it.

Liz herself explained to me that she tried to balance everyone's needs, taking into account personalities, wishes, child care, career plans and so forth, at the same time putting the good of the school first. When Kristin King was away for a number of weeks due to complications of an ectopic pregnancy, Liz commented that some people ask her why she hires women of childbearing age. She said, 'You have to expect this, that they will have children. But they do work extra hard.' Liz's own experience of being a mother and a teacher no doubt shaped her views. My observations suggested these teachers were indeed grateful and tried to repay Liz's trust in them by hard work and strong commitments to the school.

Staff deployment

Other opportunities existed for Liz to take an active role *vis-à-vis* staff deployment and development. This role was only partly visible to the staff.

Nancy Green owed her move to a deputy headship in another school in part to Liz's strategic answers to a phone call from the head of the prospective school. This head teacher had not initially singled out Nancy for strong consideration, but had then read Liz's highly enthusiastic reference, so telephoned for some less formal elaboration. I was in the office with Liz at the time. Liz stressed that although Nancy was shy and might not make an immediately electric impression, she had 'so many talents, energy, a preparedness to work'. The other head then asked what Liz called the 'crunch question', whether Mrs Clarke would want Nancy as her own deputy head. Liz explained why Nancy would probably not be right for her – Nancy's preferences for organizational order and clarity often clashed with Liz's more spontaneous style – yet she would be 'right with the right person'.

Helen Davies and Marjorie Howard both enjoyed timely sabbatical terms Liz arranged for them at the university when some danger of burn-out loomed. When Liz herself went on sabbatical, she made sure Dennis would be appointed acting head teacher and Helen as acting deputy. Later, when Dennis spent a year away on a teacher exchange, Debbie Stevens became acting deputy. Helen explained how Liz gave teachers useful experiences through delegation:

> She creates a good atmosphere . . . and she does appreciate what people do . . . she is willing to delegate, and not to delegate for the sake of it, but to delegate for people to have responsibility and she will accept the decisions they make . . . Liz looks at the people, the personality, she looks and seeks what they're good at, and she will delegate those jobs to those who are good at doing it. She boosts your ego and your confidence through that. She'll only give you the jobs she knows you can handle.

An additional element entered the calculations in 1990–91. The 1988 Education Reform Act had introduced 'local management of schools' (LMS), a scheme whereby the major responsibility for school budgets would be transferred from the LEA to individual school governing bodies. A school the size of Hillview would have several years before fully operating LMS, but some of the effects were being felt by 1990–91. School funding was based on a formula that appeared to take insufficient account of the proportion of experienced, and thus more highly paid, teachers in a school (see Chapter 11). Liz had to think hard about saving money and making sure no teacher lost her job. For the time being, two teachers' maternity leaves were saving the day, as those teachers could be temporarily replaced with cheaper substitutes.

The good of the children was a particularly important consideration for Liz in making staffing decisions. When a class of children had been disrupted because of staffing changes, Liz made attempts to give them more continuity, either by allocating a particularly strong teacher or arranging for the class to stay for two years with one teacher. Another consideration was fostering innovation in the school. In several cases, moves were made to enable teachers to work together in efforts to develop cooperative teaching. Staff deployment, to Liz, was like a puzzle or a game, complicated but enthralling. She told me: 'That is the bit of the job that I probably enjoy as much as anything, you know, solving it in the shower. It's usually in the shower that I think of something like, hey – this is the moment to move so-and-so.'

Staffing moves could have mixed consequences. Moving Marjorie Howard to reception teaching was a stroke of genius as she was brilliant with the little ones. Earlier chapters contained examples from her classrooms. I was mesmerized as I watched her make everything into a drama or a game, keeping up a fast-paced performance. Teachers knew that contrary to popular belief, reception teaching could be the most demanding job in the school. Some children came in without sufficient cultural or language resources to make the transition to school easy. Moving play equipment and repeatedly bending down to the tiny children was physically exhausting, and as was generally true throughout the school, classes were large and resources insufficient.

Marjorie initially approached the move with great trepidation. She had originally been a secondary school teacher, switching (as was common) into primary school teaching when she returned after some time away with her own children. Mrs Clarke had already persuaded her to change to full-time teaching. When Liz asked her to take on reception teaching, she was inclined to refuse. But she felt herself under pressure to accept and she eventually agreed, not without considerable anxiety:

> I lost half a stone [7 pounds] in weight, and I didn't sleep for a fortnight, when she said about going into reception. I was so worried about it, and had terrible nightmares of her pushing me, pushing the car into the dock with the handbrake off [laughs]. I really was very worried. It's a monumental jump, to me, starting off with comprehensive [high school] age children.

Moves within the school for teachers were not always welcomed. Rosalind Phillips reacted unhappily to the suggestion that she might share a particular class when her preference was to be a floater and work with small groups of children while she pursued her M.Ed.; her worries about it probably contributed to her eventual decision to leave her part-time post at the school and work full-time elsewhere. Teachers often found it hard to say no. Marjorie said: 'I don't like to ever say no to people, because it doesn't seem helpful. You try to please people and do what they want, to keep the peace.'

CONCLUSION

Few of the studies I read before beginning my observations at Hillview conveyed anything of the atmosphere and activities I was to find when shadowing Liz Clarke. Certainly other researchers' observations about brevity, interruptions and fragmentation did apply. But there were additional features: the simultaneity of events; the dramatic quality of a day at Hillview; the emotions and commitments that accompanied the actions and thoughts of the head teacher; the continuation of stories over time. It should be clear from this chapter that being a head teacher in a school like Hillview is a difficult, demanding task. Yet Liz Clarke thrived on it. She clearly enjoyed her work, despite its frustrations.

The interruptions and unexpected events were themselves exciting and lent variety and challenge to the work. Sometimes Liz Clarke spent more time than she could easily afford talking to a visitor just because she found him or her interesting. The people-oriented side of Liz's job was a key source of pleasure. When I asked in interview what the satisfactions were in her job, she immediately spoke about the children, giving examples:

> Looking at someone like Winston and James, having had them for four years, and having seen them grow from chip-on-the-shoulder, awkward, suspicious boys into nice young men . . . that is a satisfaction beyond description, really. You know, something like that.

Even the battles over equipment and the other farcical stories I have related had their compensations. There was the pride of being a political actor – of making things happen. About the 'minutiae of daily life, I can't say I find any of that frustrating because I can change it, I can make it satisfying. . . . It's my own fault that I get pulled from one thing to another . . . I mean I guess I like it like that really.' The routines, events and stories did not simply proceed on their own. There was a great deal of choice involved for the head, especially as she was an active and powerful participant in the 'stories'.

Liz was more consciously aware of the micropolitical dimension of her work than the women primary head teachers Hall (1996) studied. When she wanted to introduce a change, for example, she thought carefully about who to talk to first, when to do it, and what to say. Yet her actions were more than pure gamesmanship, as caring and compassion were evident as well as tactics and strategies. There was also great satisfaction when something good for the school was accomplished through her efforts.

Generally, Liz Clarke got on well with the teachers in the school and promoted a comfortable environment rather than an authoritarian regime. There was a domestic quality to the way in which she moved about the school. Like the teachers, she could be found doing her own photocopying, making coffee for a visitor or another teacher, watering the plants. In the office, she would be sharing tasks with the secretary, not simply issuing orders, and working in the interdependent way that Nias (1987) found for an infant school head and her deputy and described as 'one finger, one thumb'. In staff meetings, Liz de-emphasized her authority role by making jokes at her own expense, disparaging her own tendencies to forget things or get them out of order, making reference to her 'bird brain' or 'tiny mind'.

Her support for the teachers on her staff makes a marked contrast with some descriptions of principal behaviour (McCall, 1995; Troen and Boles, 1995). As we shall see in the next chapter, the teachers at Hillview worked together in a collaborative and participatory way, and Liz was scrupulous about encouraging and thanking them for their efforts for the school.

Liz Clarke's caring and supportive approach matches what one might expect from a female principal on the basis of some of the feminist and other theories about women's leadership mentioned earlier (see also Chapter 7 and the account of Debbie Stevens' deputy headship in Chapter 10). However, Mrs Clarke was still clearly the dominant figure at Hillview. It was 'her school', as several others have found in ethnographic studies of British primary school head teachers, both women and men (Hall, 1996; Nias et al., 1989; Southworth, 1995). Liz made her preferences known and teachers tried to meet them. In the cases of Marjorie Howard and Rosalind Phillips described earlier, Liz's ideas about where and what they should teach took precedence over their own. But there was room for dissent and sometimes Liz's ideas were rejected by the teachers in staff meeting discussion. In general, her power stemmed from her charisma and conviction as much as her formal position.

As I argued earlier in this chapter, an analysis of headship must take into account the gendered world we live in, while being careful about reaching simplistic conclusions about women or men – a difficult balancing act, to be sure. Mrs Clarke managed her school in a way likely to be more characteristic of women, but this does not mean all women principals will be like Mrs Clarke, or that Mrs Clarke worked the way she did solely because she is female. For example, a previous head of Hillview was also female, but teachers with long service at the school described her in very different terms. She 'liked everything to look nice, and to be quiet and orderly'. Many times I was told the story of the lights on the office door, intended for teachers as well as pupils: green for enter, yellow for wait, red for no entry. When I asked one teacher in an interview whether anyone had ever been particularly encouraging or discouraging about her career, she replied: 'Liz has been the most encouraging. [The former head] was the one who discouraged, not me in particular but I think she was discouraging to everyone. She wasn't interested; she didn't want to know.'

Neither are all men principals alike. Woods et al. (1997) give detailed profiles of three primary head teachers, two of whom are men. James is a dominant manager who enjoys entrepreneurial activity and monitors his staff at every chance he can get, while Raymond is an enabler, quick to delegate and to encourage flexibility and creativity among his teachers. James's style may well be a 'masculine-strong leadership model' (p. 117), but Raymond's is not. In other words, we cannot expect that all men will be alike any more than all women will be alike as head teachers.

In gendered comparisons, two important sources of variation have often been ignored. First, people are not 'only' male or female; they vary according to age, experience, social class background, ethnicity and a host of other characteristics that cannot simply be bracketed away when they become a head teacher or principal (Smulyan, 1996). Second, features of the environment are critical in encouraging or discouraging the exercise of a particular leadership style (Marshall and Mitchell, 1989). In Woods et al.'s (1997) study, James's 450-pupil school is on the fringe of a prosperous town and is 'monoethnic', while Raymond heads a large, inner-city, multi-ethnic school where there is a high degree of disadvantage. It stands to reason that headship style would need to be adapted to circumstances. Mrs Clarke's leadership style reflected her experience as a woman, what others expect of a woman in the role of head teacher, and the values women have often been encouraged to cultivate, such as an emphasis on interpersonal relations, collaboration and caring for others. It also reflected her political beliefs and value commitments, her own personal history, her age and educational experiences, and other features of her life. It reflected the traditions and expectations of students and parents and teachers at Hillview School.

One feature of the environment that was changing during the later part of my research was the extent of government intrusion into the primary school curriculum and assessment of the children as well as into school finance and governance. These changes threatened to detract from the enjoyment Mrs Clarke found in her job, as there were substantial pressures for the role of the head to become more entrepreneurial, more concerned with monitoring and reporting, and less involved in classroom teaching and interpersonal relations. Chapter 11 will examine some of these changes, noting their consequences for Liz Clarke.

Chapter 7

Colleagues, Cultures and Caring

It is the first staff meeting after the spring break, and the head teacher of Hillview, Liz Clarke, is newly returned from a term's sabbatical. There is a lengthy agenda. Near the end, Mrs Clarke begins to talk about staffing arrangements for the following year:

> 'The biggest problem I've got over the next two weeks is planning next session. I hesitate to take decisions too quickly; it is more irritating to have to change them. But any decent teacher starts thinking about next year now.' Helen Davies quips, 'What about the indecent ones?' Liz smiles and continues: 'The good of the children in the school is what I must think of first. A very close second is your preferences. I may not be able to give all of you all your preferences. But I'm now in a position of being able to take a global view. I also want to thank you all very much for keeping the school so well. There's a lovely feeling and the children seem very calm, very motivated and very happy.'

Episodes like this one struck me as quite wonderful: I appreciated the warm atmosphere and the caring leadership, which seemed in marked contrast to what was typical in the university where I worked. There were many contrasts between the school and the university, among them that the world of Hillview, despite the presence of one man on the teaching staff, was unmistakably female. How much did gender have to do with the warm, supportive atmosphere?

I spent much time puzzling over this question. I read feminist scholarship on the notion of a 'women's culture' or women's world. What a women's culture is or might be is construed differently by different writers, but the general idea is that 'the values that are structured into women's experience – caretaking, nurturance, empathy, connectedness' (Ferguson, 1984, p. 25) find their expression in a community of women. I tried to figure out how to incorporate this idea without ending up arguing that men and women were homogeneous and discrete categories, membership of which explained everything. I did not want a biological, or even social, determinism to enter into my analysis. Yet I wanted to foreground gender.

As I argued in my discussion of Liz Clarke's leadership in Chapter 6, the necessary balancing act is to understand that gender can be an important, even fundamental, organizing principle in schools without adding the assumption that our cultural understandings and expressions of masculinity and femininity are natural and unchanging outgrowths of biological differences. In this chapter, I want to bring together questions about gender and teachers' workplace cultures. I will show that the teachers' culture at Hillview displayed many of the features associated with a women's culture. In particular, there was a strong sense of collaboration and of caring for one another. Gender plays a part, but is not alone in creating this culture; features of the school also supported it. I begin with a review of some recent writing about women, teaching and caring.[1]

WOMEN, TEACHING AND CARING

In the work of some feminists, a perspective sometimes termed 'relational feminism' celebrates some of the traditional orientations of women, including caring. This perspective derives from research associated with Carol Gilligan (1982), Mary Belenky and her colleagues (Belenky *et al.*, 1986), Nona Lyons (1983), Nel Noddings (1984, 1992) and others who, disturbed at the privileging of men's experiences in studies of ethical decision-making, identity development and modes of learning, began to study 'women's ways', to put women's words and worlds at the centre of the analysis. An emphasis on an ethic of care and a preference for connectedness (relationships) is said to be more often characteristic of women than men.

The major difficulties with this approach are, as suggested above, its tendencies towards essentialism (the idea that women are like this 'naturally') and the difficulties of dealing with diversity and change. Norms for relationships among women change over time and there are women of many classes, races, ages and locations.

'Caring' appears frequently in discussions of teaching children. In the USA, Noddings (1992) makes caring the centrepiece of her call for school reform: '[T]he first job of the schools is to care for our children. We should educate all our children not only for competence but also for caring. Our aim should be to encourage the growth of competent, caring, loving, and lovable people' (p. xiv). Some British symbolic interactionist studies of primary school teachers also see loving or caring about children as being a mainstay of the teacher self. There seem to be a number of aspects here, including simply 'liking children' (Nias, 1989, pp. 33, 86–7), advocacy for the welfare of children (Nias, 1989, p. 34), delight and enjoyment in children's learning (Cortazzi, 1993; Pollard, 1985), closeness and warmth as part of a school's ethos (Woods, 1990).

Child-centred primary school pedagogy rests on notions of care and empathy associated with women and particularly mothers (Brehony, 1992). The ideal child-centred teacher (like the perfect housewife) becomes invisible – we see nothing but a happy bustle of active children – while her needs, her work, and her working conditions remain hidden as well (Langford, 1997, p. 17). Walkerdine (1981, 1986) sees child-centred teaching as a trap for women: it privileges the child over the teacher and assigns these largely women teachers an impossible task: 'Women teachers became caught, trapped, inside a concept of nurturance which held them responsible for the freeing of each little individual, and therefore for the management of an idealist dream, an impossible fiction' (1986, p. 55). Steedman (1987) continues the metaphor of imprisonment in describing her experience of being a 'mothering' teacher in the 'prisonhouse' school, sucked into a self-contained vortex of intense relationships with the children:

> I loved my children and worked hard for them, lay awake at night worrying about them, spent my Sundays making workcards, recording stories for them to listen to, planning the week ahead. My back ached as I pinned their paintings to the wall, wrote the labels with a felt-tip pen, a good round hand, knowing even then the irony with which I would recall in later years the beacon light of the martyr's classroom shining into the winter's evening, the cleaner's broom moving through the corridor of the deserted schoolhouse. (p. 118)

Like good mothers, good teachers find their work is never done. Broadfoot and Osborn (1988) found primary teachers in England believed they were accountable to practically everyone. Campbell and Neill (1994) reported that the British infant teachers (nearly all women) involved in the first wave of National Curriculum assessments were often 'overconscientious', spending vast amounts of time in extra preparation and marking, so much so that their health and personal lives and even the quality of relationships with pupils was suffering. Andy Hargreaves (1994) described elementary teachers in Ontario, newly granted preparation [non-contact] time, feeling guilty about deserting their classes and spurning offers for more such time. They 'appeared to drive themselves with almost merciless enthusiasm and commitment in an attempt to meet the virtually unattainable standards of pedagogical perfection they set themselves' (p. 126).

Some writers see the dedication as a consequence of the diffuse and ambiguous goals and achievements of teaching (A. Hargreaves, 1994). But when we introduce a gender analysis, we note that teaching, like mothering, has the expectations of 'altruism, self-abnegation, and repetitive labour' (Grumet, 1988, p. 87) characteristic of women's work. Its image as natural nurturing encourages us to forget that for teachers, the classroom is a workplace. McPherson's (1972) teachers described a 'good day' as 'one in which a teacher graded many papers, kept strict order, lectured to the class, and became very tired'. Steedman (1987) says about her years teaching children: 'I never left them: they occupied the night-time, all my dreams. I was very tired, bone-achingly tired all the time' (p. 127).

Teachers' caring activities, then, have from one perspective been seen as part of 'women's ways'; from another, as derived from their teacher identities; and from a third, as a consequence of the social expectations that women's caring work should blur the distinction between labour and love. The institutional contexts in which these caring activities take place are not as often explored, nor is the extent to which caring in a school context applies to relationships among adults, not just between adults and children. Extending the scope of approaches to teacher caring requires looking at real life situations such as Hillview School.

CARING IN THE CLASSROOM

What do we find in Hillview's classrooms, mothers or martyrs? Teachers certainly showed evidence of dedication beyond the call of duty. Rosalind carried on teaching even after some painful dental work: 'Give me five minutes; I'll be all right.' Debbie's husband was in Australia on business, and she joined him for the one-week half-term holiday. Even when encouraged to extend her stay to two weeks Debbie refused, as 'it wouldn't be fair; there wouldn't be a supply teacher'. Like the teachers described in other studies, Hillview teachers became very tired. Recall Debbie' s dialogue with her husband about how exhausted she was after a day with the children at the zoo (Chapter 5).

Chapter 4 contained examples of teachers' identification with their classes and caring for the children. Although, as pointed out, the negotiated order was inevitably fragile, I saw many examples of the close, warm relations between teachers and children that others have also found in primary schools (Woods, 1990). Inside classrooms, there were instances of relaxed banter between teacher and class:

> Debbie intones to her class of 10-year-olds: 'You will do silent reading when you come back in here after dinner . . . this is a recording . . . you will do silent reading when you come back . . .'

> Helen, with her 7-year-olds, praises Omar: 'Omar, well done. You are a clever clogs. What did you have for breakfast?' 'Weetabix.' 'I'll have to get some to make me clever.' Susie raises her hand. 'Susie?' 'I can read and I had cornflakes.'

Both teachers and children moved in and out of role, forgetting their dignity (Waller, 1932/1965) or their place, respectively. 'That noise is really bugging me', growled Dennis Bryan to his class. On another day, early in the term, Dennis is explaining some organizational matters and ground rules. He tells the children:

> 'Tidiness springs to mind . . . and putting things back where you got them from. Do not walk on other people's coats.' He starts to talk about arrangements for games. A child, Mark, interrupts: 'I reckon you should put that [a clock that has stopped] right because it's annoying when you haven't got a watch.'

The moments of closeness might seem to support a view of teachers as quasi-mothers in the classroom and to buttress the notion of teaching as an expression of caring. But, like real-life mothers, teachers struggled with 'their' children. There were a number of sources of stress for the Hillview teachers, as we saw in Chapters 3, 4 and 5. The characteristics of the children, the paucity of resources, the inadequacies of the physical setting, the nature of the school ethos all made Hillview a difficult, albeit often rewarding, school to teach in. What often disturbed the teachers was the sense that the children, and sometimes the parents, failed to appreciate – or even notice – what efforts they made. A discussion among the Middle Junior Unit teachers focused on this problem. Talk turned to the case of the mother who had complained to Sheila, and then to the head teacher, about the times tables testing. There were expressions of support:

> Debbie says, 'You can't win, you've got to sit and take it from all directions.' Sheila: 'Apparently I test too quickly.' 'Do you know', says Debbie, 'I do this and the class says they know their tables, then I say "two threes" and they say "oh, no, miss". They don't really know them.' The talk turns to parent interviews, and particular children, including one named Jane. Kristin says, 'She was writing with biro [a pen not allowed]. She's so rude, looking right at me, saying I don't care if I have to leave this school.' Rosalind agrees: 'She's manipulative, tries to set you up. She got her mother early in the term to believe I was down on her. Ever since then I always talk to her with Debbie present.' [Other children and their rudeness are discussed.] Debbie says, 'I'm fed up with being treated like a doormat.' 'The pleasant humanities of person to person are missing', Rosalind adds. 'I asked Harry to pick up something . . .' Debbie interrupts, 'I can tell you what he said – it's not mine.' Rosalind is nodding. Sheila asks, 'Is it our fault?'

Teachers wondered if they themselves were failing, when the children were so resistant to efforts to mould them into a caring community, as suggested by Sheila's last remark.

We see some elements of self-sacrifice, guilt and self-blame, reflecting the mothering subtext. But although the teachers cared for and about the children, caring had its limits. Teachers tried to do their best, not to work miracles. One of the ways in which teachers coped with a difficult situation was by mutual support and collegiality. The next section of the chapter explores the teachers' culture and the ways in which Hillview teachers cared for each other.

THE TEACHERS' CULTURE

As I noted in Chapters 1 and 2, a staple feature of descriptions of primary or elementary school teachers is their isolation and individualism. Usually what is meant by isolation is a literal physical separation from other adults, although it has also been used to suggest social isolation, especially for single women (Lortie, 1975). Individuality and isolation are thought to be historically created and supported by the physical layout of the typical elementary school (Lortie, 1975). Others (e.g. Feiman-Nemser and Floden, 1986) regard the immediacy, uncertainty and complexity of the classroom as demanding a teacher's full attention. Some educational reform literature advocates collegiality as a desirable alternative to individuality, but also – especially in the USA – stresses the rarity of the truly collegial school (Little, 1987, 1990).[2]

However, there are examples of primary schools in England working as 'collaborative cultures' (Campbell, 1985; Nias et al., 1989). In the schools Nias and her colleagues describe, all of which had fewer than ten teachers, teachers saw themselves as team members. They valued both the group and the individual. The cultures were maintained by celebrations, meetings, talk, humour and assemblies that reiterated school values. The leadership roles of heads and deputies were especially important in reinforcing the culture. Valentine and McIntosh's (1991) description of the work culture of a group of female nurse educators in Canada, sustained by rituals involving food and mutual support, is strikingly similar. In two other Canadian studies, one of an elementary school (Cole, 1991) and one of a new high school (Wignall, 1992), women principals were credited with creating a teacher culture with an exceptionally strong sense of community. These examples suggest that under certain conditions (often including female leadership), strong communities characterized by the values relational feminists claim are characteristic of women arise in female, or mostly female, work groups.

Here I discuss five aspects of the Hillview teachers' workplace culture.

These are: flexible roles; participation and equality; caring and mutual support; humour; and community. Together they make the culture a source of sustenance for the teachers who worked in the school.

Flexible roles

In a discussion of how adult education might be adapted to suit women's needs, Hughes and Kennedy (1985) argue that most women's lives are not linear constructions, but more aptly described as fragmented and characterized by multiple roles, creatively integrated. What I saw at Hillview was a preference for roles without clear-cut edges, a sharing of responsibilities rather than a separation of them. This preference could be seen as a weakness (diffuse responsibilities leading to no authoritative voice) or a strength (less dependence on 'expertise' in uncertain conditions, solidarity based on similarity rather than an interdependent division of labour). As we have seen, the work itself could not easily be packaged into a clear-cut teaching role. Like women's work in the home, it was diffuse and prone to expansion.

Teachers at Hillview had designated responsibilities for areas such as mathematics, science, music or special needs. A teacher with a particular responsibility would have the main input into ordering supplies and preparing inservice work in that field for the other teachers, and she might be available to colleagues for consultation. She did not usually teach that area more often than anyone else (with the partial exceptions of art, music and special needs) or have less than a full class teaching timetable in order to pursue it. Even in my early days in the school there were exhortations in the educational literature toward greater specialization (Campbell, 1985) and eventually the government reinforced that tendency by (for a time) giving teachers incentive allowances for particular responsibilities (see Chapter 10), moving the curriculum towards a subject-based conception, and requiring schools to produce curriculum documents for specific subjects. At first at Hillview, it was not very clear who had responsibility for an area such as art or science or display, but later on as a response to external pressures these roles were more clearly delineated.[3]

Chapter 5 demonstrated the extensions of the teacher's role beyond teaching as we usually understand it. Sometimes the work also went beyond what was clearly in the educational realm. The head teacher, in particular, had parents coming to her asking advice on legal or personal matters and the reception teacher also worked closely with parents, especially those with problems. Chapter 5 also described extra-educational work such as moving furniture; scouting for cheap supplies while on holiday; placing domestic or other skills at the service of the school. Often there was a domestic quality to school activity, as teaching merged into cleaning, sewing, watering plants, washing up coffee cups. This effect was intensified when, occasionally, the teachers' own children popped into the school, the older ones to help out with something or the younger ones when some caretaking arrangement might need augmenting.

Participation and equality: 'Shall we talk about Christmas?'

'It is a strength of the school', said Marjorie, 'we're willing to work as a team.' Teachers spent a great deal of time meeting and talking together, as I noted in Chapter 5. Staff meetings were scheduled for about 90 minutes once a week after school. The three infant teachers considered themselves a unit and consulted often with one another. The junior teachers tried various forms of joint planning. Teachers saw one another before and after school, during morning assembly, at morning playtime (coffee time for the teachers), and at midday dinner-time. Complicated timetable arrangements meant classes were paired for various activities or small groups withdrawn by a different teacher.

Staff meetings were characterized by a high level of participation in decision-making, even on minor matters. There were lengthy considerations of arrangements for assemblies and productions, resources, dates, projects, visits, evenings for parents, schedules for swimming or games, as well as discussion of curriculum or school policy topics such as handwriting, multi-cultural education, spelling, science, safety. Usually meetings were divided into 'domestic' and 'curriculum' portions. For example, a staff meeting in January 1989 began with a discussion of 'language morning'. The teachers involved compared notes on their groups and there was identification of children who might be wrongly placed. Next there was mention of the problem of finding parents willing to serve on the school governing body, then a discussion of arrangements for a class visit to a country school. A request from the local hospital for children's art work was conveyed. Teachers reviewed problems and procedures for supervision of children going into the hall for dinner. Sheila Jones talked about some ideas from her library course about a procedure for cataloguing posters, and teachers considered this idea along with related issues. Some health problems of specific children were reported.

The main item of business, development of a handwriting policy, followed. This discussion lasted about an hour, during which most of the teachers gave their views, speaking of how they taught the subject and which resources they found helpful. A number of issues came up, such as how old children should be before joining up letters and the special needs of left-handed children. Finally, teachers went through the alphabet letter by letter agreeing on preferred versions of each. The discussion was informal and open, and people spoke whenever they wished. It was characteristic of such meetings that all or most teachers explained their particular procedures or preferences on whatever topic was under consideration. The handwriting discussion was highly focused but some others were less so, accompanied by jokes and tangential topics.

'Shall we talk about Christmas?' ushered in lengthy discussions, carrying on over several months leading to the actual celebrations. As with other events like Harvest Festival, the plans were created collaboratively, with Helen Davies usually taking the lead. For example, in October 1988, there was a brief discussion about whether the Christmas event would be carol singing or a Christmas play. Several ideas were put forth and teachers agreed to 'think about it'. The topic recurred a month later and was tackled more thoroughly. Together they created a storyline with the theme of past, present and future, to be linked by the device of a carol singer who would fall asleep. There was discussion of carols and other songs that would fit the theme, and what each class could contribute. Marjorie then said, 'cue sheep', which referred to two boxes of fabric, enough for 36 grey sheep costumes, that had been donated.

The tendency for all teachers to express their view on an issue might be thought of as a commitment to a democratic, egalitarian way of working. One way in which teachers were differentiated from each other was by the allocation of what were called 'incentive allowances', a practice initiated by the government in 1987, though modified a few years later. Teachers wanted the recognition and the reward, but they objected to the designation of some contributions as more worthy than others. Schools had a limited number of these allowances and were expected to award them to deserving teachers on any of four grounds: extra responsibilities, good classroom teaching, difficult-to-fill positions, or shortage subjects. Extra responsibilities was the most common basis, but such responsibilities did not necessarily receive an allowance.

At one meeting, Liz Clarke mentioned that the school had received a B and two A allowances (A was the smaller, at the time worth about £600; B about £1000). In two cases, the recipient was something of a foregone conclusion, given long service and heavy responsibilities, but this left an A allowance that might have been given to any of several contenders. A remarkably open discussion ensued about who should receive the allowance, during which Helen Davies declared, 'As head of infant department, I think the reception teacher [Marjorie Howard] needs an allowance.' Liz commented that she hadn't been sure it should be discussed so openly, to which Helen commented, 'It's good that it is, open and democratic.' The head said that she could advertise and interview for these allowances, but was reluctant to do this. She also stated several times that she felt that every single one of the teachers deserved an allowance: 'You people jolly well don't need incentives.'

Caring and mutual support: 'She's so good'

Teachers showed concern and compassion for one another on many occasions. Rosalind was about to leave on one of her part-time days, but stepped in to take Sheila's class when a family emergency arose. Betty volunteered to take over the organization of the library when Sheila went on maternity leave. 'Did you ask her?' Helen enquired. 'No, she offered', Sheila replied. 'She's so good; she should have an allowance for this.'

In an interview, Marjorie told me about an episode from a few years back:

> Mrs Green at the time had been having Thomas, that group,
> with reception at the time, and once or twice I caught her
> upstairs in the staffroom crying her eyes out. They were a tough
> class, and they were really upsetting her. She'd had three or
> four years in reception . . . And I said to her one night, standing
> outside the staffroom in the corridor, 'Now look, Nancy, if it's
> that bad, for God's sake, tell me in the morning and I'll go
> straight to Mrs Clarke and we'll swap classes.' I didn't care
> about the work, I was thinking of her, really.

Problems would often be discussed by a group of teachers, sharing their troubles. The conversation among Debbie, Rosalind, Sheila and Kristin described earlier in this chapter is an example. In another case, the tradition of participatory discussion helped deal with a teacher's problems with a second-year junior class (J2) that had made a rocky start to the term. Debbie told me that Sheila, who was sharing J2 with Kristin, was 'not having an easy time'. 'It's a shock for Sheila', Kristin said, 'so different from her previous class' (see the snapshots in Chapter 4 of Sheila's inter-action with SJ, her class from the year before). Her high expectations were part of the problem, Liz explained; 'she tries to do what a full-time teacher would'. 'J2 is terrible', Rosalind said a few days later; 'I'm worried about taking them out to games, and Sheila's at the end of her tether.' Finally, the entire staff discussed the children's behaviour at a staff meeting and agreed to a plan of action.

Outsiders noticed the teachers' support for one another. When one teacher went out to relieve another on playground duty so she could come in for coffee and cake, Joan Miller, a retired teacher who did some volunteer work in the school, remarked to me:

> How wonderful it is to see teachers here caring about each other
> that way. It doesn't happen everywhere. You need that when
> the children get you down.

The head teacher also showed care and concern for her staff, as I detailed in Chapter 6. She gave teachers encouragement, praise and gifts such as chocolates after a Christmas production. In staff meetings she took the leading role but tried to draw out the quieter teachers. She gave individuals career advice, steered them towards useful courses and higher degrees, and took into consideration their domestic and child care responsibilities in making plans for the school.

Humour

Cortazzi (1991) gives many examples of primary school teachers' accounts of humorous incidents, and includes them in the same chapter as 'disasters'. He refers to these narratives as 'tragi-comedy' (p. 81). Humour was an important aspect of the teacher culture at Hillview. It was unlike the version described at Lowood Secondary School (Woods, 1979), or the schools studied by Cunnison (1989) or Coulter (1995), where sexist banter or 'gender joking' could be regarded as humorous. Jokes might have a sexual edge to them, but the largely female composition of the staff group ensured they were not sexist. Some of the humour could be described as 'jocular griping' (McPherson, 1972), but it did not result in dismissing or minimizing real problems as it did for McPherson's teachers.

Only rarely would humour take the form of set jokes. There were a few 'children's jokes' retold. The bulk of the humour arose from the school situation itself. Common were 'one-liners', on-the-spot quips. When the question of a theme for Harvest Festival came up, suggestions included 'food' and 'the Olympics', leading to ideas that combined the suggestions such as skits on 'runner beans' [a type of green bean] and 'jumping beans'. At another time the head referred to a child who was 'irremediable; down to go [to a special school]'. 'Have you tried Heineken?', Sheila queried innocently, referring to the popular beer advertisement that claimed to 'reach the parts other beers cannot reach'. There was laughter when something came out phrased not quite as intended, as when teachers were asked to name their 'two most least able children' for remedial help; or Liz Clarke firmly stamped some documents with a blank stamp; or when Liz, trying to get the teachers' attention in a noisy staff meeting, called them (unintentionally) 'Children!'

Amusing tales arose out of daily life in the school. Marjorie told us she had teased her 5-year-olds after the class Christmas party: 'There's so much food left over, we'll just have to have another party tomorrow.' 'Next day', she said, 'parents sent more food, a nan [grandmother] turned up.' A number of remarks directly or indirectly invoked the difficulty of teaching in this school or its poor resources. When Liz Clarke mentioned a school elsewhere where 'children were so listless', Helen asked with mock enthusiasm, 'Where's this school?' On another occasion, when Mrs Clarke asked for requests for resources, Sheila said 'Can I have another school?'

Stories might be at the (often affectionate) expense of the children, the parents, the head teacher or even the teacher telling the story. There was the out-of-control boy who had pushed a student teacher, then said 'excuse me' as he rushed past out of the door. Marjorie told the others about the dad whom she got to lie down on the floor in order to draw round him in chalk for a pattern of a giant: 'When he got outside his bike was nicked [stolen]. Mr Rogers [the caretaker] thinks maybe he didn't come on it. See, he knows our parents!'

Other remarks and anecdotes referred to the 'counter-cultural' or 'alternative' parents at the school. 'We must be the only school where we have to apologize to the parents for teaching their children something', Liz said to Dennis, after the visit by the parent who complained that the tables testing put her child under too much pressure. She told him the story of a prospective parent turning up on a bicycle from another side of the city. Liz asked her how she had heard of the school. 'At Greenham Common', the woman replied (referring to the anti-nuclear women's peace camp in another county).

The head teacher herself was sometimes a target, as when in an assembly she misheard Peter's reply to the question 'What's the happy part of Easter?' as 'He's alive'. Peter was extravagantly praised, although he had actually said 'Easter eggs'. The teachers suppressed giggles and later that day teased her in the staffroom. As mentioned in Chapter 6, Liz also used humour in jokingly disparaging her own shortcomings as due to her 'bird brain' or 'tiny mind', or in reference to a staff meeting discussion that had gone off track, 'We're not going to do what we planned to do, when do we ever'.

Teachers told anecdotes at their own expense. One day Helen was laughing after she had worked with a group of small children from another class:

> This child, Tom, said 'I can't write my name.' I said, 'Look at the board, there's a "T". He said, 'I can't do it.' 'Why not', I said, 'the letters are up there, T – O – M.' 'My name's Robert', he said.

Liz made an attempt to interest the older children in navigation, using some calculations from the ship's log of a boat she had sailed on. The sheets were poorly reproduced and the children, although trying to stay attentive, were clearly bored and the lesson not a great success. 'It's hard being a child', she chuckled later, referring to their putting up with the effort. It was hard being a teacher, too – and humour was a good coping strategy.

Community

There was a strong sense of community apparent among the Hillview teachers, especially in the staffroom, the private space off-limits to everyone else. Kainan (1994) sees the (secondary school) staffroom as critical in shaping teacher culture because it provides an antidote to the isolation of the classroom. Teachers can tell heroic stories and try to create positive images of themselves in front of colleagues. At Hillview the staffroom was less a site for one-upmanship than a place where solidarity flourished. There were jokes, chats, conversations both serious and light, and food. Birthdays and other events were marked by 'delicious cakes', as my notes frequently record. At the end of term, or the day after a Christmas concert or other production, there might also be sherry or other drinks. There were parties and dinners out at Christmas and the end of the school year for teachers and their spouses.

Some examples from field notes convey the sense of togetherness. On a day near the end of a term, I arrived for the staff meeting:

> Scones and tea are in the staffroom. There is a jovial atmosphere. There are two bottles of wine there, for Lisa's [a student teacher] last day. Kristin has brought in scones and jam for her birthday on Sunday. Everyone sang to her.

> Irene [a teacher on a temporary contract] brought nice biscuits [cookies] for her last day. People were laughing and joking. Dennis [who was completing a term as acting head] tries to call for some order. He thanks everyone for their support during the term. Marjorie has a child's doll's pram [buggy] which she wheels in with a big Easter egg for Dennis. She goes out again and comes in with an egg for Helen [who has been acting deputy head]. Marjorie has a poem on a card, which she reads out. Something doesn't rhyme. 'Oh well, I'm reception', she says.

At coffee the following day:

> The atmosphere is very pleasant, warm. There is a long playtime today as it is the last day of term and the assembly will be in the afternoon. Debbie is sitting on a chair, Marjorie standing behind her plaiting [braiding] her hair. She shows us how you can pin it up . . . Dennis comes in; there are jokes about plaiting his hair. This is 'toy day'; Debbie remarks that the children are no trouble at all when they can do what they want. When I leave I see Dorothy coming in with flowers for Helen and Jan [Dennis's wife].

CONCLUSION

Teachers cared deeply about the children and often had close relationships with their classes. Although these relationships resembled 'women's caring' as typified in the relational feminist literature, it was caring in a context.

As we saw in Chapter 4, teacher–pupil relationships could not be taken for granted; they had constantly to be negotiated and renegotiated. Teachers had to care for 30 children; they could not do that in the intense way mothers care, especially when in the next year there would be 30 more. Teachers taught under circumstances that made it difficult and often left them feeling angry and frustrated. These circumstances predated the additional stresses usually credited to government policy from 1988 onwards (Woods *et al.*, 1997).

Some of the difficulty stemmed from high expectations teachers held for themselves, derived in part from widespread beliefs about *women's* work and its 'labour of love' nature – set against material conditions that worked against high standards (Chapter 3). The classes were large; the resources were poor; the building created difficulties of noise and movement. The expectations of parents; the lives children led outside school; and the school ethos that children are important, that their differences should be welcomed, and that they must learn to care for one another all conspired to set up a situation where teachers needed reserves of skill, patience and tolerance.

Perhaps paradoxically, the attempt to do the impossible gave strong impetus to the development of a caring, mutually supportive teachers' workplace culture. There was much at Hillview that could fit the 'women's culture' model, including a preference for sharing rather than demarcating responsibilities; for participation over delegation; equality over hierarchy; support over competition. Humour was integrative rather than divisive. There was a strong sense of community, sustained by rituals.

My account of the teachers' culture at Hillview should not be taken to suggest that the atmosphere was cloying or cosy (Fullan and Hargreaves, 1991, p. 57). Although there were some good friends on the staff, teachers were not necessarily close. There were some teachers that would not have worked well together had they been sharing a class, and some jealousies and resentments. One heard 'grumblings' (Kainan, 1994) about the work, the children, the parents or the head teacher. There were potential lines of conflict – especially between infant and junior teachers, according to both Sheila and Nancy – and some competition for scarce resources. A distinction could be made between younger and older teachers. But the prevailing norm was to keep conflict under control and this did not seem too difficult a task. There were no deep divides like McPherson's subgroups of primary and intermediate, upstairs and downstairs, old guard and new teachers (McPherson, 1972) or the balkanized subcultures A. Hargreaves (1994) and Kainan (1994) describe.

My view is that there are certain cultural scripts seen as suitable for women in a given place and time, the caring script among them (L. Davies, 1984). Hillview teachers were not just working with any random assumptions, or even those built into the nature of teaching, but were following one (or several) of a set of scripts available to women in Western societies. It is not always possible for cultures to be organized around support and caring, even when they have women in them. For example McPherson's (1972) Adams School also had nearly all women teachers, but its teacher culture was marked by rivalries, refusal to help one another, isolation and individuality. The presence of a female leader at Hillview is certainly relevant, but simply having a female leader is no guarantee of a collegial, caring environment, as I argued in Chapter 6. In Hillview's case, the female leader had certain beliefs and practices that contributed towards the caring culture.

Just as the predominance of women does not guarantee that a collaborative and caring 'women's culture' will arise, neither does the presence of a few men prohibit it. There were no white males on the regular Hillview teaching staff. Hillview's one male teacher was black, of West Indian background but British-born. Dennis was in a position of authority as deputy head but not actually in the headship role. He was younger than many of the other teachers. He was conventionally ambitious but not without reservations about teaching as a long-term career. His motivations for entering it involved becoming a role model for black children. He was sensitive to marginality and employed more conscious anti-sexist strategies than most of the other teachers I observed. As noted earlier, he questioned whether Liz 'cared too much' – but his very concern could be seen as caring for her welfare. His presence did not appear to vitiate the 'women's culture'. The presence of a few men in elementary schools who share the general ethic of caring is not incompatible with the idea that a workplace culture will be based on a feminized gender script for all its members.

A competitive work environment, or a manager with other ideas, would work against the emergence of such a culture. Circumstances at Hillview permitted a particular workplace culture, featuring values traditionally associated with women, to emerge. The results suggest we should add to what we know about teachers' individual survival or coping strategies (Woods, 1990) some exploration of *collective* teacher strategies and the institutional conditions under which they emerge. Moreover, we need analyses of teachers' work that acknowledge the influence of gendered scripts and surroundings on teacher beliefs and ways of working, without too ready a recourse to an essentialist equation of women with caring.

We can question what consequences follow from the presence of 'women's cultures' in some primary or elementary schools. Several writers point to deleterious ones: the need for connectedness brings vulnerability (Ferguson, 1984); the ethic of care can promote self-sacrifice and martyrdom (A. Hargreaves and Tucker, 1991). Collegiality can be contrived and pre-scribed; even organic collegial leanings can be harnessed in the service of managerial ends (A. Hargreaves, 1994; Lawn, 1996; Menter *et al.*, 1997; Woods *et al.*, 1997). State interventions may take advantage of women's traditional orientations toward caring and hard work (Apple, 1988; Menter *et al.*, 1997, p. 116). Schools receive a disproportionate share of blame for economic or political troubles of a nation – sometimes as a deliberate strategy (Menter *et al.*, 1997) – and stereotypes about maternal nurturance lend themselves to a situation where 'blame is deflected from the men who establish [the] policies onto the women who teach the children who fail' (Grumet, 1988, p. 23). Thus any celebration of the women's culture in schools like Hillview must be tempered by our knowledge of the wider circumstances in which it must operate. Yet, if we are to take seriously the symbolic interactionist emphasis on making meaning, it is clear that the meanings made by Hillview teachers helped them to cope with adverse circumstances and produced a workplace culture that was mutually supportive and affirming. How many of us can make such a claim for our own workplaces?

NOTES

1. For more detail on this topic, see Acker, 1995a.

2. In contrast, Menter *et al.* (1997, p. 63) assert that pre-1988 literature on British primary schools overemphasizes the presence of collaboration and ignores the operation of micro-politics.

3. See Osborn and Black (1994), Webb and Vulliamy (1996), and Woods *et al.* (1997) for discussions of the increasing specification of curriculum coordinators' roles within British primary schools.

PART THREE

CROSSING THE BOUNDARIES

Chapter 8

School Boundaries

The horrific massacre of young children in March 1996, at Dunblane in Scotland, brought home to many how difficult to safeguard are the perimeters of a primary school. Hillview, like other such schools, was open to the public. There were worries from time to time that a non-custodial parent might snatch a child from the playground. But by and large Hillview seemed safe, protected by its out-of-the-way location and the relatively small scale of the school that supported the staff's familiarity with parents and other regular visitors. Yet in a less literal sense, there was a lot of activity around the boundary of the school. Like David, Edwards, Hughes and Ribbens (1993, p. 13), I like the concept 'boundary' for its symbolic as well as concrete meaning. We can refer to persons and groups 'on the boundary' and mean, in part, those who literally stand at, or cross on particular occasions, the territorial limits of the school premises; we can also use the concept to draw attention to the separation between the identities and understandings of groups differently positioned in terms of the school's core activities. Children and school staff, including teachers, cross the boundaries regularly, while parents and others do so less frequently and usually with special purposes in mind. Boundary crossing can be a physical act or one accomplished through a telephone call or letter.

The school may have many features of a small society (Waller, 1932/1965), but there are limits to the analogy. People did not live in the school. Staff and children alike went home and returned the next day. At any particular time, there would be many visitors in the school who were not part of the fixed staff complement. The school was involved in relationships with other area schools and subject to policies of the local education authority (LEA) and directives of the central government. Just as I argued earlier that the image of a teacher imprisoned in her cellular classroom was too simplistic, so too is the picture of the school isolated in its self-sufficiency. Along with individuals, information (ranging from gossip to cautionary tales to ideas for innovation) circulates through this web of contacts.

The discussion on the following pages is divided into two sections. First I give an idea of the relationships enacted on a daily basis between the school and its wider community, usually through visits and telephone calls. Next I look at a specific set of relationships, those with 'other schools'. I show that through 'contrastive rhetoric' (A. Hargreaves, 1984), images of 'other schools' help Hillview to define its own distinctiveness. Chapter 9 continues the focus on the boundaries and the school's 'public face' by considering its relationship with its parents, probably the most important of the players on the periphery.

WHO'S IN THE SCHOOL?

The school was a people-rich environment, filled with adults as well as children. To make this study manageable, most of my attention focuses on Hillview's six full-time and three part-time teachers and the head teacher. But for the full cast of players, we would need to add many other adults, even in this relatively small institution. Most obvious, perhaps, are the additional staff at dinner- [lunch-] time. Lunches are not cooked at the school, but delivered by the 'tin man'. Two 'kitchen ladies' serve the food to the children in the hall and later wash up the dishes, while five 'dinner ladies' supervise the children's eating and playtime before and after lunch.

The school also has to be maintained and kept clean. The caretaker, Mr Rogers, locks and unlocks the school, and looks after heating, the alarm system and general maintenance. At the end of the day, the school is cleaned by another set of workers. Cleaning was fairly unproblematic through much of my research until the point where it was 'contracted out' by the LEA. The firm awarded the contract replaced the former staff by a new crew of workers who circulated around several schools and seemed unable to cope with the job. At this point, Mrs Clarke had to make some major efforts towards on the one hand keeping parents informed and at the same time apologizing to them, while finding some solution.

There is also a fluctuating population providing classroom support for teachers. The general assistants (GAs) had the most firmly established support role in the school. As noted earlier, one of these positions was held by Dorothy Lowe, who in practice worked mostly as the school secretary, with occasional spells of assisting one or other of the teachers. The other GA, Beryl Tucker, stayed in the 'activity room' with rotating groups of children from the younger classes. For the youngest children, there was additional help on a part-time basis from 'nursery nurses', almost always women, in training at a nearby college for jobs that involve child care. One or two of the teachers would probably have a student teacher for a term. Supply teachers were also in evidence, sometimes for fairly long periods of time if there were a prolonged teacher absence. A youth training scheme might provide an additional helper. Less involved were occasional helpers such as older children from a secondary school, parents and a few other volunteers. Parental help would usually be solicited on an *ad hoc* basis e.g. for taking classes out of the school on visits.

There were regular inputs into the school from peripatetic teachers, i.e. those who moved from school to school, usually giving music lessons. Most prominent was the violin teacher, Caroline Pringle, who came once a week to give lessons to a selection of older children. There was also a guitar teacher. During my research, the local multicultural education centre added Hillview to its list of schools receiving support, and one of its staff members came to school on two half-days each week to work with certain students. After some complicated negotiations, a regular session once a week with a visiting specialist in remedial reading was set up for a small group of older children. During the time Peter was in the school, an emergency request to the LEA also produced an extra teacher who spent an hour a day with Peter alone.

Other visitors connected with the LEA were frequently in school. The most regular figures were the nurse who was there once a week and the educational psychologist. The teachers would refer children to the nurse when they thought there might be a health problem. The educational psychologist might be giving special needs training or advice to teachers or checking on the progress of a troubled child or seeking to get a child with some difficulties transferred from another school to Hillview. Other health personnel such as a dentist or audiometrician appeared on an occasional day to treat or test a group of children. Advisors from the LEA might visit either in their capacity as curriculum advisors for a particular subject or because the school was one of a cluster deemed the responsibility of that particular individual and visited a few times in each term. Advisory teachers – teachers who were seconded to work with the LEA in a particu-lar capacity for several years – were also available, usually when the school asked for help or advice. My research predated the current era of manda-tory inspections by OFSTED (the Office for Standards in Education, created by the 1992 Schools Act to replace the former system of visits by Her Majesty's Inspectors) although there were a couple of semi-formal visits by advisors or inspectors that produced reports on the school's successes and needs.

Hillview is a 'voluntary controlled' primary school.[1] 'Voluntary' means that a school funded through the LEA has church ties: this connection is stronger for 'voluntary aided' and weaker for 'voluntary controlled' schools. Voluntary aided schools include Church of England, Roman Catholic and a smaller number of Jewish schools, while voluntary controlled schools, like Hillview, are mostly linked to the Church of England. (In January 1998, two Muslim schools were for the first time approved for state funding.) Just over a third of the primary schools in England in 1987 were voluntary schools (D. Johnson, 1990, p. 37), while the other two-thirds did not have specific connections with a religious organization. However, it is important to note that *all* publicly funded schools in Britain are expected to provide religious education and a collective act of worship. The 1988 Education Reform Act specified that with certain exceptions this worship should be 'wholly or mainly of a broadly Christian character' (D. Johnson, 1990, p. 36). In practice, some schools highlight religion more than others. Like many other schools with multicultural and multifaith populations, Hillview interpreted its religious mission in largely humanistic and community-building ways, rather than as a strictly religious exercise. The relationship between Hillview and its local church was cordial though not intimate. The church vicar would visit from time to time and the school held certain events at the church.

Each school in Britain has a governing body legally charged with making certain decisions for the school. In a voluntary school, a proportion of the school governors are representatives of the particular religious organization. At the time of my research, a voluntary controlled primary school of Hillview's size would have three parent governors, one teacher governor, three local authority governors, and four church governors, plus the head teacher (who could at that time choose whether to be formally designated as a governor or not) (see Hill, 1989, p. 5). Governors and the head teacher would meet about once a month. They held an annual meeting for parents and produced a report about the school. Individual governors could get more involved with day-to-day activities within the school if they wished. In many cases, of course, full-time employment precluded any regular commitment. While some other governing bodies had reputations for internal strife and interference in the daily activities of the schools, in Hillview's case, the governors were on good terms with the head and the school, and not particularly intrusive. By and large they listened to and followed the wishes of the head teacher. Several Education Acts before, during and after my research gave governors additional powers and responsibilities over school finance, hiring, salaries and policies; in the late 1990s they are more powerful than they were at the time of my study (Lawn, 1996, p. 115).

The above description has covered the main categories of school-related personnel and visitors, apart from parents, prospective parents and certain contacts with other schools, to be discussed in other sections below and in the next chapter. However, it has not exhausted the list. On a given day, the head might see someone from the central office of the local education authority, the social services, the play scheme that operated at the school after hours, publishers' or toy companies' representatives, community groups, the traffic warden, local residents, researchers or student teacher supervisors from the universities, and miscellaneous others. As noted in Chapter 5, the teachers would move in and out of school, taking groups to sites for swimming, games, skating, library or musical activities or for educational visits. They went on courses, attended meetings and inservice training days and made visits to other schools, perhaps in connection with a job interview or to liaise with the secondary schools where children would go after leaving Hillview. Sometimes teachers had to attend to personal business such as a dental appointment or an activity at their own child's school. During the lunch break, they might dash out for some shopping or to have lunch out, although more often than not, teachers stayed in the school. The head teacher had further commitments outside the school such as case conferences or meetings with other heads. There was additional movement: the caretaker taking the mail to the authority or collecting it; the secretary delivering papers to individual governors or buying a sandwich for the head at lunch-time.

Thus there was a constant interchange of people who went in and out of the school. It is important to note their presence, because it contradicts the idea that a school is an isolated society. Although each school has its own culture, it is formed in contact with the wider society, in the particular local context. One important feature of that context is other schools, especially those in the local area.

OTHER SCHOOLS

'Other schools' was not a theme that I noticed early in my field work, nor one I had anticipated. It truly emerged from the data. When doing preliminary analysis of field notes I began to notice how often there was talk of other schools, usually in or near the city. After a while, I decided that this talk had some purpose beyond just casual conversation. I now see it as helping to define what Hillview is and is not, through a process similar, though not identical, to what Andy Hargreaves (1984) called 'contrastive rhetoric'. Hargreaves analysed a series of taped curriculum discussions held by teachers at a middle school in England. 'Contrastive rhetoric' was defined as follows:

> Contrastive rhetoric refers to that interactional strategy whereby the boundaries of normal and acceptable practice are defined by institutionally and/or interactionally dominant individuals or groups through the introduction into discussion of alternative practices and social forms in stylized, trivialized and generally pejorative terms which connote their unacceptability. (p. 218)

For example, in the middle school discussions, some alternative ways of approaching education were raised, linked with a well known 'progressive' school. Discussion turned into laughter at the supposed extremes carried on at that school. Hargreaves refers to images of (in)famous schools becoming deeply embedded in teacher folklore, having potential to trigger strong feelings, along with exaggeration of the differences between the teachers' current situation and the (threatening) alternative. What is produced is a 'sometimes humorous but always dramatic definition of normality by reference to its opposite, deviance. And thus the demarcation (albeit a hazy one) of the outer limits of existing practice' (A. Hargreaves, 1984, p. 220). Hargreaves goes on to look at additional functions of contrastive rhetoric and also finds that in his transcripts, the defining statements were generally introduced by the persons in power – the head teacher or the deputy head teacher. He believes that their dominance is not only due to their formal position but to their greater access to knowledge about educational alternatives. Experience was considered a better guide than theory, and these individuals could call on more experience than could their teacher colleagues.

There were several differences between Hargreaves' observations and my own. At Hillview, talk about other schools might be initiated by anyone, not just the head teacher or deputy. Perhaps the difference stems from different observational methods, as my field notes incorporate informal as well as formal situations. Most of my notes on this topic did not come from staff meetings. Perhaps also the Hillview teachers were not as limited in their experience as those in Hargreaves' middle school. What I think is similar is the use of statements about other schools to heighten what is special about one's own school. As the contrasts could be either flattering or deprecating, it was not clearly defining the normative against the deviant. But there did seem to be a cumulative effect of fragments of conversation incorporating comparisons, which was the spelling out of what was unique about this particular school, Hillview. Through talk about other schools, 'this school' and thus its teachers could be positioned somewhere comprehensible in the wider scheme of things.

The comparisons helped teachers analyse their own levels of satisfaction, assess how well they were doing, decide whether they were working harder than they would elsewhere, ponder whether to go for promotions or transfers to other places. They gave a framework, albeit loosely constructed, with which to think about one's own school's ethos, the idiosyncrasies of its children or parents, the head's management style, collegiality with other teachers, and adequacy of resources and facilities in the school. Teachers' approach towards their school as a place to work, with virtues and vices, is constructed largely at the workplace level, through a discourse of comparisons and contrasts.

Secondary versus primary schools

Some of the references referred to the divisions between primary and secondary schools. Primary school teachers knew that their contributions to a child's life had a temporal end, and that the secondary schools inherited all of their efforts. Generally, they suspected that the secondary schools were not up to the job. An added level of distrust was created by the difficult system in operation at the time in Wesley for allocating children at ages 11 to 12 to secondary schools. Although parents certainly made choices, choices might not be honoured. The situation was complicated in several ways.

One complication was the existence of a few state schools in the area that were still academically selective to some degree (called grammar schools), and thus required a passing score (different from year to year) on an examination given to the children in their last year of primary school. Tests were not normally a feature of life at Hillview, and this particular one was seen as not only ideologically unsound but an intrusion into school life. Parents had to opt for other choices in case the children were not admitted into the grammar schools, but there was always a slight risk that their preferred comprehensive (non-selective) school might not have room for them by the time the test results were known. The school also found itself helping children and their parents appeal for places if they were not initially admitted. Another complication was that children at Hillview came from a scattered geographical area already, and so some would wish to attend secondary schools nearer their homes. A third one was that there were also selective independent schools in the city, requiring fees as well as entry examinations, and some parents wanted their children to attend one of these schools.

The last year of primary school, then, when the children had achieved their most socially mature and academically successful status, was shadowed by the prospect of the peer group being about to be broken up and by the uncertainty about future placement for some of the children.

> Liz shows me the list of children and schools. More have applied this year so the cut-off score was higher. Only six got into Kingston [the local state grammar school] right away. They are down to go to nine different secondary schools. She is upset to see this group broken up. She takes the envelopes into Dennis's class. She tries to explain the system to the class. She suggests they visit the comprehensive school on their letters; some are very good. If they are not happy, they should appeal straight away. Some will be going to private schools. Where you go is mostly to do with where you live, no matter how high you are on the test, she reassures them. She tells them not to open the envelope now but take it home for their parents. A few children follow her, looking worried, to ask her about things. They ask her about individual schools and what they should do in particular cases. Liz says maybe next time she should have a meeting with the parents. I see the list of children and their

scores. The highest are 125 and 126; the cut-off for Kingston is 99.

So, although there were liaison activities and visits to local secondary schools, the whole transfer process was an awkward one for Hillview. But beyond the specifics of the situation, there seemed to be other reasons for what may well have been a mutual distrust. The 'top class' was about to be redefined as the bottom, age-wise. In one conversation I commented about how mature the older children were becoming. 'Trustworthy, too', Liz added. 'It's a shame the secondary schools assume it [their transition] will be traumatic, treat them like babies.'

Another source of resentment was the better working conditions secondary school teachers enjoyed, namely more 'non-contact' [preparation] time. At an inservice training day that brought together teachers from a number of primary schools, one of the speakers spoke of primary teachers as 'very, very unfairly prejudiced against' for this reason, linking the situation with the new expectations for a National Curriculum to be delivered despite inadequate planning time for primary teachers. After another inservice training day that mixed primary and secondary school teachers, several of the teachers came back to Hillview, upset at what they had heard. They thought the secondary teachers were disaffected and aggressive; some, mostly men, 'just sat back'. 'They just want us to ask how we can prepare children for them.' Judging from the speakers, 'all of the exciting work was on the primary side': 'I was proud to be part of the primary group' said Debbie.

Other primary schools

Positioning Hillview

Most references to 'other schools', however, were to other primary schools. Some conversations drew on what could be thought to be an implicit typology of primary schools. Hillview was positioned somewhere between 'real inner-city schools' and 'leafy suburb schools' (sometimes 'posh schools'), not quite at home with either group. Many of the references in my field notes were to schools that were relatively close geographically. Among these are the four schools that most often lost students to Hillview (see Chapter 9) and three others that served a somewhat more affluent group of students and parents than Hillview's. Probably all of these schools could have been placed on a continuum of average parental affluence, with Hillview in the middle. An occasional shorthand for referring to the two groups (augmented by several other schools in each case) was 'down the hill' and 'up the hill'.

Liz Clarke belonged to two area heads' groups that represented 'down' and 'up' respectively, symbolizing Hillview's ambiguous status in the middle. These were unofficial groups, each containing head teachers of six or seven schools. Hillview was the only school to belong to both. This positioning could cause difficulties, such as the time when bids were taken from clusters for funds for projects, and Liz chose to cluster with the more middle-class schools for the purpose. The inner-city group was successful, the middle-class one was not. From an interview with Liz in 1991:

> I imagine that it's been rejected purely because it's being assessed that the needs of the schools in that cluster are not as great as the needs of the schools in the other cluster and I can't argue that, I can't fault that, except that I am the idiot who's clustered in with the wrong group, because my needs are very intense . . . my needs, *our* needs, we actually have 25 per cent special needs children, that's a quarter of our children and that is a very high percentage and that's certainly not true of the other schools I've clustered with, but I preferred to fly high rather than to fly low. I think it's better for the school, I think it's better for the aspirations of all our parents that we look to the middle classes and don't sort of bewail our situation.

My field notes suggested that being in the inner city did not have a single meaning, either:

> I asked if there were any other schools over where the prospective parent who wanted to move her child from Martindale lived. 'Only Rivertree', Liz says, 'and it's even more a sink school, without the inner-city élan.'[2]

To 'up' and 'down' we would need to add a category for the additional schools that entered into comparisons but were not located near Hillview. Some might be 'out' – rural, or located in a very different area of the city – but encountered through teachers' past careers, interviews for future jobs, or in the neighbourhood where a teacher lived. Others could perhaps be described as 'elsewhere', schools that were in other parts of the country entirely, but perhaps had been part of a teacher's earlier career or encountered for some other reason.

Sources of teacher knowledge about other schools
Teachers made many comments about other schools, basing their information on a range of sources. One such source came from teachers who were also parents. They would compare what they knew of their own children's schools with Hillview. So Sheila said about her daughter's school, 'it's quiet there'.

Teachers would contrast Hillview with the schools they had worked at in the past:

> Liz was reminiscing about her [former] country school. 'It's now closed. It was in a beautiful setting.'

> Debbie says: 'In my last place I was a Scale 2 for computers. Everything was so organized. I hate to think what needs doing here.'

Teachers came into contact with other schools either directly or through talking to teachers from those schools whom they met on courses, joint inservice training days, or through associations. They sometimes had friendships with teachers in other schools or relatives who were teachers. A teacher might visit other schools in an organized fashion, for example as part of a sabbatical. An informal exchange was arranged between Marjorie Howard and her counterpart at a rural school. Teachers who were looking for promotions to deputy headships went to other schools before making formal applications and when called for interview. They shared their perceptions with other Hillview teachers afterwards. Sometimes teachers took groups of children to a setting where they would see those from other schools, for example sports events, joint concerts, country dancing, and other competitions and special events. Teachers who had moved on to other positions sometimes came back to visit:

> Mr Benton is there today. He says how different it is [in his new school, in a village] – how the children lack spark. He's working on it. Some have learning difficulties. They're all so quiet. The classes have 11 or 17. The secretary has a completely quiet Tuesday to catch up as everyone is off for games.

Another major source of information about 'other schools' came from those individuals who passed through the boundaries of Hillview. Parents, especially those who had moved their child from somewhere else to Hillview, might talk to the teachers about the other school. The educational psychologist, an advisory teacher, a reading specialist, the violin teacher, the teacher from the multicultural education centre and other visitors all shared with me or with the teachers their experiences elsewhere and underlined the contrasts. The same was true with student teachers who might be working at Hillview after a placement elsewhere, and supply teachers who might work in more than one school. Here is a conversation where we see Hillview compared to schools that are 'up', 'down' and 'out'.

> Adrienne, the teacher who came in to work individually with Peter [see Chapter 4], told me about the different schools she knows about. For a while she worked in Outbury [an outlying, working class area of the city]. 'You can manage there if you're single, but it's so draining, you can't do justice to your own children when you get home.' Now she works at Hillview, St

Augustine and Brookline. I ask about the differences. 'They are very different. Brookline is very organized, with great curriculum plans for a term all posted up . . . The parents are in all the time. The resources are much better. The parents contribute and they can raise loads of money. St Augustine is like Hillview, though the parents include more teachers, are slightly more professional . . . Outbury is real deprivation. If you take the children on a trip with parents along, it's the parents who need the supervision, they're the ones who go off into the lake.' I ask 'What do you prefer?' 'Hillview and St Augustine, the middle ones.'

One of the student teachers in the school, Karen, told me about her previous teaching practice in an area much like Outbury. She couched her discussion in comparative terms, telling me that it is very different here (at Hillview) because parents care, are involved, while at Allton (an infant school, i.e. with children aged five to seven), some wouldn't turn up to pick up their children. The children were already 'hard' at a young age, she said. 'Every time they'd change for PE we'd have to check for bruises – there was a terrible case with barbed wire.' I asked her what she found hardest about Hillview. She replied: 'Days when I'm feeling a bit low, some of the children take advantage, play you up.' 'What do you like most?' 'They make me laugh, their quirky sense of humour, for example in the aquarium there was something like a leech and one of the boys wanted to have it suck his blood.'

On another occasion, in a staff meeting, Liz asked Colin, a teacher working temporarily in the school, what his impressions of Hillview were.

> Colin said he hadn't really seen a nasty class. He talked about his experiences at Edgewater, where 'you're really talking violence'. He said he'd heard of or seen children stabbed, children who slept in their clothes, urinated in classrooms. At Hillview, he thought that the children, despite their freedom, were under reasonable control. It was difficult when there were not enough resources like pencils, though, he said.

Comments of Karen and Colin contrast with those of Joanne, a student teacher who had started out in a more affluent school: 'It was a real culture shock when I first came here . . . Parkside was very different, a very organized school.' Similarly, Simon, another student teacher, told me 'My last school was easy, this one is hard.'

Content of comparisons
The quotations above suggest that not only do these and similar statements place Hillview in a status hierarchy *vis-à-vis* other schools, but they

131

differentiate it from the other schools on a number of dimensions. One might be something elusive, ineffable, perhaps best titled 'cachet'. Compared to Overbury, Allton or Edgewater, schools on outlying estates created by urban redevelopment and devoid of charm and amenities, Hillview had much to recommend it. It had good academic results, an interesting mixture of parents, including some who were well educated and/or in professional occupations. It had an attractive ethos, as described in Chapter 3. In contemporary parlance, it had 'attitude'. At the same time, it had enough structure to avoid the ever-present possibility of attitude tipping over into chaos.

Cautionary tales from other inner-city schools told of the dangers of chaos. The remedial reading specialist who visited Hillview once a week told me: 'A chaotic school is Oak Grove. Nothing is "together", there's a new head from within who's not up to the task.' Charlotte, the educational psychologist, remarked that Hillview was 'not a typical [inner-city] school: it's cosy and well run. You should see the chaos at Martindale.' A more detailed story about Martindale came from Debbie, who had been talking to Dennis's wife, Jan, who was doing supply teaching there:

> The whole school [Martindale] was in the hall and were meant to sing something. Four or five boys refused. They were massive, streetwise boys. The head asked them to do it alone. They did it with stupid voices. The whole school was rolling around, in hysterics, out of control. One boy said 'You can't make me – I've hit you before and I'll do it again.' She got hold of him and a male teacher came to help – the boy grabbed his tie but they got him out. The teachers were fuming . . . The head came back in, lectured the children. Just then a parent came in and picked up her child, saying 'who do they think they are, speaking to children like this'. She went around telling other parents. The head rang Jan, knowing she was married to Dennis, and Jan said she wouldn't say anything about it. She said 'I don't mind you mentioning it, I'd rather have the true version get round.' Debbie said it's like one of her nightmares.

A certain amount of chaos might not be too bad, though, if combined with other virtues, like 'élan' or 'bonhomie'. In an interview, Kristin talked to me about her search for a deputy headship:

> About six deputy head jobs came up . . . There was a job at Dockside. I looked – I was not at all impressed. It was similar to Hillview but without the bonhomie, the charisma, the comforting buzz of semi-chaos.

A related dimension is the difficulty of working in one school rather than another, often coupled with notions about what and where would provide satisfaction. One teacher, Rosalind Phillips, was working part-time in each of two schools. She talked repeatedly about the contrasts between Hillview and her other school, Queen's Park.

> Rosalind thinks perhaps she's coming down with a virus sweeping through Queen's Park. She says she could do Queen's Park without trouble when she's not well, but is worried about being here [at Hillview]. 'I work harder here', she said.

Recall, too, Simon's characterization, quoted above, of his student teaching schools as 'easy' and 'hard'. Schools such as Queen's Park that served affluent populations were thought to be easier to teach in. Descriptions of more affluent schools tended to stress their academic results, good organization or controlled behaviour. In an interview in 1991, Liz Clarke noted about another nearby school: 'Parkside is much more middle-class, infinitely more middle-class and infinitely more competitive and pushing. Our parents . . . are non-competitive for their children. They're assertive but they don't want them to see them succeeding at the expense of others, they really don't want that.' The year before, Marjorie Howard had visited Orchard Road, well known for being an exemplar of 'High Scope', an approach to primary schooling that involved children choosing and negotiating their activities, with careful preparation, including different activities set up in different places in the classroom: 'Orchard Road was High-Scoping away. I had tears in my eyes, it was so well organized. I had to walk out.' My own notes on Rosemont produced many contrasts to Hillview. One day at Hillview I wrote:

> The difference between schools is powerful. This noise, mock fighting would never be allowed at Rosemont! This 'quiet room' is not very [quiet]! . . . By and large the children [in Dennis's class, the oldest group in the school] are very self-directing. Nearly all want to get on and do something. They are very similar at Rosemont in George's room [the equivalent age group], but it's at their own tables, directed at their own work, with little movement.

Nevertheless, teaching in a difficult school was not necessarily to be avoided. There was satisfaction in coping, in doing a challenging job well. Such work could also be perceived as noble:

> The teachers are talking about Nancy's impending interview for deputy head in an infant school. They pass around the list of local vacancies. Helen comments about a job in a special school – if you could get through [to the children] it could be really rewarding. Marjorie talks about looking for a job in secondary remedial, now that she knows more about teaching to read.

Comparisons with other schools anywhere on the socioeconomic continuum suggested that Hillview was superior in several respects. One was collegiality, explored in Chapter 7. Helen came back after a visit to the school she would shortly be joining, as acting deputy head. My notes say: 'Helen is very depressed. She says they all have their own mugs there, do their own washing up. "It really came home to me that here we are all one big family", she said.' Hillview's teachers perhaps also held the edge on creativity:

> Rosalind says that what Debbie and Dennis are doing would be wonderful at her other school. There they are dull and traditional. She wishes she could get teachers from each school into the other one.

And although teachers might be critical of Liz Clarke's management style on occasion, comparisons with other head teachers usually favoured her:

> Rosalind talks about the head of Queen's Park in a very critical way. She says it's made her realize how good Liz is as a head. He keeps his door closed, doesn't make an effort to communicate with the staff or ask them about themselves.

On the other hand, comparisons regarding the state of decor or resources were inevitably detrimental to Hillview (see also Chapter 3):

> Liz comes back from a meeting at St Luke's: 'What we could do with a building like that . . . what we have to offer is just as good, or better.'

> Rosalind tells me she brought in the plates from home, the glue stick from Queen's Park. Hillview is so poorly resourced compared to Queen's Park, she says. I ask why. The children there bring more things from home, she suggests, and the priorities for ordering resources may be different.

> Liz discusses the cleaning problem [caused by the county putting cleaning on a contract basis]. 'Other schools look so beautiful', she says. 'We're in a terrible state of decoration, however hard you work.'

CONCLUSION

Hillview, like other schools, has its own staff and its own children, but there is a fluctuating population of persons on the periphery. Some might be designated support staff, as they help teachers, prepare lunches, supervise children and otherwise contribute to the life of the school. As well, agencies or groups like the church, the local education authority and the school governing body all have an impact on the functioning of the school.

Teachers carry on a public and private dialogue that attempts to place Hillview in a wider network of schools, in order to assess its attractions and difficulties as a workplace and by extension set standards for their own practice. Their impressions are formed in a mode of contrast with 'other schools'. Information for that process can be gleaned from multiple sources, including teachers' past experiences, the schools their own children attend, conversations with other teachers, parents and other individuals. Through this process, we (and the teachers) learn that Hillview is an inner-city school, but with 'cachet' or 'élan', and it is 'well run' rather than mired in chaos. It is less organized and less calm than some schools, especially more affluent ones, which generally possess better resources and facilities. Hillview is also unlike the schools on outlying estates, with their poverty and bleakness. The staff see Hillview as a hard, but rewarding, venue to work in, and benefit from the collegiality and generally good management they find there.

Important in the life of the school is another group – the parents. The next chapter looks at the multiple ways that parents influence the workplace culture of the school.

NOTES

1. At the time of my research, state schools could be county, voluntary or grant-maintained (GM). Under the Labour government's new legislation in 1998, the system is to be reorganized into three categories: community (the former county schools), voluntary and foundation. Grant-maintained schools (more often secondary than primary schools) were encouraged by the previous Conservative government. They were schools that had 'opted out' of local education authority control and were funded (more generously) by central government. Initially, GM schools will be designated foundation schools, receiving their budget from LEAs, but with somewhat greater independence than the other schools. The distinction between voluntary controlled and aided schools is supposed to remain.

2. Please note that school names referred to in this chapter are pseudonyms.

Chapter 9

Parents

CONCEPTUALIZING PARENTS

This chapter, like the previous one, deals with the 'public face', featuring here the relationship between the school and its parents. Much, although by no means all, of the boundary work involved fell to the head teacher. Woods *et al.* (1997, p. 88) refer to this function as 'gatekeeping'. In both of my research schools, relationships with the public, especially the parents, were a major concern. Well before the *Parent's Charter*, open enrolment, league tables of test results or rules about reports to parents were introduced through government reforms, creating a good public image was important for the survival of the school as a tolerable environment and for the peace of mind of teachers, pupils and parents.

I begin this chapter with a brief review of some of the literature about parent–school relationships. I then move into the specifics of the Hillview situation, considering parent–teacher and parent–head teacher relationships, parental activism, and the process of recruitment and retention that was vital to sustaining the balance of client groups at Hillview.

Parents: natural enemies or partners?

Parents are a prized but problematic part of schools. Sara Lawrence Lightfoot (1978) refers to families and schools as 'worlds apart', and in his classic account of the sociology of teaching, Waller (1932/1965) went so far as to call teachers and parents 'natural enemies' (p. 68). What Waller had in mind was a fundamental difference in the way teachers and parents looked at the child. The parent had a specific interest in the welfare of his or her own child, while the teacher had to balance the needs and wishes of each such child against those of the others. When that balancing act produced a less than ideal result for the parent's child, strife was a logical outcome.

Almost 60 years later, Cortazzi (1991) found parents figuring prominently in the narratives of primary school teachers, so much so that he devoted one chapter out of seven to narratives about 'awkward parents'.

Just as Waller noted, the fundamental tension was one of numbers, parents being primarily concerned with their own child or children, teachers with a class or the whole school. One such narrative involves a parent happening to walk across the playground (suggesting that the territory is easily breached) and noticing that her child is out in the rain. The teacher's attention is taken up with trying to get 'three hundred children into the building' when the parent 'came sort of storming in and really went hammer and tongs' at the dinner ladies and then at the teacher for leaving her boy exposed to the weather (Cortazzi, 1991, p. 105).

Since around the mid-1960s, a prominent image found in the literature, and in the schools, is that of parents as *partners* to teachers, jointly interested in the welfare of the child (Epstein, 1995; Vincent and Tomlinson, 1997, p. 366; Webb and Vulliamy, 1996, p. 122). Teachers at Hillview did see parents as partners. They enlisted their help when a child was in difficulties and saw them for regularly scheduled parent conferences. For their part, parents often came to see the teacher or the head teacher to explain about a family or health problem that might influence the child's learning or behaviour. Webb and Vulliamy (1996, p. 125) comment that the 'social work' or counselling aspect of the primary school head teacher's role is virtually ignored in the literature. Like Liz Clarke, the head teachers they studied spent many hours helping parents in need and for some it was their most time-consuming task. For families in trouble, the head teacher, especially when female, may be the only professional who is accessible, reliable and concerned. There are echoes here, of course, of the 'caring' expected of women teachers and explored in Chapter 7.

Which parents?

One way to avoid overgeneralizing the category 'parent' is to consider different groups of parents according to characteristics such as social class and ethnicity. Social class influences have been most widely identified as the source of major discrepancies in children's school performance and parental involvement in the school. Working-class parents have on average less time available for school visits – they may be at work, or lack child care for other siblings – and are less comfortable in the school milieu. However, an uncritical absorption of this body of work into teachers' commonsense knowledge has led, some charge, to low expectations for working-class children and a consequent effect on performance (King, 1978).

Perhaps surprisingly, middle-class parents are not an unalloyed delight for teachers either. Teachers in schools with upper-middle-class populations report parents (usually mothers) critically eyeing displays, engaging the teacher in learned discussions of reading or mathematics schemes, rifling through papers on the teacher's desk, exerting efforts to get children transferred from one teacher to another or a teacher moved out of the school (Biklen, 1995; Cortazzi, 1991; Lareau, 1989).

Like class, race or culture can influence parental relationships with schools. For some groups, there may be cultural discontinuities or mismatched expectation between home and school (Casanova, 1996; Heath, 1983; Henry, 1996, p. 94; Ogbu, 1974; D.J. Smith and Tomlinson, 1989; Wells, 1996; Wright, 1992). Sally Tomlinson's (1984) review of British studies finds that regardless of social class, minority parents held high expectations for their children in the school system.

Another way of deconstructing the category 'parent' is to distinguish between mothers and fathers. Lightfoot (1978) observes that the 'natural enemy' thesis is further heightened by the implicit competition between mother and teacher when both are seeking to nurture and educate the child – she uses the phrase 'the other woman'. Very striking are the studies that have uncovered the intensely gendered nature of parental involvement in schooling (Biklen, 1995; David, 1980, 1993; David et al., 1993; Evans, 1988; Griffith and D.E. Smith, 1991; Lareau 1989, 1992; D.E. Smith, 1987; Walkerdine and Lucey, 1989). What this body of research demonstrates is not just the input of mothers into the school, but the input of school into the lives of mothers (David, 1984, 1985, 1993). Lareau (1989) comments: 'The coordination and supervision of their children's educational activities often demanded a major portion of mothers' waking hours' (p. 87).

PARENTS AND TEACHERS AT HILLVIEW

Relationships

Hillview's varied parent groups made it difficult to generalize about parental involvement in the school. Certainly, there was little sign of the interference and monitoring documented in upper-middle-class schools. Many families seemed content to leave professional decisions to the teachers and head teacher. Few parents helped on a regular basis in the classrooms. Only a small number turned up for the governors' annual meeting with parents. Curriculum evenings were also indifferently attended for the most part. Yet school events such as concerts and fairs were well supported and most parents came in for the twice-yearly formal conferences with their child's teacher. A subgroup of parents was active in the Parent–Teacher Association.

It was not always easy to label Hillview parents according to class. For example, there were a number of single-parent mothers who might have had middle-class backgrounds and good educations but whose current financial resources were sparse. Put differently, many Hillview families had more intellectual or cultural capital than economic capital. Recall the head teacher's characterization of her middle-class parents as the 'deviant middle class' (Chapter 3). Parents might be community activists, or might be exploring alternative lifestyles.

Days observing Liz Clarke always contained many interactions with parents. She regarded contact with parents as a satisfying part of her job. Parents came to see her with complaints or problems, including family or personal problems. Sometimes they approached other teachers, too:

> Helen Davies is talking to Marie Young [a parent]. From what I can overhear, Mrs Young seems to be pregnant, is thinking of having an abortion, can't get the girlfriend away from her husband.

A parental presence was more evident in the infant than the junior classrooms and was especially prominent in the reception class. Reception teacher Marjorie Howard believed parental contact was an important part of her responsibilities.

> Marjorie tells me she has a new Arab child in the class. 'I said his mother could stay with him in the mornings, that it will teach her English. She is swathed from head to toe. She put jigsaw pieces everywhere, in the wrong place. I had Denise [a helper] show the child how to do a puzzle so that the mother could see; we have to be careful not to be insulting; she didn't know how to look at the straight edges.' Marjorie also remarked on another child in the class from an African country who needs help with English. She worries she can't give her enough help.

Teachers frequently talked about parents. Debbie Stevens told me about her dream: 'It was parents' evening; they were coming in and I wasn't prepared. The times had gone wrong, and there were all sorts of complications. Normally it's the children rioting [in a dream]; this time it was the parents.'

Teachers were often critical of parents, especially in a few cases where the parent appeared feckless or even dangerous. One of the teachers said to me about her class: 'I love the class – though I could tear my hair out . . . There's not a child in there without some kind of problem', and proceeded to name individuals. 'Even, say, Nigel: his mother's a teacher . . . and yet he can't read very well. His father is this important [local] figure but hasn't much, no time to hear him read. Jana stays up pub hours. Kay's home background . . . Selina's mother brawls in the street. Ann – look at her mother.'

Tommy's mother was observed heavily petting with a boyfriend during a school event in the church. The story of 'snogging in the church' became a shared, rather rueful, joke among the teachers. Another time, Mrs Clarke threatened Tommy's mother with the social services when she failed to pick up her child after school. Melvin's father tried to get Marjorie to go out to dinner with him, saying parents' evenings were too formal. She refused, saying she had to be home to cook dinner for her husband and family, but finally agreed to a half-hour lunch-time meeting in the pub. Melvin's father was said to be aggressive towards Melvin's mother, who was 'desperate, phoning Liz'. Marjorie said she felt she should meet him or he might take it out on Melvin's mother. After the rendezvous, Marjorie was still talking about Melvin's father. He's 50 and has left two wives already, she told us. Marjorie's sympathies are entirely with the mother, she said.

Underlying these discussions was a concern for the welfare of the children. Perhaps lost in the debates over parent–school partnership is the question of who stands up for the child. Statements critical of parents often came from teachers' worries about the children, not from a family-home background ideology used as an excuse for poor school results. Parents do not always know best (Henry, 1996, p. 54). Where there was a conflict, teachers tried to advocate for the child. For example, the teachers avoided telling Beth's mother just how disruptive she was, for fear she would be punished with physical abuse. They might worry about a child who seemed undernourished or to get too little sleep. But there seemed to be an invisible line drawn so that teachers did not often intervene in such matters.

Certainly, teachers sometimes felt unappreciated by parents. They noted that parents had greater access to teachers than to other professionals – the boundary was uncomfortably permeable.

> Ian Connell's mother comes in carrying her baby. She is obviously expecting to see Debbie; Debbie knows nothing about it. Mrs Connell says she made the appointment through Dorothy Lowe, and it is in the book. Mrs Clarke is out of school so not available to cover. So Mrs Connell waits briefly until Debbie can get the class into the TV lounge to see *Zig Zag* and then have a word with her.

> I chat to Rosalind who is working through her lunch-time in her room as usual. She tells me Jane's mother didn't come to the parent interview appointment; instead she turned up one lunch-time while she was eating her lunch.

Some parents, perhaps especially the middle-class mothers, tended to initiate contact when they had a complaint:

> Liz came into the staffroom with a letter from a parent, Marcia Perrin. It was a nicely written complaint re the fact that only some children can go to camp. Bart and Edward [her sons] were upset they couldn't go, but one line the parents took was that it would be a nice small group with their teacher . . . she was then sorry to learn that what happened instead was that they had been divided up and left with the middle juniors, to 'do the

Saxons' which they had done before. Liz said children from the posh group weren't chosen for the camp experience but she should have thought of compensation for them. She put the letter on the bulletin board. [Next day] Liz still seems to be smarting about the Marcia Perrin letter, that it was 'Dear Mrs Clarke' instead of 'Liz'.

Parents could hurt teachers' feelings, as in the case of Mrs Perrin's formal letter to Mrs Clarke, or in Marjorie Howard's case, when she told me unhappily that 'two white parents came in complaining that their children were coming home saying that black child means naughty child. I don't even know how many minority children there are – they are all my children.' On the other hand, teachers were glad to see parents, especially when they could correct misunderstandings or enlist parental support:

> Debbie says: 'Mrs Connell said she didn't want to talk about Ian's behaviour but about his work. Then I realized she thought we weren't doing the work. It's him, he does very little. I showed her Kathy's tray to show her the work a normal third-year has done. I explained the timetable to her, she was pleased with that. But he doesn't produce. She went home worried. It's all very negative.'

And parental praise meant a lot:

> Liz talked about the Smiths, 'my favourite parents'. Sam Smith had called Hillview the 'Mozart of primary schools'.

Activism

The illustrations above mostly concern individual parents and their relationships with teachers and the head teacher. An alternative type of parent involvement can be collective, which has been seen both as empowering and as dangerous (Casanova, 1996; Fine, 1993), perhaps depending on which parents get involved and for what reasons. One way parents can be involved is as members of a school's governing body. But physical presence does not guarantee empowerment (Deem, Brehony and Heath, 1995; Fine, 1993; Vincent, 1996; Wragg, 1989).

From time to time, a temporary alliance of parents at Hillview led to collective voicing of views. In one case, a small group of parents began to push the school to be more overt in its anti-racist stance. In the terminology of Chapter 6, this story could be considered a 'saga'.

In the spring of 1987, some parents were said to be asking about anti-racism and anti-sexism in the school. Next, I heard that the topic came up at the governors' annual meeting for parents in July. In the autumn, the issue arose again in a PTA meeting. The school responded to the expressed concern by ordering multicultural materials recommended by one of the school governors, celebrating holidays such as Divali and the Chinese New Year, and talking in assemblies about important non-white figures such as Mary Seacole. In February 1988, a multicultural curriculum evening was held at the school. In attendance were twenty parents, eight teachers, one governor, the head and myself.

At the end of that meeting, it was decided there should be a school policy on anti-racism. Liz said: 'This is very stimulating for me, including this idea of ancillary staff training and the children being involved. It's really helpful.' Then one of the parents asked 'What is going to happen now?' and another said she'd like to see follow-up on a very productive evening. She would like another forum. At this point, Liz responded that she had to balance many priorities in the school and added 'There's a limit to the amount of time I can ask teachers to commit outside working hours.' After some further discussion, it was decided there would be another meeting the following term.

Anti-racism was discussed again in the annual governors' meeting for parents a few months later. It also came up at the next PTA meeting. Debbie Stevens told me over the phone what happened there:

> There was discussion of the school's anti-racist statement. A parent asked 'What's going to happen about this meeting on racism?' Dennis was quite angry, saying it's time to concentrate on something else now. The atmosphere was difficult and tense. 'We want this', one of the parents said. How many really want it, it was asked. Only two put their hands up. Liz said 'Don't you trust we're doing what we say? If you tell staff you don't it will make everybody demoralized.' . . . They [parents] called for 'more staff input'. Oh we just can't – Dennis and I looked at each other. We couldn't believe it. You don't understand what pressures we're under, we told them. Dennis said we're miles ahead of a lot of schools. We're very pleased and can't understand why you want more teacher time.

The parents' vision of what the school should do contained little understanding of the pressures the teachers met daily, the fact many were extremely stretched already, that resources were poor and beyond their control, that there were many other areas of the school's provision that called out for action. The school and the head tended to see anti-racism or multiculturalism as a curriculum issue, while the activist parents took the curriculum largely for granted and wanted 'action'.[1]

On my visit in 1991 I asked Liz what had happened to what I called the multicultural saga. She replied:

The multicultural saga has died down because it's no longer an issue. It's been replaced by other issues. I think people believe that we have got a multicultural policy and have got it in place . . . we do refer to it and we do our best to combat any kind of prejudice.

Only a small number of parents were involved in the activism over anti-racism. Few black families took part. The one black teacher in the school – Dennis – was not especially sympathetic to the protest. In keeping with the literature on mothers and schools, few fathers were in evidence. The protagonists were mostly educated white women. Some had black children.

For the Hillview teachers and the head, it was confusing to have one aspect of their work examined within this magnified framework of critique, as if nothing else they did – their worries over mathematics, handwriting, technology, behaviour, children's problems, resources, cleaning the school and so forth – existed or mattered. Here they were correct, as few parents were in a position to know much of the hidden workplace culture of the school. There was a clash of priorities and of discourses – in the struggle over boundaries, the activist parents won concessions but not control.

SCHOOL RECRUITMENT

The saga described above suggests that organized parents have some potential to influence school priorities through activism, though whether that influence can be fairly ascribed to all parents in a school is doubtful. The indirect effect of parents through their influence on the ethos of the school, as described in Chapter 3, is greater. What Hillview was like depended in great measure on the communities who provided the children. We must add to the image of parent as partner or protester the more recent, and controversial, image of the parent as *consumer*. Parental choice was indeed implicated in the formation and survival of the school, although – like the parent activism – not in precisely the way politicians may have intended.

As consumers in the new rhetoric of 'parentocracy' (Brown, 1990; David, 1993), parents are meant to insist on high standards in the school, either directly as school governors or by taking their patronage away from an unsatisfactory school and to a better one. In this model of parent consumerism, standards will supposedly rise through the application of market forces to school choice and through heightening teacher accountability. After the 1988 Education Reform Act introduced so-called 'open enrolment', a system whereby schools were required to admit students up to their physical capacity, local education authorities could no longer even out school populations in different schools. Schools were meant to compete and unsuccessful ones eventually close (Hellawell, 1992).

As these ideas have moved into the public spectrum, a number of good discussions of the available research and issues around parental choice in Britain have entered the literature (for example, David, 1993, 1996; David, West and Ribbens, 1994; Gewirtz, Ball and Bowe, 1995; D. Johnson, 1990; Munn, 1993; Stillman, 1994; Vincent, 1996). School choice has also been an issue in the USA (Chubb and Moe, 1990; Fuller and Elmore, 1996; Wells, 1996), Canada (Dehli, 1996, 1997) and elsewhere. Research in Britain continues to document the processes involved when families 'choose' schools and the consequences of government policies on parental choice (e.g. Ball, Bowe and Gewirtz, 1995; David et al., 1994; Gewirtz et al., 1995), as well as examining the changes in the head teacher's role that these policies have brought about (Grace, 1995; Jones and Hayes, 1991; Webb and Vulliamy, 1996; Woods et al., 1997) and the vexed nature of the concept of 'choice' (David, Davies, Edwards, Reay and Standing, 1997; Reay, 1996).

At Hillview, parent meetings with teachers or the head teacher were usually woman-to-woman, although there were a small number of regularly involved fathers. By and large, children's problems in school led to negotiations with mothers rather than fathers. With particularly disturbed or difficult children like Peter, Dale or Ian, the mothers were frequently in the school and efforts were made to work together to find solutions. When the difficult behaviour went too far, mothers were called to remove their children for the day or for a short period of suspension.

It was mostly mothers who did the work of negotiating entry to the school. For local families, entry was a matter of knowing early enough that they needed to put a child's name down on a list of children due to enter school at a particular date. For many families, there were several schools within walking distance, and parents (mothers) would visit them, talk to the head teachers, talk to their neighbours and their children's friends, and make a decision. During the period of my research, there were LEA rules about who got first preference for a school, based on geography and having siblings in the school, but there was not a rigid restriction to a local catchment area. In fact, Hillview often took children from some distance away. Getting into a school might be more difficult for families who had just moved to the area, were in transit, or who wished to attend an oversubscribed school in a different geographical area, or for families who were unhappy with the school their child attended and wanted to make a change. The impact of the open enrolment policy after 1988 was to force the school to take in more children up to a level set by its physical capacity rather than its historic organization; thus by counting, say, the hall – a large space used for games and dinners – as potential classroom space, the number of places the school could fill rose. It was in the school's interests to keep admission high so that the number of teachers would not be forced down.

But from my earliest observations at Hillview, even before government policy changed, I saw complicated negotiations over entry to and exit from the school. Many of my days with Liz Clarke featured visits by prospective parents. For all sorts of reasons, parents might hope for a place for their child. Although formally the school was simply required to take children up to a particular number in each age group, there was room for negotiation. The head teacher could help a prospective parent appeal against a decision or apply for entry. Entry and exit were not simply *parental* responsibilities or choices; they were critical processes *for the school*. Maintaining Hillview's 'mix' of children was a major priority and at times a challenge for the head teacher. Moreover, Hillview's recruitment processes were interwoven with those of other schools. Hillview's gain would be another school's loss, and vice versa.

Some additions to Hillview's roster came through the educational psychologist, Charlotte Edwards, who thought highly of Hillview and seemed to believe its atmosphere could help certain troubled children who were not flourishing elsewhere. Peter (see Chapter 4) had found his way to the school through Charlotte. Also through the auspices of the educational psychologist, two children with serious developmental disabilities had been added to the Middle Junior Unit around the same time as Peter's entry. At break one day there was intense discussion among the teachers about the consequences of taking so many children with special needs into the school:

> Della [supply teacher] came into the staffroom with concern
> about the children in Nancy's class who weren't getting
> anywhere but had special needs; one or two were not native
> English speakers. Marjorie said she thought Mohammed was a
> slow learner, but he was just waiting to learn English. Debbie
> [who held the special needs responsibility in the school] and I
> had just been talking about a girl called Kirsty and how often
> she can get to her for extra help – maybe once every three
> weeks. The new children take her time and attention away. It
> seems a cycle of failure – the reputation for coping with difficult
> children is good so Hillview is sent more of them and then can't
> cope [my comment]. Debbie and I just listen as the others get
> into a heated discussion. [They talk about the special needs in
> their classes and their strategies for working with children with
> a range of abilities.] 'Beth', Helen says, 'she gets so frustrated. I
> have to sit with her to build up her confidence – then I turn
> away and she's lost it.' Various other children are named and
> discussed. 'This is an impossible job', Helen says . . . Marjorie

145

and Helen suggest to me that it is the time of year (mid-June)
that brings on these thoughts – earlier on, you could think
you've got another term.

Children found their way into the school through other means than an
educational psychologist's intervention. It was very interesting to see how
parents made efforts to change schools in mid-year when their child was
unhappy. School moves went mostly in predictable if unacknowledged
patterns, somewhat analogous to Ball, Bowe and Gewirtz's (1995) notion of
'circuits of schooling', although the parents did not divide neatly into the
categories Ball *et al.* identified of locals (working class) and cosmopolitans
(middle class) in their choosing behaviour.

Four schools, all in communities similar to or more disadvantaged than
Hillview's usual intake, produced most of these cases (see the discussion of
'other schools' in Chapter 8). Parents might feel that Hillview would offer
more academic chances for their child. They might hear that it was a
better-run school than their own, with a more approachable head teacher.
They might learn of its reputation for doing well with difficult children. Or
they might be trying to remove their child from a situation where she or he
was experiencing bullying or racism. Liz Clarke had to tread a careful line
in agreeing to take these children into her school. If there were vacancies
in the appropriate age group, she was supposed to offer places, although
she could argue that some spaces had to be left open for children who
moved into the local neighbourhood. She also had to be aware of the
difficulties adding more children might cause for other children or for
teachers. If the children happened to be disruptive, other parents might be
unhappy with the effect. Last, but not least, she also had to watch out for
the sensibilities of other head teachers.

The mother of a child called Patrick contacted Liz with her worries
about his situation at Martindale School. Liz had several phone conversations with Lillian, Martindale's head, while the transfer was being
negotiated, offering other forms of help to her (a suggestion for a supply
teacher) in order to smooth over the awkwardness. From my field notes:

> Walking with Patrick and his mother (and me) around the
> school, Patrick's mother said to Liz, 'I feel great [that] I've
> actually done it.' She told her that up to two years ago, she felt
> welcome at Martindale. I like to be involved, she says. Liz says,
> tactfully, that when there are new heads, schools change
> regimes; some like it and some don't. The parent says that
> Patrick dreads going to school and his school personality is
> changing. He has nightmares. She says she is going in and
> getting no joy [response] and that there are racial tensions in
> the school (Patrick is mixed race).

About two weeks later, another prospective parent appeared, having heard from Patrick's mother that there was space in the school. In this case there were no obvious racial overtones in the situation but simply a desire to find a better school for her child. On the tour round the school, this parent recognized Peter, who had also been a pupil at Martindale. These are 'small worlds'.

My guess is that even in the current era of 'parentocracy', of schools competing for children and parents reading league tables of test results in the local papers, these networks are still functioning. Once a school gets a reputation for being good with a particular type of child, or open to a particular set of parents, the tendency intensifies, and more of those children appear. Liz's openness and acceptance of diversity was a great draw for parents who would have been marginalized elsewhere. For example, several lesbian couples with children found a welcome at Hillview. There were stories of continuity, of parents who themselves had attended Hillview as children, or those who after starting second families later in life sent their small children to the school where their now-grown children had once been pupils. There was a tale of a couple who kept their child out of school until they could get into Hillview: 'true Hillview parents', Liz called them, pleased. Liz summed up her style with parents: 'I just treat them all as people and they don't get that everywhere.'

A major task for Liz Clarke was the maintenance of Hillview's ethos and its balance of diverse groups, requiring her to pay attention to children both entering and leaving. Although children might come or go at any time, there was a greater intensity of concern at the beginning and end of the school year. One reason for this concern was that staffing was contingent on the number of children in the school. In the first weeks, it was hard to tell whether children had gone away or were just late arriving back in town:

> [In early September] Liz looks worried, says we'll lose half a teacher at this rate. She speculates on whether the Bridges have gone. Leonie Bridges will never learn if they go to Italy again. They may not tell me so we can keep her on roll, Liz speculates. Another family has gone to an evangelical school. A child expected to start in reception has gone to the Waldorf school instead. There was a discussion of children who come from or leave Hillview to go to the Waldorf school. Another child's family has been rehoused so moved away.

At the close of the school year, there could be some unpleasant surprises, as parents came to say their children were being moved elsewhere through parental 'choice' rather than, for example, because they were changing residence. Near the end of the 1987–88 year there were several such defections, and it seemed that the children the school was losing were its middle-class component. In a conversation I had with Liz Clarke, she wondered whether the school was not doing its best for middle-class girls. She remarked: 'The worry is that we'll lose that middle-class nucleus while catering for our socially disadvantaged pupils. That we have almost no parent volunteers for the zoo trip is worrying for that reason.'

A few weeks later, I was told by Dorothy, the secretary: 'The office's off limits, the Bakers are in there.' Mrs Baker had been an active parent at the school, even serving on the governing body as a parent governor. A few months ago, she had phoned Liz to resign from that position and despite Liz's best efforts, could not be convinced to stay on until the end of term. Nancy Green came by, summed up the situation and gave Dorothy and myself a meaningful look. Dorothy said, 'We don't do enough maths'; Nancy pointed out who was leaving: a bright, middle-class child. A few days later, Liz confirmed the story of 'not enough maths'. 'They should have understood', she said, 'I was very hurt.' Noel Baker will be going to a school in a middle-class neighbourhood for his last year at primary school. On another day, Liz told me that the fact he can cope with it is due to what we've done. It's particularly hurtful his going at the end of this term, before his last year at school. 'The thing is, he'll go to Millway School and do brilliantly and they'll get the credit.' Normally buoyant, Liz was still brooding a few days later. There were seven or eight children leaving. Liz tells me she could understand the others going, but not the Bakers.

This incident reveals a less-remarked aspect of 'exit' (Hirshman, 1970; Vincent and Tomlinson, 1997) as a form of parental choice. Entry and exit from schools is not as simple as changing to a different brand of soap. There are human relations involved. The intensive interpersonal relationships that primary school head teachers sometimes forge with parents – part of their 'social work role' (Webb and Vulliamy, 1996) – needs to be factored into decision-making. In this case, the parents had been heavily involved in the school, to the extent of Mrs Baker sitting on the governing body. When they came to say that they were moving their bright son to another school it was seen not only as a betrayal of their commitment to school, but a betrayal of friendship as well.

In the long run, though, the lack of loyalty to the school that the exits represented was more important than the personal relationship between parent and head teacher. Schools are vulnerable to the exercise of choice and exit by even a small number of parents (Dale, 1994; Menter *et al.*, 1997, p. 28). As discussed in Chapter 3, the character of Hillview always rested on a precarious balance of different pupil groups, maintained with the aid of a large dose of head teacher charisma. Attracting the middle-class achievers was harder than gaining the difficult, disaffected or disappointed pupils from other schools. The school had to be vigilant about how it was seen from the outside. A concern with image – the public face – was even more evident in some of the other schools I visited, especially Rosemont, where open houses, gymnastic displays, concerts and fairs seemed to provide a never-ending demonstration of a 'successful school' for its upper-middle-class parents.[2] At Hillview, the extent of the poor repair and lack of resources was generally not brought to the attention of parents, even though the better-off among them might have been in a position to donate materials or contribute time had they been fully apprised of the need. But to reveal that much need would have been risky behaviour, as it might have triggered more exits by middle-class parents, off to the schools like Rosemont or Millway that could put on a better show.

NOTES

1. As is the case with this study generally, the saga is described from a teacher point of view. No doubt, an activist parent would describe it differently, highlighting for example the critical importance of anti-racism work for the experience of the children and for social justice, rather than the calls upon teacher time and energy.

2. In the 1990s, publication of test results in the newspapers and inspections by the Office for Standards in Education are likely to have escalated tendencies to construct carefully the public face of schools (Menter *et al.*, 1997; Woods *et al.*, 1997).

PART FOUR

CHANGING PEOPLE AND PLACES

Chapter 10

Teachers' Careers

Children are not the only persons to enter and exit the school. Teachers also join or leave, in response to changes in their professional or personal lives or in pursuit of career opportunities or new and different challenges. 'Career' as a concept is at once an individual construction and a structural constraint and approachable at several points in between (Acker, 1989a, b; Acker, 1992). At the individual end of the continuum, we can consider how teachers make decisions, how they interpret and negotiate their choices, shaping and reshaping the 'teacher self' (Nias, 1989). At the structural end, we can examine social, political and economic constraints that control and limit teachers' careers, and how these constraints have changed over time. In between the extremes of the spectrum lies some less explored territory, including the workings of the internal labour market for teachers (Evetts, 1989) and the ways in which teacher careers are influenced by workplace experiences. At all points on the continuum, feminist scholars call for better reflections of the realities of women's lives (Acker, 1989b; Biklen, 1995). The next section of this chapter briefly sketches in the structure of opportunities for primary school teachers like those at Hillview, working in England in the late 1980s and early 1990s. The main body of the chapter explores the career experiences and plans of the Hillview teachers. I focus on the individual decisions but seek to place them in the context of school processes and interactions as well as gender relations. As the teachers' careers develop over time, so the school will change as well.

TEACHER CAREER STRUCTURES

During the late 1980s and early 1990s, while I was conducting this research, teachers in England and Wales were paid on a main professional scale or grade, also called the Standard Scale.[1] They moved up the scale with annual increments. Some teachers received, in addition, one of a series of 'incentive allowances'. Although school governors were responsible for the allocation of these allowances, head teachers usually had considerable influence. The allowances available for distribution depended on the size of the school. In theory, allowances could be given for teaching excellence, shortage subjects, or difficult-to-fill posts, as well as for extra responsibilities, but the latter criterion was by far the most common (School Teachers' Review Body, 1993, p. 17).

Primary schools usually had only A and B allowances, the smallest ones, to offer, and the proportion of primary teachers receiving any allowance was smaller than that of secondary teachers, about 43 per cent for primary and 69 per cent for secondary in 1992 (School Teachers' Review Body, 1993, p. 65). These features of the system represented a hidden disadvantage for women teachers, who are represented more heavily in the primary than the secondary teacher workforce. In 1993, the system was replaced by an alternative that abolished incentive allowances and instead gave points for a number of possible achievements and responsibilities on a common scale. Some points are mandatory, and some discretionary, their award determined by the school governors. The extent to which points are awarded is constrained by the school's overall budget.

Much has been written about teaching, especially at elementary or primary levels, being a 'careerless' occupation (Lortie, 1975, p. 84). Nevertheless, promotion opportunities certainly existed within the system, for a teacher could acquire an allowance (or in the replacement system a higher place on the pay scale), as well as contemplate the possibility of going for a management position. Management posts – deputy headships and headships – did not always require additional paper qualifications. At the time of my study it was possible for a good, experienced teacher to apply for and be awarded a deputy headship or even a headship. Men sometimes made this leap even without much classroom experience. However, a trend towards expecting additional qualifications, such as an M.Ed. in educational management or some type of headship training, was becoming apparent.

Let us imagine that teachers from Hillview sought statistics on teaching careers in order to estimate their chances of promotion. They would already know, from looking around them, that the great majority of primary school teachers (81 per cent) were women. Some would also be aware that women were under-represented at management levels compared with their proportions in the teaching force: about 49 per cent of primary headships in 1990 were held by women (Acker, 1994, p. 108; Department of Education and Science, 1992, p. 36). About a third of schools like Hillview, with children from the whole primary age range of 5 to 11, had women head teachers. Junior schools (ages 7 to 11) would be less likely to appoint a woman to headship, going by the statistics that showed only a quarter of these schools were headed by women. Infant schools (ages 5 to 7) provided better opportunities for ambitious women teachers (Evetts, 1990), as they were almost entirely female territory, headships included (Department of Education and Science, 1992, p. 36).

The proportion of head teachers who are women gives a public message as to who leads the schools. When nearly half of the primary schools in the country are headed by women, that message would seem to say that it is not a rare event to see a woman head teacher in the primary phase (especially when the pupils are younger). Despite their under-representation in headships, there are clearly many women primary school head teachers around – potential role models and mentors to their women staff.

We can also arrange the figures differently, to show what proportion of each sex achieves higher ranked positions. In 1991, women were concentrated in the lower categories. Over half (51 per cent) of full-time women teachers in primary schools were on the standard scale without an incentive allowance, compared with just under a quarter (23 per cent) of the men. In contrast, 51 per cent of all the men in primary schools but only 16 per cent of the women occupied headships or deputy headships (School Teachers' Review Body, 1993, p. 66).[2]

The message for primary school teachers in this set of statistics is that men have a better chance than women for promotion; but again, women's chances are not negligible. About 16 per cent of women will be heads or deputy heads. A woman primary school teacher could conclude that women who want (or are enabled to try for) promotion have a chance to attain it. In practice, most teachers, including those at Hillview, will not catch sight of these tables, and thus rely on observation of schools around them. The results of this observation will be altered by local circumstances, as some regions offer women more opportunities than others do (Grace, 1995).

CAREERS IN THE SCHOOL WORKPLACE

Workplace experience is a largely missing level of analysis in the literature on teacher careers. Hillview teachers' career stories illustrate ways in which careers combine elements of chance, intention and experience.[3]

The role of chance

Although teachers planned careers, the plans were provisional. Several responded to my questions about intentions in ten years with humour: 'sunning myself on a lovely beach somewhere', 'haven't got a clue', 'running a charter yacht business in the Caribbean'. Some wanted incentive allowances or deputy headships or to change schools. Dennis Bryan expected to head two or three schools in the next ten years, then do something else, perhaps becoming an advisor. 'I'd hate to think I'd still be a teacher in 20 years' time, when I'm 50', he said.

A major source of hesitation was what I came to think of as simply 'life's unpredictability' or 'accidents'. During 1987–90 at Hillview, to my knowledge, among teachers and general assistants there were two children born (with two maternity leaves), one ectopic pregnancy and three miscarriages, one husband's death and another's heart attack, a marital separation, and several deaths of parents and grandparents. Added to these serious life events, was a stream of 'everyday' illnesses, injuries, car breakdowns, house moves, problems with children and so forth. Three long-serving teachers left the school for promotions elsewhere. Part-time or fixed-contract staff moved on more frequently. Teachers attended courses or in a few cases took paid sabbaticals.

Teachers' past careers also carried themes of accident and unpredictability. This was especially true for the older teachers, who were likely to have taken time out from teaching for child care, an option less available to the younger teachers, who encountered a less hospitable job market for re-entrants (Grant, 1989). Returning to teaching after starting a family provided complex stories. Marjorie Howard explained in a lengthy interview how she had started out in secondary teaching, later moved into junior school teaching, stopped when her children were born, then came back first into supply [substitute] teaching, then part-time teaching and eventually a full timetable. During her whole career, she had never had an interview. It was always a telephone call, a chance meeting in the village, someone who knew someone:

> Anna [her daughter] was born in December 1969. I never actually expected to go back to teaching, I don't know why, it just never occurred to me then. I had this idyllic thing that I would be like my mother, stay home and bring up my children, spend all my time with them. That's what people did, and that's what I thought I would be doing . . . Then after a couple of years, there was a knock on my back door one day. I was playing in the kitchen with the girls and it was the headmistress of St Hubert's, Sister Teresa, at the door and she said could I come up quickly: Mrs Brown, a teacher of the second-year infant class had bent over the bath rinsing out her tights and couldn't get up, she'd slipped a disc or something. 'I'm desperate, she can't come in, she's in Valleyton, and she's bent double . . .' and I said, 'Well, look, I've got to bring the girls, because I've got the children here, I can't just leave them . . .' so I gathered up the girls, and I just managed.

She did two weeks' substitute teaching then, after which she would be telephoned for 'odd bits of supply', and later, when a teacher left suddenly, she taught a junior school class for the year at St Hubert's. Then there was a lot of publicity about pupil numbers dropping in the schools and teachers being unemployed. Marjorie concluded that she wouldn't work again:

Then the phone rang, and it was Mrs Temple who was the [then] head of Hillview. [This statement is followed by a lengthy explanation of how Mrs Temple knew someone who knew Marjorie.] 'You don't know me, but I know you; you were at Lilymead. Can you come and do three days a week for me?' I said, 'Nope, I can't drive to Wesley, I only ever work in Bayview.' 'Of course you can work in Wesley.' She wouldn't take no for an answer, she just would not.

Marjorie explained how her husband showed her how to drive to Wesley, and how she insisted on doing only two (later three) days a week. A few years later, Liz Clarke replaced Mrs Temple as head teacher and talked Marjorie into 'going into the infants'. She also asked Marjorie to do it full-time. Marjorie resisted and then agreed to a compromise, that she would do four days but plan the fifth; however, Liz soon convinced her to teach all five days.

Generally, teachers believed that career changes were their own responsibility, although they recognized the role of chance. The tendency to look at one's own experience rather than analyse structural constraints led some teachers to highlight 'mistakes' they had made in the past. 'Staying too long' in a school was a typical 'mistake', one that haunted Helen Davies, who had great difficulty securing a deputy headship elsewhere because she had spent her whole career, then nineteen years, at Hillview. During that time, she had worked under five different head teachers and seen many other changes at the school. 'Helen is the school', Liz Clarke told me. But her repeated efforts to move into a deputy headship were thwarted by the convention that one's experience had to be gained in more than one school.

Helen's career-mindedness came relatively late when it appeared she would not after all have children of her own. When she became seriously ambitious she found opportunities blocked:

> I felt very frustrated. I had got as far as I could and I couldn't do anything, because I hadn't moved in my career at all. And they were saying well that's it, you've had it. And I felt very depressed.

She was rescued from this low ebb by Liz, then newly appointed to Hillview (see Chapter 6). She encouraged Helen, organized a term's sabbatical for her to study at the university, and asked her to reorganize the infant department of Hillview. Eventually she set in motion a train of events which was at last to lead to a move for Helen. Liz's own sabbatical was taken on condition that Dennis, the deputy head, be made up to acting head and Helen be acting deputy. This extra experience helped her case and an advisor from the local education authority subsequently suggested she take over an acting deputy headship in another, troubled school where the incumbent had a serious long-term illness.

Helen became acting deputy and then acting head teacher at that school. A few years later, when that school was amalgamated with another one and the new headship was advertised, she was unsuccessful in the interview for the position. Although Helen had reportedly excelled in the position, and proved her worth in practical terms, the successful candidate had experience in a bigger school and possessed an M.Ed. degree in educational management. As, technically, she was still 'on loan' from Hillview, she had little choice but to return there. She was looking for other headships when she told me this story in 1993. It still hurt her chances, she said, to have taught in so few schools.

Sponsorship: labels and triggers

After several years as a researcher in the school, I could see that some teachers had gradually risen in the esteem of the head. A subtle labelling process appeared to be at work. In the schools I studied or visited, heads, including Liz, rarely did any systematic observation of teachers actually teaching classes, although they would pass by or through the classrooms frequently. Judgements about teaching competence were not necessarily arrived at by direct empirical evidence derived from the classroom.[4]

On the other hand, the role the teacher took in the wider life of the school was more visible; for example, taking responsibility for writing a policy in a particular curriculum area, giving a talk to parents, organizing a school concert or fair, general participation at staff meetings, or working with the head or other teachers to plan some other aspect of school work. Mrs Clarke had clear ideas about who was 'like a rock' or 'a good, average teacher' or 'a brilliant teacher'. Evetts (1989) argues that sponsorship has to be triggered by appropriate behaviour. Somehow a teacher has to show that she is able and willing to benefit from special efforts on her behalf.

Debbie Stevens' progress through the school illustrates the labelling process working successfully for a teacher. Right from their first meeting, she and Liz got on well. Hillview was Debbie's second teaching job. She had spent several years in an inner-city London primary school. She moved to the Wesley area when her husband changed jobs and their first child was only a few months old. She told me how Liz had taken her on a tour of the school and asked her some questions.

> I didn't mention that I had a baby who was six months old, I thought I'd keep that [to myself] . . . I think at that time she didn't really think that I was what she was looking for, because I really played on the computer things that I'd done and she kept saying 'it's a shame we're not looking for somebody for computers, because I really feel that you would fit in'. And when

I got home, and I thought about some of the things I'd said, or really the things that I hadn't said, I was kicking myself because I had done so much work with special needs [which was what the school was looking for] . . . and I didn't mention [it]. So I wrote another letter and then sent it, and I got a letter asking if I wanted an interview . . . In the second letter I said 'Thank you very much for showing me around the school today. On reflection, there are some points I think you should know about my past teaching experience', and then I listed about six things that I hadn't mentioned that were very important.

Later, after working in the school for a while, she was amused to come across a note made by Liz after their first meeting that said 'pretty blonde and very sympathetic'.

Debbie began her appointment at Hillview teaching the 'special class', soon to be mainstreamed into the Middle Junior Unit. In her second term at Hillview, Debbie became the only full-time teacher involved in that experimental team-teaching effort. Thus she found herself in a leadership role, which she handled ably. Liz sang her praises to me on several occasions. She admired her gentle style, her competence and commitment, her grace under pressure. In her early months at the school, Debbie had problems getting her child care sorted out and arranging a house move. Her child woke frequently in the night, and her husband gave relatively little support with housework and child care. Debbie's ability to cope with these multiple pressures probably increased her value still further in the eyes of the head teacher.[5]

Generally she was amenable to the head's ideas. When Liz suggested it would be good for her to get experience teaching a class of younger children, she said she 'wouldn't mind'. Despite the complications of her domestic arrangements, she managed to put time into the school well beyond the minimum, staying late when necessary, coming into school before and after the term to sort out materials, going on short inservice training courses as well as working on a master's degree. During the years of my research, Debbie had two more children. While on her maternity leaves she kept in touch with the school and attended weekly staff meetings. In January 1990, Liz mentioned that she might try to get her an acting deputy headship if Dennis's foreign exchange materialized. By September 1990, at age 29, Debbie was teaching the oldest children (a traditional position for deputy head) and acting as deputy head, after only three years and a term at the school. In interview, I asked Debbie whether she thought that Liz was looking out for her career:

Oh she is. I think [that's] one of the things she enjoys doing . . . all the [younger] teachers except Sheila have gone on to headships or deputy headships.[6] I actually feel that she's paving the way for me in a way. You know, she's actually directing me. This year [as acting deputy head] – what I've learnt and what I've actually done is going to mean more than any M.Ed. that I could get . . . and it's only because she's given me the opportunity to do it, so I feel really privileged that she's singled me out. I know in the future that when I look back that it'll be Liz that has actually made me realize that I can do it because I wouldn't have actually said myself that I could have done it but she obviously saw that I could do it.

In contrast, Sheila Jones was less successful in triggering sponsorship efforts. At the start of my research in 1987, she was a part-time teacher in the school, with one young child. Sheila said she had been ambitious in the past and would have liked to have become a head teacher. She was becoming less certain of this goal, but was edging closer to full-time work. Sheila had been 'secondary trained'. Generally this seems to be thought (by other teachers) to be a disadvantage in English primary education, as it is assumed to be synonymous with being less flexible, more didactic and less child-centred. Some of the other teachers had 'overcome' their training to become adept at primary school pedagogies. But Sheila, who had also held several jobs outside teaching, and spent ten years teaching at a more traditional primary school, sometimes felt uncertain about her ability to produce the type of primary practice favoured at Hillview.

Sheila hoped for an incentive allowance but did not manage to achieve one. She embarked upon a course in library management and got recognition from the head and others for her excellent efforts to reorganize the school library, as she did from successfully running the school fair. But then she had a second child and her hopes of moving into full-time teaching suffered a further setback. Coming back after maternity leave, she 'took groups'. For a teacher to take groups means that rather than have her own class, or a shared one, she works with small groups of children who need extra help, or, alternatively, takes another teacher's class to permit that teacher to do some other work. After a year, she decided to leave teaching entirely. Liz Clarke told me how sorry she was that Sheila was leaving:

> She has not enjoyed the last twelve months. Being a relief teacher is not an enjoyable experience in a primary school, because you get all of the hassle and none of the satisfaction. We've not developed Sheila. That is partly because of having the children, and her family situation. She's given up on her career now. Maybe when the little one is in school . . . she could still do it, although she'll be that bit older. She is someone who could easily be in a position of authority within a school, and she is not going to move on. So I'm sad about that.

It is important to realize that the images head teachers have of their teachers are not fixed. The teacher's behaviour – and indeed other factors such as her family phase – can alter the 'label'. Debbie said this herself, commenting that she and Kristin 'perhaps gave off vibes that we were willing to be manoeuvred in that way, whereas Sheila perhaps didn't'. She also noted that both she and Kristin benefited from having spouses who were keen to see their wives develop careers.

Women's careers

Teachers were asked in interviews if they thought there were any particular advantages in being male or female teachers in primary schools. Most (although not all) stated that men had a career advantage. Helen Davies believed that women had to work harder than men for equivalent rewards. Several teachers had concluded that the crux of the problem was the scarcity of men and the surfeit of women. Every school wanted some men, so men got preferential treatment in hiring and promotion. Teachers thought that appointing committees, especially the parents and school governors on them, were working from stereotyped ideas such as women inevitably leaving to have children or not having the strength or strictness to keep the school in order. Some teachers had been to look at schools or attended job interviews where 'it was quite clear they wanted a man'. They, or their friends, were asked questions such as how they would manage when their own children were ill.

Women who had children were thought to experience further disadvantages. Either they carried on, with only a short break for maternity leave, or they were faced with returning to a lower-status, often marginal, position. Grant's (1989) review of studies of women teachers' careers identified the 'career break' as particularly deleterious to women's chances of career advancement in a system where 'promotion is tied to age-related norms' (p. 44). Nias (1989) discusses sources of satisfaction and dissatisfaction for primary teachers she interviewed. Those who were temporary, supply or part-time were particularly likely to express 'disappointment, resentment or frustration' (p. 127). Chessum's (1989) interviewees voiced similar sentiments, one terming herself a 'part-time nobody'.

Certainly, such teachers provide flexibility for the *schools*. For the teachers there could also be advantages. Marjorie Howard said, looking back, 'it suited me beautifully, doing part-time, with two children and a home to run'. Yet frustration and insecurity were evident, too. Helen Davies explained how difficult supply teaching is when you don't know where the staffroom, the lavatory and the office are. The children are hard to control and you have nowhere to keep your resources and records. Fixed-term contract teachers were by definition only temporary. Part-time teachers were subject to sudden changes in routine. It is important to realize these teachers are nearly always *women*. The problem is not only instability and lack of job security. These teachers, like the others, had high standards. It was not unusual to hear a remark that a part-time teacher was trying to do a full job in half the time. It is not surprising if they feel, as Nias (1989) suggests, that there is a discrepancy between their desired self-images as teachers who should work hard and make a difference, and the reality of limited relationships and smaller accomplishments imposed by their position.[7]

The teachers did not usually self-identify as feminists nor did they adopt a feminist interpretation of inequalities in the teaching profession. It was difficult to feel discriminated against, as Cogger (1985) also found in a study of Welsh teachers, when the *choice* to have a family is believed to be the cause of career blockage. In interviews, several teachers said that women were less likely than men to seek promotion because of their dual role:

> *Question*: Why do you think there are relatively few women primary heads?
>
> *Helen Davies*: Well, either because they've opted for their families and think that they shouldn't have a career, either they think or they've been told that it doesn't go hand in hand, and the pressures of life are so much that you can only do one or the other.
>
> *Rosalind Phillips*: Often they are trying to do two things, aren't they, they are trying to hold down family responsibilities and do their work on a par with their male colleagues.
>
> *Betty Chaplin*: You've got to be able to get over the problem of a family, and . . . for some women it's not always easy to be able to have a family and then leave it and go back to work.

Betty Chaplin was one who believed that there was little discrimination in primary schools, because 'it's always been women in primary schools'. She thought that women's preponderance, in fact, kept salaries down because so many women, at least in the past, were second earners. She pointed to a change in society's tolerance of women at work:

> I think it's going to be easier now, because I think this generation of teachers are a lot more organized at getting their families organized . . . [in the past] Mum stayed at home, it was the general thing to do. Debbie and Sheila, they don't see it like that at all . . . If you don't give up for ten or twelve years, there's more chance that you will go on and aim higher. I suppose this is where the attitude to women has changed a lot, hasn't it, in

the last ten years. I think a lot more women have decided that they can do it, and they'll jolly well have a go.

Moreover, as I showed earlier, there *are* significant numbers of women in primary headships, even if they are under-represented. People tended to look at their schools and their own experience for guides, not to national statistics or feminist literature. At Hillview, the presence of a woman head teacher gave teachers a successful role model.

There were signs later in the research of a rising feminist conscious-ness, although still not labelled as such. Amanda Prentice, who had been appointed to replace Nancy Green, was particularly interested in encour-aging girls to do science. The school followed up an anti-racism policy with an anti-sexism one. During Debbie's 1990–91 year as acting deputy head, she began to notice how she was treated differently from Dennis in the role and how she herself acted differently. When Dennis was there, Debbie (his team partner with the Older Junior Unit) would keep track of dates for him, act as a sounding-board, and bring him a sandwich when he was unable to leave the office at lunch-time. No one was backing her up in the same way, although she realized that colleagues would do so if she asked for help.

Sometimes she saw herself as at a disadvantage through being a female in the role:

> There are situations in which I find myself thinking – for example with that difficult parent – if I'd have been *Dennis*, perhaps the situation wouldn't have arisen. The father wouldn't have dreamt of threatening Liz, because Dennis would have been around . . . Just the simple fact that he's a very charismatic, prominent male figure and I will never be that [laughs] . . . I don't know if I feel I've got to do everything twice as well, but I do know a lot of parents look around and assume that a man's got better discipline and assume that he's not as approachable as I am, that they haven't got the right to encroach on his time . . . There are things that people come and perhaps talk to me about that I think Dennis wouldn't have got . . . So, if, say, dinner ladies would come up and mention to me a problem that they had . . . or if a teacher has come up and said to me about something they've been concerned about, actually they will be more frank and honest with me because I am a woman than they would be with Dennis. There are a lot of things that go on that Dennis never knew, or will never know, because people don't unburden themselves to him . . . [It's] not because they don't feel that he was approachable but because they wouldn't have thought of approaching him in that way.

> Liz's got the same with being a woman head. I do think that if a
> man was sat in the chair down in the office, that there would be
> fewer interruptions. I mean, I know it's awful and perhaps I'm
> just – no, I do think it's true – if Ronald Grant [head of a
> neighbouring school] was sat in that office downstairs, people
> wouldn't come and knock on the door and say 'so and so's just
> tied my shoelace together'. Even for the children, I think there's
> this sort of distance thing about it and it's a protection for a
> man, in a way, that they can get away with not having to be
> this sort of nurturing, helpful type of character in the school.

Debbie recognized that there were exceptions, women who did not make
it comfortable for people to approach them. She continued the theme,
however, noting also that while Dennis could bring his children into school
when there were problems with child care arrangements, she went to great
lengths not to do the same because she felt she had to prove that her family
life did not get in the way of her job. Even when she was in hospital with
pregnancy complications, she found herself thinking

> Well, this is it, you know, people can now say there you are, you
> see, she's lying in there in hospital with this pregnancy, and, I
> thought . . . I've let people down, because it's only because I'm a
> woman that I'm actually lying here in hospital. If Dennis was
> doing this job, he wouldn't be here at the moment [laughs].

She noted that the school has had a male deputy for at least 20 years and
she wanted not to let anybody down, not let Liz down, to show her that
she'd made the right decision. Although she normally felt accountable to
others, being deputy head had made the pressure greater: 'The deputy head
level has made it more acute than any other job that I've done . . . I feel
I've got to be everything to everybody . . . it's a really giving job all the
time. You have to give out, which is quite easy for women to do; I suppose
they're quite used to that in a way [laughs].' Later in the interview, she
explained how a priority for her in the job was making sure the staff felt
'happy'. She was pleased when Marjorie thanked her for keeping the staff
happy and giving them a stress-free year. Debbie commented:

> I've seen situations arise before where people have been
> unhappy about something . . . they haven't been given
> information on something or they've asked for something and
> they haven't got it yet, and it was really getting them down, and
> I didn't really want that, I wanted to try and make sure that
> everyone felt that I was able to provide them with something or
> I could do something for them. So when Marjorie wrote that on
> the report, I was quite pleased because that was something that
> I was really aware of, keeping everybody feeling happy and

stress-free in their job because I was actually sorting something out in the background or the sidelines.

Debbie's comments illustrate Grace's (1995, p. 182) observation that head teachers might not embrace feminism directly, but often expressed views or advocated ways of working that others might see as feminist. They also give support to those who argue that the role of the deputy head is ambiguous and overloaded (Southworth, 1994a,b; Purvis and Dennison, 1993; Webb and Vulliamy, 1996). At the time Debbie held this position, she was pregnant with her third child and she also had a full class responsibility for the most difficult class she had so far encountered at Hillview. Her scheduled non-contact time (by then one morning a week) was taken up in the school office, so she found it even more difficult to do class preparation and relate to the children. Her account is also reminiscent of narratives of Canadian women academics in another study, who feel on the one hand that they are trapped into taking on all of the nurturing and service work in their departments, but at the same time take pleasure from living out that image of themselves (Acker and Feuerverger, 1996; see also Chapter 7).

CONCLUSION

Teachers make active choices in constructing a career. To some extent, their choices are constrained by structures – the social arrangements largely outside their control – such as the size of steps on the pay scales, the number of teaching vacancies in a locale, the probability women will be appointed to senior posts, even the configurations of national political and economic systems. But structures are difficult to fathom, and in the process of constructing a career, the teachers are guided by their immediate experiences in the workplace culture of the school. The culture not only provides sustenance, but also a framework for creating and sharing of views and interpretations (Metz, 1989; Rossman, Corbett and Firestone, 1988).

When someone went to look at another school, or for an interview, the other teachers got detailed feedback. Teachers could see by looking around them how careers would be affected by time out for childrearing or what advantages men had. They could find out how a man and woman in a deputy head role might be treated differently by the children, parents and other teachers. They could work out at what age a promotion could be expected. They could see that it was possible for women to become head teachers. The sponsoring process made a big difference to teachers' career chances; but the process did not operate independently of the teacher's efforts, for teachers could trigger sponsorship by demonstrating their commitment, ambition and potential. In sum, careers are provisional, kaleidoscopic constructions, made up of everyday events and interchanges, surrounded by dimly perceived structural constraints and characterized by change which – by definition – never stops.

My next chapter deals directly with change in another sense, considering the effects of educational reform on Hillview as a workplace culture. In the last chapter, I will pick up both themes – careers and change – and explain what happened to the Hillview teachers in the mid- and late 1990s.

NOTES

1. After a prolonged and unsuccessful period of teacher 'industrial action', the government passed legislation in 1987 that withdrew the negotiating rights of teachers' unions and gave the Secretary of State for Education, aided by an appointed Interim Advisory Committee, the power to set salaries. The School Teachers' Review Body makes recommendations each year to the Secretary of State for salary increases or changes to the system. There are various points of consultation with teachers' organizations and others.

2. The pattern was very similar under the system that replaced incentive allowances. In 1994, 51.7 per cent of women but just over a quarter of men (26.9 per cent) were at points 0–9, the lower end, on the pay spine. Men still held their advantage in attaining headships or deputy headships in the primary phase (49 per cent) while women's chances remained at 16 per cent (8.4 per cent held deputy headships and 7.3 per cent headships) (Department for Education and Employment, 1996, pp. 26–7).

3. An earlier article considered career patterns for teachers at both Hillview and Rosemont (Acker, 1992).

4. Although teacher appraisal was required from 1986, and operated in some schools, including Hillview, it was not formally implemented until 1992.

5. See also Chapter 5 for an account of Debbie's domestic routines.

6. See Chapter 12.

7. See also Damianos (1998), Galloway and Morrison (1994), and Office for Standards in Education (OFSTED) (1994). Little research attention has been given to supply teachers or others on the periphery of the school.

Chapter 11

Change at Hillview

CHANGE FROM WITHIN

In the previous chapter we saw how teachers' career pursuits were in part shaped within the school. The child population of the school is constantly changing, as some leave and others enter, and those who stay get older and move up the school. Together the changing staff and clientele contribute to a sense that the institution and its culture can never be wholly captured on paper, as it is constantly evolving (Nias *et al.*, 1989).[1]

There are sources of change other than shifts in personnel. The teachers and head teacher initiate many of these, as they try for an alternative way of celebrating Harvest Festival, a new arrangement of chairs in a class-room, a different procedure at dinner-time, or a more complex innovation like the Middle Junior Unit. The Middle Junior Unit, an innovation that formed the context for many of my observations, was not generally thought to have been a success in and of itself. There was no evident decline in pupil learning, but the teachers were unable to find a satisfying way of coordinating such a complicated entity. Three of the four teachers were part-timers, and there was only one afternoon when all four teachers were present, and only thirty minutes set aside for joint planning by the full group. Other disruptions and dilemmas came from teacher illness, from the introduction of Peter into one of the classes (see Chapter 4), and from chronically inadequate resources (see Chapter 3). The head teacher, stretched by other commitments, was unable to give the Unit as much support as it needed.

The Unit was thus labelled a failure in its original aspirations to create an innovative team-teaching situation. Seen over a longer timespan, how-ever, the Unit no longer looks quite the same. In an interview in 1988, after commenting that the children were not harmed by the experiment, Liz Clarke continued:

> The other good thing is that I think the teachers, whether they
> wanted to or not, had to think very hard about how they related
> to other teachers, and I think that's going to have knock-on

effects, hopefully for this school, and certainly for them as teachers in their own teaching careers, that will be hard to estimate; unless you followed teachers for the next fifteen years, you will never know. So I think it's had a very good training input to the teachers, even though it's been frustrating and even though they've not succeeded, or by their criteria they probably feel they haven't succeeded, in creating a unit. From the school's point of view, we've found one way in which *not* to set up a unit, but it hasn't removed the desire to have a unit, to have unit type teaching.

Looking back now, several years later, it is as if there were indeed a ripple effect, with lessons learned from the operation of the Unit influencing other innovations over the next few years. Dennis and Debbie were able to teach an Older Junior Unit the following year with fewer difficulties of coordination (although resource shortages and teacher absence through illness also affected this iteration of the unit idea). The three infant teachers already worked closely together and were sometimes referred to as the 'Infant Unit'. At the point when the National Curriculum was introduced, the unit idea took on new life, as teachers with adjacent age groups began regularly to plan and work together. A scheme was devised for a teacher to stay with a group for two years, with each pair then exchanging places, in an effort to aid continuity and progression towards the testing stages. Another kind of ripple effect was the influence on teacher careers. Most of the teachers involved in the Middle Junior and Older Junior Units have been unusually successful in acquiring deputy headships and headships.

As of the late 1980s, Hillview was a developing and changing professional workplace, where experiments were tried and teachers worked closely together for the improvement of the school and the good of the children, though often thwarted by the material conditions under which they laboured. At this point, another source of change entered the picture, as central government interventions created a new context for teachers' work in England and Wales.

CHANGE FROM OUTSIDE

In the 1980s and 1990s there have been determined efforts to use legislation and other forms of persuasion to alter the ways in which teachers approach their work.[2] Despite the enormity of the changes imposed in this period in Britain, there are always signs of contradiction, struggle and contestation, such as the teacher boycott of Standard Assessment Tasks (SATs) in 1993 and 1994. For a few pages, I shall move away from Hillview to describe the reforms in general terms and note their particular impact on primary school teaching. I concentrate on the events between 1988 and 1991. Then I shall return to the story of Hillview to document the effects of the early stages of these reforms on the Hillview teacher workplace culture. Hillview also provides an example of how the existing occupational and workplace cultures of teachers significantly influenced the fate of the changes central government hoped for.

Controlling teachers

It is well known in the literature on educational innovation that top-down efforts to bring about change frequently fail. One reason for their failure is the classroom focus of teachers; because it is impossible to have total surveillance of every teacher in every classroom, there is plenty of scope to sidestep unreasonable prescriptions. Teachers are thought to accept innovations when they can see sufficient potential and practicality to make the effort worthwhile (Doyle and Ponder, 1977).[3]

Over time, teachers in Britain strengthened their claims to professionalism, despite the well-known divisions among them, given concrete form in multiple and competing teacher unions. By the 1970s, however, relationships among central government, local government and teachers' unions had begun to show signs of strain (Grace, 1987). In the 1980s, teachers demonstrated their disaffection by a lengthy and bitter phase of industrial action from 1984 to 1986 (Pietrasik, 1987).

The Conservative government's response was to weaken further the occupational autonomy of the teachers. In the previous chapter, I noted that teachers' bargaining rights were withdrawn in 1987; power to establish pay and conditions went to the Secretary of State, aided by an advisory committee to whom he would appoint members. In 1987, the government also specified teachers' hours and responsibilities. Details of new contracts and conditions were announced, setting a fixed number of days for teaching and inservice work and dividing teachers' time into three categories, including 1265 hours per year that would be 'directed' by the head teacher. Head teachers and deputy head teachers had specified responsibilities. This was also the time when the salary scale for teachers was revised from its previous version into a Main Professional Grade (later called the Standard Scale) that could be topped up with one of five levels of incentive allowances, a limited number available for each school. Since that time, teachers have also been subject to new requirements for appraisal, and the pay scale was revised yet again with incentive allowances deleted but points given on the scale for various qualifications and responsibilities. The next stage was new requirements for teacher appraisal and removal of incentive allowances with an alternative scheme of extra points for qualifications and responsibilities. Most recently, the government's Green Paper on teachers

(Department for Education and Employment, 1998) stresses standards, incentives and opportunities. Many of its arrangements would have the effect of differentiating between teachers, and among them are proposals linking salary increments to satisfactory appraisal, introducing a perform-ance threshold above which teachers can gain higher salaries, and allowing small numbers of teachers to enter a 'fast track' or be designated 'advanced skills teachers'.[4]

Teachers' work is, of course, not only affected by legislation that directly targets pay and conditions but by changes in curriculum, assessment, finance, management and other features of the education system. For example, decentralized management and financing of schools, one of the features of the 1988 Education Reform Act, had serious effects on teachers' work and career opportunities. Because schools were funded according to average teacher salaries but forced to pay actual ones, older teachers became less desirable in the job market. Schools were tempted (or virtually forced) to hire 'cheaper' teachers, including those who were less experienced or were on short-term contracts, to save money (Jones and Hayes, 1991; Hellawell, 1992). The current Labour government has now offered LEAs the chance to fund schools on a basis that reflects the actual costs of the teachers in them (Lepkowska, 1998). Another theme in reform efforts has been to give more responsibility to school governors and to encourage parents to become more involved in school matters.

Introducing the National Curriculum and assessment

The 1988 Education Act gave a broad outline of the curricular framework to be used in all state schools in England and Wales. Nine subjects (plus religious education) were required in primary schools: English, mathemat-ics, science, technology, geography, history, art, music, physical education. (Later, technology was split into two – design and technology, and infor-mation technology – making ten subjects.) Details of the process by which the framework was developed and how the details of the curriculum for each subject were specified can be found elsewhere (e.g. Acker, 1997; Webb and Vulliamy, 1996). Much controversy focused on the plans for systematic testing of children in order to assess their knowledge of the new curriculum. A decision to begin the introduction of the assessment procedures with 7-year-olds shone an unaccustomed spotlight on infant teachers and on primary schools. It was widely believed, by parents as well as teachers, that the age of 7 was too young for testing and might have traumatic effects on sensitive children, yet the scheme went ahead as planned with pilot SATs for mathematics, English language and science in 1990, and expecta-tions for all schools to conduct and report teacher assessments and SAT results for 7-year-olds, starting in 1991.

Results of individual schools were not made public in 1991, but some summary figures for local education authorities were reported, accompanied by widespread protests about both the lack of standard procedures from one classroom or school to another, and the difficulties of interpreting raw data without controls for factors such as socioeconomic disadvantage. There were also many complaints about the extended time and energy required for the administration of the SATs. The 1992 versions cut the number of attainment targets to be covered, and more of the assessment was designed to be done with the whole class.

Throughout the first years of the implementation of the National Curriculum and assessment, advice was liberally provided to schools instituting the changes. As well as receiving the 'Orders' that gave details of the curriculum, schools were showered with additional documents from various sources, clarifying or changing requirements or assisting in implementation. The underlying problem was that if taken literally, the new work required of teachers, especially in revising the curriculum and recording children's progress towards hundreds of attainment targets, would be impossible to accomplish within any semblance of a normal day (Acker, 1990b).

The credibility of both the advice and the arrangements for the curriculum and assessment were also undermined by the frequency with which alterations were made, itself due to the rush with which most of the reforms were being implemented and the under-representation of practitioners among those devising the policies. Moreover, the changes themselves were repeatedly 'altered, amended and reoriented' (Ball, 1992, p. 2). The documents and politicians' pronouncements showed little recognition of the variation among schools. In the real world of schools, as we have seen in previous chapters, children can be disruptive, plans come unstuck, spare time is scarce, equipment breaks down. Not all children have English as a first language; not all children turn 7 at the same moment of the year. Some schools have such high pupil turnover that the children entering at 5 are not the ones being tested at 7, let alone 11. In contrast, guidance in the advice manuals appeared to be most suitable for a relatively small, quiet, stable, middle-class classroom setting (Osborn, 1996a). Through this period, an overloaded curriculum, oversize classes and inadequate resources were not taken seriously as constraints, reinforcing the impression that the individual teacher is the sole agent of bringing about or thwarting children's learning (Woods and Wenham, 1995, p. 123).

Targeting primary pedagogy

In the later months of 1991, perhaps stimulated by the imminence of a general election (Woods and Wenham, 1995), there were a number of attacks by government figures on 'standards' in primary schools, culminating in a statement (Clarke, 1991) sent from the Secretary of State for Education to all primary school head teachers, announcing the appointment of a body dubbed the 'Three Wise Men' to produce over the next few months a report on the current state of primary education.

Clarke's statement was very negative about the 'dogmatic orthodoxy' of discovery methods and child-centred teaching. It urged greater consideration of 'more effective' traditional methods of formal, didactic and whole class teaching; specialist teachers; increased use of setting or other methods of ability grouping. The subsequent report (Alexander, Rose and Woodhead, 1992) also criticized 'highly questionable dogmas' and advocated more subject-based and specialist teaching. It called for a better balance among modes of organizing teaching such as individual, small group and whole class teaching. The document noted difficulties teachers experienced in implementing the new curriculum and assessment procedures, but tended to regard them as temporary troubles rather than indications of flaws in the procedures themselves.[5]

Attacks on primary pedagogy were supported by the appearance of a discourse that applauded moves towards tradition and away from progressive styles of teaching and school organization. The tone of much of the press coverage of educational matters around 1991 exemplifies what Ball (1990) called the 'discourse of derision'. Education professionals were dismissed as having vested interests and therefore unable to contribute to the debate; teachers in general came under suspicion for being insufficiently rigorous and politically suspect. The government reforms were presented as an inevitable result of decades of too much teacher power and too little concern for conservative values. The workings of this discourse of derision can be seen particularly clearly in the efforts to influence pedagogy in primary schools. Brehony (1990) describes the phenomenon as a manufactured problem, a sense that 'something is wrong' created by repeated statements in the press made by government figures. Whatever the shortcomings of child-centred teaching, the form taken by the critique suggested an ideological rather than an educational impetus (Acker, 1997; Brehony, 1990).

Perhaps the primary school was simply seen as an easy target. It is, after all, the province of female teachers. Almost all of the pronouncements on primary school pedagogy were made by men, few of whom were likely to be intimately familiar with child-centred, topic-based practices in nursery or primary schools. The campaign can also be seen as an attack on values traditionally associated with women, and perhaps even an attack on women themselves. Some of the most scathing sneers were directed at 'Plowden' – the Report that was said to put the seal of approval on progressive, child-centred education in the 1960s, or at Lady Plowden herself (Hofkins, 1992, p. 11). We see a familiar phenomenon of men controlling the work of women teachers, and as Grumet (1988, p. 23) puts it, 'blame is deflected from the men who establish [the] policies onto the women who teach the children who fail'.

IN THE SCHOOLS: RESPONDING TO REFORM

Thus primary schools and teachers had to respond not only to the details of the National Curriculum, assessment and other changes, but to widespread charges about their supposed dogmas, excesses and failings. Whether or not teachers were being deskilled, they were certainly not being empowered. Yet they were not without resources for resistance. I locate these in the culture and structure of primary school teaching as an occupation, and in the local workplace cultures where teachers discussed events of the day.

Culture, structure and gender

Although all teachers suffered from the pressure of new expectations and the problems associated with lack of clarity and frequent revisions of guidelines, primary school teachers faced several additional difficulties with the National Curriculum. One stemmed from the typically generalist nature of their work. Primary school teachers were expected to become competent practitioners of every subject in the National Curriculum – a recipe for anxiety, especially about some elements of science teaching and about technology, areas that were not always part of the teacher's own training (Bennett, Wragg, Carré and Carter, 1992).

The other major problem for primary school teachers, especially infant teachers, was the ideological clash between their child-centred tradition and the subject model upon which the National Curriculum was based (Osborn, 1996b). While teachers did not always in practice adhere to a progressive model of teaching (Galton, 1989), neither did they typically divide the day rigidly into chunks designated 'geography', 'history' or 'science'. Project-oriented work often combined several subject areas. Perhaps more important than their actual practice was the widely shared ethos that revolved (at least rhetorically) around the needs of the child. It was a strong plank in the occupational culture, not easily dislodged, to which we could add the preservation of classroom autonomy, i.e. relatively unimpeded decision-making in the classroom by the individual teacher. Ever since the demise of the 11-plus examination and the competition for entry to selective secondary schooling, primary school teachers in Britain had enjoyed a level of classroom autonomy far above their counterparts in many other countries.

Also significant, as suggested above, is the fact that almost all teachers who were to begin the assessment of the National Curriculum were women. In 1990, 81 per cent of teachers in nursery and primary schools in England and Wales were women. In separate infant schools (with children aged 5 to 7), the percentage rose to 98 per cent (Department of Education and Science, 1992; Acker, 1994). What is important is not so much that these teachers are women *per se*, but that they are influenced by social expectations about caring, nurturing roles for women.

Working hard, doing good, feeling bad

If I extrapolate from my findings and those of others such as Osborn (1996b), the group of teachers who were to spearhead the National Curriculum and assessment were female, child-centred and highly conscientious. In some respects they suited the government's purposes perfectly, as they could be relied on to try hard to do what was expected of them, even against the odds. The cultural script for women caring for young children leads to an ethic of putting others first, even to the point of self-sacrifice (see Chapter 7). Overconscientiousness on the part of such teachers, and the resulting fatigue and exhaustion, has been noted both in the context of the National Curriculum (e.g. Campbell and Neill, 1994) and outside it (e.g. A. Hargreaves, 1994; McPherson, 1972).

There is now considerable evidence that the curricular and assessment reforms increased teachers' workloads and heightened their stress and anxiety levels (Acker, 1990a; Bowe and Ball, 1992; Broadfoot and Abbott, 1991; Campbell and Neill, 1994; Chard, 1994; Osborn 1996a, b; Pollard *et al.*, 1994). Infant teachers interviewed by Campbell and his colleagues (Campbell and Neill, 1994) welcomed and supported the National Curriculum and found that their professional skills were being improved by implementing it, but nevertheless believed that what they were being asked to do was 'simply not manageable, even for experienced and able teachers' (p. 182). In adjusting to the new requirements, teachers were not just acquiring technical skills, but making a 'major reconstruction of their self-identity' (Stone, 1993, p. 188).

I too found teachers becoming increasingly anxious over the period 1987–91 (see also Acker, 1990b). Although praising certain aspects of the draft specifications for technology in the curriculum, Dennis Bryan commented, 'It's ridiculous to expect ordinary mortals to do this.' Rosalind Phillips provided an example of what Campbell and Neill (1994, p. 166) call the 'running commentary syndrome' when she remarked: 'To do all that's expected is impossible . . . you've got to come to terms with that. You're always looking at components . . . you can't remember it all. I'm enjoying what I do, but if I look ahead I panic. I wander around with a book in my hand trying to work out what attainment target something is.'

Hillview teachers found themselves spending large amounts of time recording children's progress. Betty Chaplin, the teacher responsible for the class that took the first round of SATs in 1991, estimated that she was spending an extra hour and a half working on records every weekend. During the weeks when SATs were administered, each school had to find ways to find cover for the children not being 'SATed' at any given time. The class teacher might be listening to a child read, or working with a small group investigating which of a number of items would float or sink (a science SAT), but meanwhile the other children needed looking after. Broadfoot and Abbott (1991) noted that arrangements varied so much from classroom to classroom and school to school that serious questions might be raised about the validity of the testing practices (see also West, Sammons, Hailes and Nuttall, 1994). For the main teacher involved, as Betty said, 'it was just my life for six weeks'.

By 1991, Betty Chaplin and others in the school had come round to accepting much of the principle of a National Curriculum and regarding systematic teacher assessment as having some positive features. This outcome might be predictable as a means of reducing the cognitive dissonance produced by beliefs at odds with actions. The SATs were regarded as a good experience for the children who were doing them at any one time, who enjoyed getting so much of their teacher's attention, but as problematic for others. Keeping any kind of effective instruction going during those weeks was difficult. Having a supply teacher take the class for long periods of time led to a restless class of children who lost several weeks of learning time and were difficult to settle down afterwards. The teachers believed they learned little from the results that they did not already know.

Hillview teachers' concerns went beyond extra work. They worried about the curriculum becoming unbalanced: 'Music's gone by the board completely', Betty said in a 1993 interview. Mathematics, science and English were the core subjects in the National Curriculum and introduced first, with technology, history and geography following. Mathematics and English were familiar territory for infant teachers (Bennett et al., 1992), but the science curriculum brought new challenges. Bennett et al. (1992) found that primary school teachers' confidence in science increased considerably between 1989 and 1991. Betty suggested that science (a subject that had been relatively de-emphasized in my 1987–88 observations) was now taking a major role in the curriculum. She explained how at one point, worried about neglecting the rest of the curriculum, she finally 'abandoned' science to do a history topic. Liz Clarke feared that the arts and the 'affective curriculum' were being crowded out. The teachers were also concerned about how the school could afford to purchase the necessary materials for areas such as technology.

Other activities traditionally promoted by the school were difficult to maintain. Comments I recorded in meetings in 1990 and 1991 included: 'There's no way we're going to have a concert, we just don't have the energy'; 'We'll have a deliberately low-key Christmas this year'; 'I can't face another Harvest Supper'. And Liz Clarke told me in 1991, 'For the second year, we've not had a big celebration in summer.' Osborn (1996b) reported similar findings, commenting that there was 'clear evidence that KS1 teachers[6] felt compelled to narrow their priorities to concentrate on basic skills at the expense of broader academic and nonacademic activities'.

Doing it all

Teachers tried to square the circle: adapting to the new requirements while preserving their traditional ideologies. The effects could be seen in schools such as Hillview. In Chapter 7, I described the workplace culture of Hillview teachers as close, warm and caring. Collaboration and partici- pation were highly valued. Roles overlapped and responsibilities were shared. The school ran on a model that was more like a family than a corporation. Humour, shared in the staffroom or staff meeting, lightened the mood of the teachers. The head teacher looked after the interests of the staff as well as the children. Chapter 3 described the school ethos, featuring tolerance and the social as well as the intellectual development of the children. At Hillview, there was 'never a dull moment', as teachers and the head teacher coped with equipment breakdowns, coaches not turning up, visitors arriving unexpectedly, television programmes not as advertised, children with leading roles in a production falling ill, new children arriving with little or no English, and numerous other events for which the most sensible response was to be very flexible and able to change plans at short notice (see also Acker, 1990a). Throughout the period covered by my research, teachers retained this ability to tolerate ambiguity and switch gears rapidly.

Yet a number of changes could be discerned over the period 1987 to 1991 in the direction of structure rather than spontaneity. There was more delegation and less whole-staff discussion of matters such as setting up the timetable and making arrangements for taking children to local swimming pools. Individual responsibilities for aspects of curriculum were delineated more clearly. Staff meetings were more orderly; curriculum reviews more systematic; record keeping procedures clarified and agreed upon by all. Ways of keeping track of materials and identifying those in need of replacement were suggested. Resources in the staffroom were reorganized. The secretary finally got a computer. Curriculum policies were written down and accessible. A helpful booklet for new or temporary teachers was produced. The requirements of the legislation were responsible for at least some of these changes, as schools were now being asked to produce systematic records, school development plans, reports to parents and so forth.

Finding a way to record progress in the many statements of attainment for all the subjects taxed teachers at Hillview, as it did teachers in primary schools across the country. Much discussion concerned the best ways of making such records and what procedures should be adopted across the school. Comments such as 'We've got to start being more disciplined' appear in my notes of meetings. In July 1991, Liz Clarke said to me, 'The assessment process is very much more clearly defined in our minds' and, in March 1992, 'We have been forced to plan more carefully.'

At the same time, staff tried hard to preserve the ethos of the school and the aspects of their workplace culture that they most valued. There was, for example, continuing emphasis on the child-centred, socially concerned agenda of the school. In a 1989 staff meeting discussion of special needs, Liz Clarke said 'Everything we do should aim to give the children a positive self-image.' The school developed anti-racism and anti-sexism policies and an elaborate strategy to improve behaviour in the school. In a 1993 interview, Liz stressed continuities that were still evident:

> Well, we're still doing what we've always done. We still have a mixed approach to our learning. We still expect our children to develop independence in their learning. We teach to the needs of the child. We believe in child-centred teaching. We believe in experiential learning, you know, that you learn by doing. We believe in questioning. And we believe in the didactic mode sometimes. I mean we always have done. We've always had a mixed approach.

Another continuity among the Hillview teachers and head teacher was their participatory, democratic, collegial and caring way of working together. When interviewed in 1991, Debbie Stevens believed that colleagues were busier: 'People always seem to have a backlog of paperwork to do, things that need sorting out.' For example, in her position as acting deputy head, 'I can't remember taking a lunch break . . . I haven't actually gone out myself just to go to the shop or go to lunch for the last year.' Nevertheless, 'I still think that the staffroom is a very happy sort of place. I think staff relations are very good, and people do really work together and there's a feeling of support . . . so, although the staffing's changed, it hasn't had any detrimental effect upon the relationships or ways that the teachers support one another.' Aware of Little's (1990) findings in the USA that teacher collegiality is more often congeniality than true 'joint work', I asked whether the talking together was chat about general topics or about work. Debbie responded:

> I think, actually we've talked more now about the nitty-gritty of the work than we do about anything else. I mean, we don't have much chance to sit and have idle talks about where we do our shopping and that sort of thing [laughs]. It's very rare that we all come in and sit down and talk about anything apart from work. But we do talk about work quite a lot and there are feelings of support around, you know, people know what other

people are doing and what other people's concerns are and which children are causing concerns around the school.

I commented that I had always noticed talk about particular children but that it was harder to see talk going on about issues like the curriculum, apart from staff meetings. Debbie replied:

That is 'snatched'. There are the bits in the curriculum meetings that we have . . . regularly throughout the year and the inservice days but curriculum issues are snatched, really. Kristin and I will meet each other in the office and spend five minutes talking about something and then get interrupted, but it started the conversation up and we'll pick up [later]. Like we've been talking about this assertive discipline recently, and we started talking about it about four weeks ago, and then Kristin brought in a paper that looked interesting for me to read about it, and then I managed to say a few words to her about that a few days later in the middle of another conversation, and then we met in the car park and talked about funding, and . . . it's a bit like ongoing sagas of curriculum issues between two members of staff . . . We 'snatch' conversations. You know somebody might be doing something on the photocopier curriculum-wise that looks interesting and then you say 'Oh, what's that?' and it starts something off, you know, or 'This is the new maths thing that I've looked at' or 'This is the new science thing, have you seen this new science thing?' We've got the structures as well; we've built staff meetings into the term, mainly for language this year and for science the year before, so there are some structures but there's also a lot of unstructured discussion going on around the place.

One of the positive side-effects teachers have applauded about the new requirements is greater collegiality (Osborn, 1996b). At Hillview the workplace culture already promoted collegiality, and Debbie's reflections indicated that it continued into the 1990s on issues such as curriculum, though discussions might have to be in 'snatched time'. Nevertheless, although later staff meetings retained the collaborative approach to planning major school activities, developing a school policy or solving a major problem such as children's bad behaviour at lunch-time, minor and administrative matters were less often tackled collectively.

The determination to preserve valued elements of the culture, combined with the newly systematic approach, was evident with the hiring of Amanda Prentice, who entered the school (as a replacement for Nancy Green) with the clearly delineated responsibility for developing science activities. Differentiated responsibilities for subject areas were becoming more common in primary schools and have increasingly become institution-alized since that time (Osborn and Black, 1994, 1996; Webb and Vulliamy, 1996; Woods *et al.*, 1997). In 1989–90 Amanda conducted a number of staff meetings to introduce aspects of the science curriculum to colleagues and to work with them to shape the school science policy. She prepared carefully for the meetings and used flip-charts and handouts. At the same time, she was at pains to encourage teachers not simply to accept what was on paper, but to voice their own priorities, so that policy would not simply come from 'on high'. Similarly, the school worked to develop records of children's achievements that not only met the criteria set down by government but allowed other accomplishments of the children to be displayed. Reports to parents did not simply follow the approved format but were modified to incorporate the kind of communication the teachers believed was important.

These examples show an intensification of teachers' work beyond the extra hours needed to study, teach and assess the National Curriculum, one that appears almost paradoxically self-induced (Campbell and Neill, 1994). Yet it seems less freely chosen when one notes it is consistent with efforts to preserve the teacher 'self' (Nias, 1989; Pollard, 1985); with the culture of teaching in this school and more generally; and with the cultural script for women noted above. Moreover, the necessity to adapt policies to suit a school with a large ability and social-class range, together with poor provision of material resources, was not internally generated. As Woods *et al.* (1997) note, what may have been dilemmas for primary teachers can easily tip over into tensions or constraints when their freedom of action becomes circumscribed by material circumstances or legal requirements.

For the head teacher, there were many sources of strain during this period (see also Grace, 1995; Jones and Hayes, 1991; Hellawell, 1992; Southworth, 1994a, 1995; Woods *et al.*, 1997). Perhaps even more than the teachers, the head needed to develop a new style, one that departed in significant ways from her preferences. In British primary schools, at least up to the reforms of the late 1980s, head teachers often did some class teaching, perhaps one afternoon a week to relieve a teacher for another task, or to substitute for a teacher who was away. Liz Clarke had enjoyed making some teaching input into the school, both for the closeness it gave her to the children and for the credibility it might give with the staff. The very term 'head teacher' suggests a first among equals, a model teacher, rather than one who simply administers or manages. Yet the introduction of the new curriculum meant that many head teachers were no longer experts, for they had not actually had the personal experience of teaching it.

With the increased pressure brought by other aspects of the 1988 legislation, Liz found less time could be made available for teaching. Debbie commented 'Over the last few years . . . I think her job is changed out of recognition. She's not able to teach. Teaching now is actually a burden for her because it takes her out of the office when she's just got piles of stuff to do. And I can see that because I've spent a lot more time here [as deputy head] . . . There are just times when you just have to say "go away" – which she's done with the note on the door today [laughs].'

Liz was also out of the school more often, as the LEA sent head teachers on short courses in management and various aspects of the new procedures. New responsibilities for financial management had to be shouldered by the head teacher and the school governors, taking time and effort, although bringing a positive pay-off as well when repairs and expenditures could be made more expeditiously than in the past when cumbersome LEA procedures had to be followed (see Chapter 6) or when supply cover could be acquired for whatever reason Liz chose rather than according to strict and inconvenient rules. At a staff meeting in February 1990 she set before staff the parameters of their new partly delegated budget, explaining how staff numbers might have to be reduced under certain conditions. She said she would try to increase pupil numbers even if it caused the teachers hardship with larger classes, because she would rather say 'your job is secure, not I'm sorry you have to go'. Local management 'is going to change the way we relate to people', she commented. 'We're forced into an approach to life we'd never had.'

Liz Clarke also spent time reassuring the staff about their ability to cope with the pace of change (see also Webb and Vulliamy, 1996). The new system of open enrolment and the concern to keep teacher jobs meant the school was growing. Increased numbers of children in the same space brought additional control problems, especially for the dinner-time staff. In September 1990, Liz commented after a meeting with other area primary school head teachers that they were 'a group of tired-looking ladies, just like me'. Her main regret was greater distance from parents: 'I'm no longer Mrs Available Clarke who is there whenever you want to call in about anything.' By 1991, she was thinking seriously about retirement at age 60, four years away. In 1993, she had firmed up her decision to retire in 1995. Yet she was as intensely involved in the school as ever: 'I don't feel any different about the school, I feel just as motivated and just as involved.' The overload of paperwork and government directives was disturbing:

> I cannot be as closely personally involved either with curriculum development and the teachers or with the families, the pastoral side of the school. I mean, I just can't. I mean, you take a decision. You either do what has to be done, or you do the paper about it, and I decide to do what has to be done and I leave the paper, so I'm constantly being hassled by people who say 'Send me that form. Send me this, that' . . . It's just preposterous, the increase in bureaucracy . . . You have to justify everything . . .

That's how my job has changed. I find it even more difficult to be proactive than I did before. Before, the reactive behaviour that I had was to incidents with the children. Now just at the point where we as a group managed to control that, through applying a planned discipline system, just at that point, I start getting all this rubbish – look! look! [gestures round the room].

CONCLUSION

In trying to get to grips with the effects of the reforms, it is hard not to overgeneralize about 'teachers' and their response. Osborn (1996a, b) and McCallum, McAlister, Brown and Gipps (1993) remind us that there are a range of possible responses, even among apparently similar teachers in the same school. Moreover, there are changes over time in such responses, parallelling changes in the politics and policies surrounding the reforms. Osborn's (1996b) work shows that anxiety and concern among primary school teachers rose from 1990 to 1992, then declined again by 1994, although the introduction of rotating privatized school inspections again raised anxiety levels and reinforced order, organization and tradition rather than flexibility, child-centredness or creativity (Osborn, personal communication; Woods and Jeffrey, 1996; Woods et al., 1997). As interactionist theories in the sociology of education would predict, teachers respond to imposed reform creatively with a certain amount of agency (ability to take individual action), rather than mechanically and as victims of forces beyond their control. On the other hand, it is unlikely that there is simply an infinite scatter of possible responses, or that individuals can wish away the real constraints and consequences caused by the policies and other features of the British educational system.

What can we learn from the stories of teachers' responses to the government interventions into the curriculum and other aspects of schooling in Britain in the late 1980s and early 1990s? We learn that changes in educational policy have their counterparts in changes in the nature of teachers' work, but that there is no simple correspondence. We learn, not for the first time, that hegemony is never total; that in the world of education, the outcomes are rarely quite what was intended – itself not always obvious or agreed upon (Bowe and Ball, 1992; Woods and Wenham, 1995). There is no possibility of policing every classroom every minute of the day, and modifications of the original policies are bound to occur as they are shaped and stretched to fit realities of school and classroom life.

We learn, or should learn, that stereotyped ideas about teachers' inevitable reluctance to collaborate, or women teachers' domestic responsibilities and lack of job commitment, or the ease of teaching young children, are difficult to reconcile with what we see around us. We learn that there are different interpretations and different responses to what seems the same event, and that we need ways to conceptualize these individual and group differences. We learn that school cultures cannot survive untouched by imposed change, but that material realities and school cultures influence the form taken by innovation. We have, in effect, a case study of the intricate and changing relationships of agency, culture and structure.

The struggles of teachers such as those at Hillview did not go unnoticed. While the 'overconscientiousness' of the mostly women infant school teachers appeared in the first instance to work in favour of government reform – a more substantial revolt was to await the disaffection of secondary school English teachers (Waters, 1995) – it had paradoxical consequences. The caring script also stood in the way of simple acceptance of the reforms: child-centredness was hard to reconcile with testing, subject orientation, and regimentation (Osborn, 1996a,b). Teachers in schools like Hillview insisted on holding on to the values they cherished, even at personal cost. Gradually the media, parents, heads and others came to show some respect and sympathy for these dedicated teachers who were clearly trying so hard to make sense of the challenge with its many impossible expectations and built-in flaws. The Conservative government, its popularity on the wane, would be forced to make some concessions, and eventually it would be supplanted by the Labour Party, which came into office in 1997.

The Labour government appears just as interested in bringing about educational reform as the Conservatives had been, although they have backed away from the Conservatives' insistence on market forces such as open enrolment. Their focus so far has been on 'standards' with a special interest in improving numeracy and literacy. A daily 'literacy hour' and 'numeracy hour', with rather rigid specifications, have been recommended. Local education authorities and schools are required to set tough achievement targets. Baseline assessement of reception children has been introduced. League tables of test results are still being published and schools are still being inspected.

The National Curriculum had already been made somewhat more manageable by changes in 1995 stemming from the 1993 Dearing Report (Dearing, 1993; Webb and Vulliamy, 1996, pp. 15–16), but schools were still finding it nearly impossible to teach everything well in the time available. At the beginning of 1998, the Labour government proposed a radical change: primary schools would only be required to follow national programmes of study for English, mathematics, science and information technology. The other subjects – geography, history, design and technology, music, art and physical education – should be taught, following government guidance, but with the details at the discretion of the schools. Not surprisingly, these proposals have been met with mixed reactions. On one hand, they appear at last to recognize the overload on primary school teachers and to restore a certain amount of trust in teachers' decision-making. On the other, they appear to promise a back-to-basics curriculum that disregards the achievements of the National Curriculum. Betty Chaplin's comment in 1993, 'Music's gone by the board completely', sounds like a prediction for the future. A leader [editorial] in the *Times Educational Supplement* comments:

> So let us say a requiem for the national curriculum. It caused primary teachers countless hours of anguish, but most would probably not want to turn back the clock to the days before its introduction. Here are some of its accomplishments: whole school planning, better skills for assessing each child's attainments and needs, a specific and wide-ranging entitlement for every child, a vision of high standards and progression in subjects such as art and history. ('Reforms and regrets', 1998)

Whether teachers are to be further controlled, trusted, or simply trusted to control themselves, remains to be seen.

NOTES

1. Chapter 7, 'Change and continuity', in Nias *et al.* (1989), gives a vivid picture of endemic change in five primary schools.

2. More detailed accounts and critiques of the reforms and their consequences can be found in a number of sources, including Acker, 1997; Campbell and Neill, 1994; Croll, 1996; Galton, 1995; Gewirtz *et al.*, 1995; Helsby, 1999; Helsby and McCulloch, 1997; Pollard *et al.*, 1994; Webb and Vulliamy, 1996; Woods *et al.*, 1997.

3. Wideen (1994), however, argues that the practicality ethic may operate only for top-down innovations; in his study of an innovation devised by a school, practical problems were regarded as a challenge (pp. 96–7).

4. A Green Paper on the future of the teaching profession was published in late 1998. It is difficult to anticipate changes that might be in place (or discarded) by the time this book is in the hands of readers. See Chapter 12 for comments on the problem of dealing with 'time' in writing a study like this one.

5. Woods and Wenham (1995) provide a fascinating account of the 'career' of this document, from inception to implementation. Some of their material is based on interviews with the three authors, who are quite disparate in their own ideologies and agendas. The role of the media (to which the document was released several weeks before it was made public) is highlighted in the article. See also Alexander's (1997) reflections on the events and the document.

6. KS1 stands for Key Stage 1, meaning the years up to the end of Year 2 (approximately age 7) – analogous to the infant years, using the older terminology.

Chapter 12

Conclusion

Some time ago, I realized that my research would be inevitably frozen in time. There was no chance of fully appreciating the impact of educational reform efforts as they would continue to unfold, or judging whether teachers' work was beginning to take on new forms that parallelled changes in industrial work in 'post-Fordist' times (Menter *et al.*, 1997), not only because I had left Britain, but because I could not continue the research indefinitely. The best I could do would be to depict 'Hillview' as a school in the late 1980s and early 1990s. Even so, it would be a construction dependent on where I was, what I noticed, what caught my interest. We ethnographers are perhaps not as full of hubris as in the past, having learned that 'the real' is impossible to convey given that there is no such thing as an agreed upon, definitive 'reality' (Britzman, 1995). In this concluding chapter, I begin by following the fortunes of Hillview and its teachers beyond the main years of my research. I then look at some of the 'lessons' this volume contains for future educational policy-making. In the final section of the chapter, I raise some questions of 'time' and 'place' that arise in the effort to generalize about the realities of teachers' work.

UPDATE ON HILLVIEW

My first research observation at Hillview was in the spring of 1987. My last visit to the school – on one of my trips to England from Canada – was in June 1993, over six years later. In 1993 I spent time in the school over a span of a week, as well as talking to teachers, meeting them for a meal or visiting them at home, going to a staff meeting. Some extracts from field notes may convey both the difference and sameness that I found.

> I came into school in late morning, June 25th. I see that cars are no longer parked in front of the school but on a piece of land along the side that had belonged to the university. A barrier keeps the cars out of the playground area. Picnic tables have replaced the car spaces. I learn later that thanks to some clever

negotiating by Liz Clarke and a 'deal' made between the local education authority and the university, an adjacent university car park is also going to be turned over to school use and will be professionally landscaped as a school playground and meeting area.

I went directly to Liz's office, where I found her doing an 'appraisal discussion' with Debbie Stevens, now deputy head teacher. The office has been rearranged, with a corner turned into a desk area for Debbie. Two steel bookcases hold a series of box files with labels like 'government', 'National Curriculum' and 'governors', and other government documents and publications are stacked up. Larger binders with curriculum materials are on a shelf over the secretary's desk. Dorothy, the secretary, now has a laptop computer, connected to a monitor and a printer. Liz stated 'You've very welcome to look at anything.' She started to tell me what she would be doing that day, including taking a teacher's class. There were several interruptions and the recounting of the schedule was never completed.

Some use of 'assertive discipline' techniques in the school may have contributed to the fact that, according to Liz, 'we are a much calmer school'. While traditional middle-class white children were growing scarce, there are larger numbers of middle-class black children, well-educated 'alternative' families, and New Age travellers now attending the school.

I took notes on staff changes. After 35 applications and 6 people interviewed, a new young probationary teacher had been appointed. A teacher who had been on a temporary contract was now full-time in reception and Marjorie Howard was teaching a junior class instead. Dennis's wife Jan had joined the staff. A teacher who had done supply work when I was in the school was now on fixed-term contract with a class. Amanda Prentice (see Chapter 11) was part-time now, after having had a child, and was substituting in Debbie's class to allow her some time for deputy head work, and Sheila Jones was doing supply work in the school as well. Another teacher, who had been hired when Helen Davies first left the school (see Chapter 10), was on sick leave, very ill with cancer. A young girl on a training programme was giving some help to the secretary, Dorothy Lowe.

Several anecdotes were related to me. In one, some of the children had been recruited to sing for something on television. Apparently a patronizing lady had asked them if they had travelled to other countries, and they had obliged her by making up extensive tall tales about travel to France, Germany, America and Jamaica.

While I was in the office, a child was sent in for bullying. Two more boys came in, and then a further two were sent for to get clarification of the story. Liz and Debbie played hard and soft police. Words like 'disappointed' and 'not acceptable' were used frequently. Dorothy's questions and observations punctuated the morning, as they had in the past. After a call from the LEA: 'I put Stacey [a new teacher] out sick in February and I haven't put her back.' There was a conversation about some records not sent on for a child who had left the school. And just as in Chapter 9, a woman came into the office to ask if her sister could change from her current 'rigid' school to Hillview. Another pending case was a child appealing to get into Kingston Secondary School (see Chapter 8); Liz said she was getting fed up with the constant problems of that transition.

In the afternoon, it was quiet, and Liz and Dorothy both worked at their desks. I noticed a pile of items in an in-tray. Dorothy said things go in there 'and wait'. Liz wrote a couple of sympathy letters to parents: in one case a husband had died, in another a grandfather.

A few days later, Liz was out of the school in the morning, at a heads' meeting. Everything was quiet. Some classes were away on trips. One of the coaches had been late arriving. I went over to Debbie's class, Year 6, in the newer building. I recognized some of the children who had been in the reception class I had visited in my first weeks of research – now the oldest in the school. I realized my research has spanned a complete school generation. The class worked quietly; there was a buzz when working but not too loud and the children appeared to be on task. They were working on a collage with pictures of women and men as portrayed in the media.

After school, I attended a staff meeting. There was a visitor who was a music specialist, and the main agenda was a discussion about music in the school and how to identify composing talent. The staffroom looks better: it has been painted a light blue, and space opened up by moving a table that had an old mimeograph machine on it – it is now flat against the wall. A microwave oven has replaced the mimeograph and there is a small fridge wedged under the table. After the meeting, several of us waited a while, as one of the coaches still wasn't back. Liz was cross – said she wouldn't use that company again.

The next day, Liz seemed distracted, distant, busy. She commented that you can tell when her stress level is up when she starts arranging the flowers. Dorothy was out with a virus. Her helper was also ill, as was the other general assistant.

Marjorie Howard is now teaching in two of the rooms occupied by the Middle Junior Unit during my research. She has Year 3 (first-year juniors) and will take them on to Year 4 in September. I noticed some changes – there is a door between the rooms where there had been only an arch before (though it is wedged open and a display table occupies some of the space). The worst wall – the one that Dennis had tried to disguise with paper (Chapter 3) – has been covered with some kind of panelling. Windows still looked rather cloudy. Marjorie sat on the edge of a table in front of a group. Each child held a map of the area they visited and she went through it with them, asking questions, keeping up a version of the patter used with the reception class years before. The children were attentive; then they broke into groups at tables to work. The work was about the Angles and Saxons, and seemed to be geography, history and art, linked together and to a trip the class had made. Life-sized drawings of the children as soldiers and other characters decorated the walls.

There is a new child who speaks Chinese but little English. The child whose sister had inquired just a couple of days ago about her joining Hillview is already here, too. Marjorie told me about another child in the class, whose family is very poor; he makes his own food and looks after himself and also his mother in some ways. He came into her class unable to read; she tells me how she has worked with him and what progress he has made. He reads everything now. She got his mum to take him to the library. His writing is still not good, though. She said she'd overheard one child asking another why Mrs Howard was so strict; the answer was 'because she wants us to go to college'.

We discussed 'whole class teaching'. Marjorie said she did it in the reception class and though it's old-fashioned, it is coming back into style. I think perhaps the teachers feel vindicated in such cases; the suggestion is that they always have done what they think is right regardless of official sanction. She doesn't get as tired as she did with reception: 'I used to crawl up the stairs at home on Friday night.'

These field note extracts may be enough to suggest the pattern of different-yet-the-same. The school seemed quieter and the children more likely to be concentrating on their work. There were signs of a more organized school office, with better technology and devices like an in-tray and document files, though their contents were not as neatly organized as their labels suggested. Teacher appraisals had become more formalized. The staff meeting did not seem to try to cover as much territory. Some improvements in decor were noticeable and the playground problem was on its way to a solution. There had been staff changes and those who remained were in some cases teaching different classes. But reorganizing the office and the staffroom could not make them any larger. Although the head could now deal directly with coach companies rather than going through the LEA, chronic problems with coaches were still in evidence. Children were still moving from school to school, and teachers dealing with difficulties of English as a second language and children from poor families, with little extra help. The head teacher was trying to do many things simultaneously and was interrupted frequently. Hillview had undergone changes, but was recognizably still Hillview. There did not appear to be many 'dull moments'. The biggest source of change was related to teacher careers. Had I revisited the school in 1996 or 1997, my sense of recognition might have been weakened, as by then some key players had left Hillview.

UPDATE ON TEACHER CAREERS

My extended association with the school was a strength of the research, as it enabled me to see changes over time that other researchers would not have noticed. However, it made for certain unanticipated difficulties. One problem in writing about the careers of the Hillview teachers was that it sometimes seemed they would not stay still long enough for me to capture them on paper! Teachers' expressed intentions were sometimes a good guide to what would happen a few years hence, sometimes not.

For example, in Chapter 10, Dennis Bryan was quoted as hoping for headship within a few years. In 1992, he left Hillview for such a post in another school. This time, it was no longer simply assumed, as it had been in the past, that the new deputy would be a man, and in fact Debbie Stevens was appointed to the post. I learned of the event through a fax she sent to me in Canada in June 1992, using the pseudonym from my research and announcing 'Debbie Stevens is new deputy head of Hillview'. Through Liz Clarke's efforts, the ground had been paved for these moves by the term in which Dennis had been acting head while Liz was on sabbatical; and the subsequent year when Debbie was acting deputy head while Dennis was on a foreign exchange. By this time, Nancy Green had moved to a deputy headship elsewhere (see Chapter 6). Helen Davies had become an acting deputy and then acting head teacher in another school, but eventually had returned to Hillview (see Chapter 10).

In a staffroom conversation near the start of my research, Rosalind Phillips told Debbie Stevens and myself that she had held a management position in a secondary school before her children were born. 'I'll never get there again', she commented, 'my age is against me'. But she didn't mind, she said, she was religious and believed things would work out. Debbie agreed, saying that when she had her daughter Katy and her husband moved jobs to Wesley, she thought she'd never be working again – but here she was. During my observations, Rosalind Phillips first juggled two part-time teaching jobs, then moved to a full-time position in her other school in 1989. Despite her earlier fatalism about her future prospects, she had taken up a deputy headship at a different school by 1991, helped in her quest by a strong reference from Liz.

When I visited England in 1993, I talked informally to most of the teachers in my original research. Sheila Jones, as noted in Chapter 10, had left teaching. Kristin King, a part-time teacher during my original observations, had become a full-time teacher, taken on extra responsibilities in the school, and had now had secured the deputy headship of a school that was undergoing a certain amount of 'turbulence' (Wallace and McMahon, 1994).

While the younger teachers were moving on, the older teachers were also developing professionally. Liz noted that the 'old stagers' in the school – herself included in the description – had found their intellectual capacities flowering alongside the younger teachers who 'are intellectual about what they are doing'. Betty Chaplin provides an example. At the start of my research, she was clearly a committed classroom teacher but without any strong career ambitions. Her family responsibilities were dominant. When I interviewed her in 1989, she observed that her colleague Helen Davies was spending her evenings doing work for her diploma course but 'I couldn't cope with all that – not at the moment, perhaps in another couple of years when the kids have gone'. By 1993, her children were older and she had more time and energy. I wrote in my field notes that Betty looked younger every time I saw her. As some of the other teachers left the school, Betty took on more responsibilities, and she now held a temporary incentive allowance. The age group she taught was the one that went through the first national testing following the 1988 Educational Reform Act and she was able to explain what was happening to meetings of parents, school governors and colleagues. Liz spoke to me of Betty's contributions in highly complimentary terms and Betty knew that Liz had appreciated her efforts.

By 1996, my next visit to England, there were further, major changes. Nancy, Dennis and Rosalind remained in their 1994 posts, although Rosalind had been seconded to work with an OFSTED team of school inspectors, while Marjorie and Betty were still at Hillview. Helen, too, was at Hillview still, but had been appointed deputy head. Sheila had after all returned to supply teaching at Hillview in the interim, though looked set to leave again. Kristin was now a head teacher. And both Debbie Stevens and Liz Clarke had left Hillview.[1]

A few years before, Debbie and her family had moved to be nearer to her parents and live in the country. Both Debbie and her husband commuted to Wesley. Debbie had to be even more organized than before (see Chapter 5) in order to add several hours' driving to her day. She began to look for headships nearer her new home. Although by this time she had an M.Ed. in educational management [administration] and experience as a deputy head, moving into a headship did not come easily. She was interviewed for several positions, but others (usually men) secured the posts. Ironically, the school where she was finally successful was the largest school at which she had been interviewed, about the same size as Hillview but in a middle-class, semi-rural setting. Hiring procedures were very complex, with candidates being interviewed several times, taking a psychometric test, and being given problematic situations to respond to in simulation exercises. Still in her early thirties, she was the youngest woman head teacher in that county. I visited her school, set in a picturesque village. The buildings, like Hillview's, were a mixture of old and new. There was more space around the school. Many parents delivered and picked up their children by car and there was a large car park. The strong hold of tradition on this school was evident in the children's school uniforms, no longer a widespread feature of English primary schools. Debbie looked relaxed. She said that for the first few months she waited tensely for 'something to happen', but the crisis never materialized. Looking at her smiling and chatting with her staff, wearing an attractive suit, moving confidently around the school, I thought how much she had gained in both poise and experience since our first meeting nine years earlier.

As Debbie's career as a head began, Liz Clarke's ended, with retirement in 1995. She had accomplished much of what she wanted for Hillview, especially the large new playground. The school had its centenary celebrations, and she shared with me pictures from what must have been a stunning event. She, too, looked more relaxed, though I suspected separation from Hillview had not been easy. I decided not to visit the school. A head teacher from another county had been appointed as Liz's replacement. It would take her some time, I thought, to put her stamp on Hillview School. One of the problems with charismatic leadership, as Max Weber noted long ago (1922/1978), is finding ways to pass it on to a new leader. Hillview School might take some very different directions in the future.

LESSONS FROM HILLVIEW

My purpose in writing this book was to engage with the literature and popular conceptions of primary or elementary teachers and teaching, through the medium of a study of the teachers' workplace culture at Hillview. Hillview tells us many things about reshaping our preconceptions and misconceptions. We need to start thinking of teaching as difficult work. We need to deconstruct the gendered underpinnings of our expectations for teachers, whether exalted (teachers as natural nurturers) or demeaning (teachers as unintellectual babysitters). We need to understand that teachers in a given school form a community who develop a particular set of shared understandings that give their work meaning. We need to revise our assumptions about inevitably isolated teachers in closed classrooms and self-contained schools.

While I have not been expressly concerned with school improvement or pupil outcomes, there are lessons here for policy-makers and politicians. I discuss these areas under the following set of headings: re/forming reform; improving conditions; supporting strengths; and recognizing the school as a workplace. These 'lessons' are heavily intertwined. To change matters in one area impacts upon the others.

Re/forming reform

I start with 'reform' because it is so much the motto of recent educational policy-making. It is a slippery term. We now tend to think of it as synonymous with government-imposed change. Because it connotes change-for-the-better, it has been a powerful word in the hands of politicians. If reforms make things better, then resistance on the part of teachers or unions can be and frequently is constructed as standing in the way of progress (Acker, 1988).

It seems to me that there is no doubt that imposed reform works, in the sense that teachers have no choice but to do it or resign. How they do it is another matter, and Chapter 11 showed that the Hillview teachers made efforts to make the government reforms of the 1980s and 1990s fit their vision of what the school should be like. Clearly, however, the school changed under the impact of the reforms. In the long run, the change could be very great indeed. Yet as many others have pointed out, the cost of imposed reform is, at the very least, teachers who feel that their experience and opinions have not been taken seriously and that the public (through its politicians) has expressed its lack of faith and trust in their professional judgement. Teachers like those at Hillview are committed enough to teaching and to their school to do whatever is necessary to sustain their vocation. Yet it would not seem unimaginable that reforms could be arrived at in consultation with teachers. The British government chose the strategy of coercion and shaming, rather than (in the rather overworked cliché) empowering. Many teachers and head teachers have left the system, often through early retirements hastened by stress, and it is impossible to know how many prospective teachers have turned away before entering the occupation. Not only would teachers be happier had they been praised and consulted, but the whole reform programme might have been considerably improved and there would have been less need for the constant changes of direction that characterized this particular reform agenda.

Thus a clear lesson for reformers is to consult the experts – the teachers – rather than to deride them and deny their competence. The portrait of Hillview teachers begins to give us some appreciation of what primary teachers actually do, and under what circumstances, a realistic look conspicuously missing in the reform agendas of recent British governments as well as many others. Every school has its unique features as well as those shared with other schools. What works well in one school may be chaotic and counterproductive in another. One-size-fits-all solutions simply do not make sense. For example, advice manuals for testing that assume the teacher can work with a small group while the other children get on quietly with seat work, perhaps supervised by a parent volunteer, do not succeed in situations where there are too many children, in a small and noisy space, and no parent volunteers. Thus reforms need to be more like guidelines that can be moulded to fit the particular school culture and community by the teachers who are the resident experts on that culture.

In many reform agendas, parents have been seen as a potent force for altering schools. But as Dehli (1994) points out, it is too easy to generalize wildly about parents and their wants and needs, or to assume that parental involvement can accomplish miracles. Some of the literature on parents and schools hints that the category is not homogeneous, that parents differ in their relationship with the school according to social class, ethnicity, and gender. My account of Hillview's interactions with parents (Chapter 9) suggests that even those dividing lines may be too crude to describe fully the variations of parental response to and impacts on schools. Only a relatively small, unrepresentative group of parents participated in the 'anti-racism saga' yet they had a strong (though not determining) effect on the direction taken by the school. Other parents had an impact far beyond what they knew by trying to get their children into Hillview and away from another school, or deciding to leave Hillview in search of a more middle-class school atmosphere. Politicians who see parents as a counterweight to teachers, a group that can whip school standards into shape, must realize that parents are not homogeneous across schools; that they are not even homogeneous within schools; and that they cannot be counted on to be inevitably in sympathy with government-desired projects and priorities. Increasing parental power in schools may be increasing unpredictability.

We must also recognize that, as I have argued earlier, change is a constant in schools. The children come and go and they grow older; teachers join and leave a workplace or move within it from one age group to another, one set of responsibilities to another. Individual teachers innovate when they decide to assign children to different seats or call the register in a different fashion, as well as when they make deliberate changes in their pedagogy. Groups of teachers or whole schools experiment with team teaching or mainstreaming, as in Hillview's 'Units', or introduce a new code of behaviour or a policy on anti-racism. It is a conceit of governments to act as if they are the only initiators of innovation. Instead, teachers need to be supported so that they are encouraged to experiment and improve what they do.

There is a role here for universities. In my account of Hillview teacher careers, there were several points where teachers followed courses, sometimes for master's degrees in education; or were able to have a short sabbatical for a particular purpose such as looking at assessment practices; or in one case participated in an exchange programme to another country. All of these experiences, which are not always easy to come by, benefited both the individuals and the school. Other teachers were able to get additional experiences as acting head or deputy head teachers during those times as well. No doubt these enriching activities helped Hillview produce an extraordinary number of teachers who secured promotions in the system. At the same time, fresh ideas were brought into the school.

The trend in Britain has been away from supporting teachers to follow advanced education courses (teacher education has shared in the derision directed towards teachers as a whole) and towards short school-based inputs specific to curriculum needs and reforms and government-determined priorities. In my university in Ontario, we are seeing drops in graduate school enrolment of teachers, too, as provincial reforms take up their energy, and increases in the cost of tuition add a further disincentive. The chance to do a higher degree is denied to many teachers, and there is little public concern about it; yet such opportunities for professional development are important for the teacher's career chances and sense of professional self-esteem as well as for infusing into their schools current educational thought and a link with the wider scholarly community.

Improving conditions

Accompanying the general disrespect that leads governments to ignore teachers when making policies is the neglect of the conditions under which these teachers toil. One of my recurring points in the book has been the paucity of physical resources encountered at Hillview. Teachers at Hillview did not have enough space, materials, money or help to do the kind of job they wanted to do (Chapter 3). Student teachers are often shocked when they go into schools (especially if they have worked in another job first) and discover that teachers do not have telephones, offices, computers and sometimes even a place to hang a coat. There is simply no privacy. Primary schools seem more disadvantaged than secondary schools, where there may at least be a shared office for teachers in a particular department. The conditions are not peculiar to Hillview, nor to British primary schools. Susan Moore Johnson (1990) makes the same point about American schools when she comments: 'No one would ever surmise that teachers' work is crucial to the future of the country from the physical features of their workplaces, the condition of the buildings that house instruction and the supplies that support it' (p. 58).

It is a pity that so much of the money spent on enforcing reforms could not have been spent on making schools more tolerable workplaces for professionals, not to mention comfortable places for children to spend many hours each day. Here again the uniqueness of each school needs to come into educational planning: what may look like a fair distribution of funds may ignore the greater needs of schools serving more disadvantaged communities or those that require extra support for other reasons such as higher proportions of children with English as a second language. Some formulas for funding do aim to redistribute finances with some attention to differential needs, but there seems little awareness of the precise situation of each school and a studied ignoring of the huge impact that parents with deeper pockets can make on the resources available to a school. Teachers in schools like Hillview subsidize the school with their extra labour and their 'make do and mend' credo, while their schools, seen as workplaces, remain highly inadequate.

Supporting strengths

Was Hillview a 'good school'? I thought so. It was not a perfect school, if there is such a concept. Sometimes it was noisy, semi-chaotic, confused by its competing attachments to academic excellence, child self-esteem and social justice. Yet for every drawback, there was an advantage. What one person might describe as disorganized another would see as lively and imaginative. Certainly, the school benefited from strong yet compassionate leadership and a caring community among the teachers. Several of its features would help anyone trying to put together a model of a 'good school'.

Among those, I would include the relatively small size of the school, around 200 children. This size may seem small to some readers but it is an average size for a British primary school. The size of the teacher population was also small, in part because of the tradition of every teacher being a class teacher. So these 200 children were taught by just 6 full-time and 3 part-time teachers, with help from two general assistants and the head teacher. As I have commented in the study, there were also other adults in the school for many purposes, perhaps more than one would find in a more isolated community (Chapters 8 and 9). So although Hillview was the 'small society' of sociological descriptions of schools, it was not by any means in a separate world. Active engagement with the world outside was part of the strength of Hillview.

Such a small group of teachers, facing common challenges and opportunities, could bond together in a work group that 'worked'. Another factor that undoubtedly influenced the closeness of this teacher community was the system in place for hiring teachers, which gave the head teacher considerable influence in each decision. Liz Clarke, over time, could create the community of teachers that she wanted: teachers who would be loyal to her and share her vision for the school. By genuinely caring about her staff and enabling them to do their best (Chapters 6 and 10), she inspired allegiance both to herself and the school philosophy.

The fact that most of the teachers were women was also one of its strengths. Many of the women had in the past, or were having concurrently, experience in managing homes and families and balancing competing commitments. They seemed well adapted to the flexibility and tolerance for change required for a successful teacher at the school. Their support for one another, as well as Liz Clarke's support for them, seemed in part to rest on an understanding that women may well have responsibility for the domestic scene and a willingness to work with and around that. For the head teacher, a few concessions for women with children was repaid many times over by the extra work and loyalty these women showed to the school and its leader. In the past, women with domestic responsibilities were thought to be by definition not committed to their careers (Riddell, 1989) and the whole social structure reinforced that difficulty of becoming committed by making it hard for women to move into more than a narrow range of occupations and to break through the glass ceiling into managerial responsibilities, even in those occupations where they were welcome. While discrimination against women is still in many ways alive and well, there is more scope for career progress and choice of occupation than there was in the past; the careers of the younger staff at Hillview exemplify some of the changes. They still needed to struggle with child care and intermittent part-time employment. Yet they were pursuing higher degrees and taking minimal time out of the full-time labour market.

Put a different way, the particular 'patriarchal bargain' (Kandiyoti, 1988) that had obtained for women teachers in the past was that in return for giving up intentions to lead in the field, they might be allowed to have a circumscribed role within teaching, often finding fulfilment in classroom teaching but without becoming 'extended professionals' (Hoyle, 1974). Teacher shortages meant that they could usually find a way back into teaching after a break for child care if they needed and wanted it, as Marjorie Howard's story (Chapter 10) showed. This trade-off was the only way that many women could manage the full gamut of home responsibilities and yet work outside the home. The younger teachers at Hillview still had major domestic responsibilities, but they were expected to be fully involved in the workplace culture, to develop professionally through courses or other means. They no longer gave up their ambitions in return for a modest level of expectations for school participation. Debbie Stevens even continued to attend staff meetings when on maternity leave. The younger women teachers were supported by social changes which gave more credibility to women's ambitions and made it less obligatory that child care be provided solely through the mother's full-time involvement. The school survived – and even thrived – because of the intensity of the commitment of its teachers. They did not have to feel that they were second-class citizens, or serve as a foil to a powerful male father-figure in the role of principal (Alexander, 1984).

The question of whether women have an affinity to more participatory, caring ways of working has come up at several points in this book, and I have cautioned against an essentialist and simplistic equation of femaleness or maleness with any particular leadership or collegial style. Yet one thing elementary or primary schools have going for them is the tradition of caring with its strongly gendered character (though applying to persons of both sexes working in these schools). The danger is that caring for others and not oneself can become self-sacrifice and a recipe for exploitation. In the situation of resource deprivation that many primary schools fall into, there is a dangerous reliance on women's willingness to sacrifice for the good of the children and the institution (Acker, 1995a). Persons working in the so-called caring professions are described over and over again as being exhausted and overstretched. Caring is 'work' and we must stop thinking of it as a natural, unrewarded, adjunct to women's work. To the extent that women have other choices, they may be less and less willing to work selflessly in the service of a mission (teaching included) that does not include their own best interests.

The 'lessons' we can derive from the forgoing discussion include the virtues of small school size; engagement with the community and concerns beyond the bounds of the school; control over hiring by the principal or head teacher and strong charismatic and caring leadership. Policy-makers should also be fully aware of the gendered subtext of primary school teaching as work and prospects and problems if they continue to rely on unrewarded goodwill and sacrifice by women.

Recognizing the school as a workplace

The point that ties together all of the above arguments is the need to recognize that communities of teachers in schools are adult working groups. We are so obsessed with schools as places for children that we forget they are workplaces for adults. The conditions under which teachers work are full of contradictions. Teachers are charged with improving society through preparing the next generation, yet treated as if they are little more than children themselves and expected to spin gold from straw. Their jobs are hard in so many ways, yet socially defined as easy and natural, for women at least. If children spend 15,000 hours in schools over their school careers (Rutter, Maughan, Mortimore and Ouston, 1979), how many hours do teachers spend in these venues over their total years of service? Why do we persist in assuming that what is good for children must be bad for adults and vice versa, to put their respective needs in competition? As Peter Woods (1990) reminds us, for children to have opportunities to learn, teachers must have opportunities to teach. Rather than belittling, deriding, or deskilling our teachers, we must trust those to whom we entrust our children and create enabling conditions to encourage the best from them; otherwise primary teachers' work risks being love's labour lost.

TIME AND PLACE

I began this work in one place, England, and concluded it in another, Canada. There are 11 years to account for between the start of the study and the delivery to the publisher of the manuscript. That meant 11 years to change the way I approach research, theory and writing; and 11 years for the teachers and the school to change. I have had to struggle with finding 'time' to write up this study. I have also had the difficulty sometimes encountered by doctoral students – as time goes by, one begins to think the product must be ever-better to justify such a long period in its making – and the end-product recedes a little further with each such thought.

Taking my time has been an advantage in several ways. First, my study is unusual in following the lives and work of teachers and a school over such a long period. The most interesting effect of time was on teacher careers, as I showed earlier in this chapter. Most of the teachers I worked with achieved promotions and moved into deputy headships or headships in other schools over the 11 years, in a process that seemed to blend accident and intention. I was also able to see how the school responded to the effects of the government's sweeping legislation of 1988, as it happened in the middle of my study. Another positive effect was that over time – and having moved to a different place – I have been exposed to North American perspectives, more literature and theory, and can write a book that to some extent draws on these wider perspectives.

These benefits are somewhat double-edged. I cannot get the teachers to stop making career changes by the time the book goes to print. I can document the early responses to legislation, but not the later ones, the ones today – or tomorrow. I am conscious that if I write about government policy, it could be altered, extended or even rescinded before the book comes out in print. Had I finished the book a little earlier, I would have been writing about a government as 'the government' when it was no longer in power. Many of the writings about recent educational reform in Britain have dated very quickly and are nearly incomprehensible outside of the country, as they rely so much on a knowledge of current events. I have tried to avoid this outcome by assuming less, explaining more, and setting my objectives beyond the analysis of a particular set of reforms and their context.

On balance, perhaps paradoxically, I think in the end the time gap works *for* me. I look at much of the research published on teachers' responses to the National Curriculum and reform and think: I can be less parochial, less time-focused; I can say something broader, something more transcendent about 'teaching'. But only with caution – in the years since I started the research, we have begun to be suspicious about overarching claims to understand 'women' or 'teachers'. I want to write about 'the nature of teachers' work' without claiming that there is a universal form of teachers' work. It helps to be modest in my claims, to say: This is what teachers' work is/was like at this time, in this place, in this constellation of political, demographic, economic influences. To think about teaching and teachers' work in a way that transcends time and place, while not making claims that all teachers are the same, is a tricky balancing act. There is a sense of perpetual uncertainty that follows many writers today, when we are increasingly conscious of issues such as diversity and the impossibility of identifying one true ethnographic story. I have offered one ethnographic story in this volume, as 'true' as I can make it, bounded in time and place. Through it, I hope, readers can reflect on their own stories and expand their understandings of gender, culture and work in the lives of teachers.

NOTE

1. I received a letter from Liz Clarke after the manuscript had gone to press, with more recent news of the teachers. Dennis Bryan, Debbie Stevens and Kristin King continue to work as head teachers, and Dennis has also trained as an OFSTED inspector. Since I wrote Chapter 12, Nancy Green and Rosalind Phillips have become head teachers, Shelia Jones is working as a consultant to schools setting up libraries, and Helen Davies has taken early retirement from Hillview, leaving teachers Marjorie Howard and Betty Chaplin and secretary Dorothy Lowe the only three of my original staff (see Table 1, p. 6) still in the school.

APPENDIX

Appendix

Method

There is a long tradition of consigning detailed discussion of methodological issues and choices to an appendix. Of the six chapters in *Journeys through Ethnography*, edited by Annette Lareau and Jeffrey Shultz (1996), three were originally appendices to ethnographic studies. It should not be thought that what follows is less important than the material in other chapters. It appears here rather than in the main text in order to aid the flow of the ethnography itself, so that readers can move more quickly to learn about the teachers' work and turn to this section if and when they wish to understand my role more clearly.

'The researcher' is very much an actor in this particular drama – in the sense of taking an active rather than passive observer role during my time in the school, and as the chronicler of the story, or more accurately one of the stories that might be told. In the next sections, I describe decisions and dilemmas that occurred throughout this qualitative research study. I conclude with some reflections on whether I might have 'done things differently'.

ACCESS

As indicated in Chapter 1, my entry into Hillview was fairly informal and negotiated solely through the head teacher. At least until the late 1980s, British head teachers were typically rather powerful figures in their own kingdoms (Alexander, 1984), and Mrs Clarke was the obvious gatekeeper for me to satisfy. I wondered from time to time whether I should have formally cleared my study with the local education authority (LEA). Mrs Clarke mentioned my presence to several key LEA individuals such as the advisor liaising with the school, and it seemed that was clearance enough. After two terms in the school, I gave a talk to the teachers on my research during an inservice training day, and sometime later did the same for the school governors.

At my current university in Toronto, there is a complicated procedure whereby ethical clearance must be obtained for research. In contrast, I made relatively few promises and had to rely on my own sense of right and wrong rather than on formal guidelines. 'Access' and 'negotiation' were processes that continued, in obvious and subtle ways, throughout the research and with many persons. In the early days I tended to work through the head teacher, who would decide whom I could see and arrange it with that teacher. During that term I managed to observe all but two of the teachers for at least a day. I missed the deputy head teacher, Douglas Benton, who was about to leave the school for a headship elsewhere and had little interest in being shadowed.

Once I began to be a familiar figure around the school, I could make these contacts for myself. Although one or two teachers were somewhat cautious about being observed, others had no apparent difficulty and welcomed my appearance, whether prearranged or not. I was not the only adult to be moving round the school. One of my first surprises at Hillview was the large number of people who appeared in the school each day, especially but not exclusively to see the head teacher. Teachers were regularly interrupted in their classrooms by parents, other teachers, the head, children bearing messages or collecting something, and others. It was easy for me to join this circulating population.

Even in my early days at the school, I was allowed further into the teachers' world than many of the more casual visitors by being invited into the staffroom. The staffroom holds a particular status in studies of the school as a workplace, as the backstage where teachers can unwind, away from children and parents (Cortazzi, 1991; Kainan, 1994; Pollard, 1985). At Hillview, the small size of the room reinforced efforts to keep it a private space. Children knocked when necessary to contact someone inside. Special visitors might be invited in for a cup of coffee. During teaching times, some activities such as remedial teaching or guitar lessons might take place there, given the absence of alternative venues. Student teachers generally joined the teachers for their breaks in the staffroom, but other helpers such as nursery nurses or youth trainees did not. But although I had almost immediate access to the staffroom, shortly thereafter even joining the coffee pool with a monthly contribution, I was kept away from staff meetings. I did not begin attending these meetings, which were taking place one day a week, until a year after my initial entry into the school. Frequently I had the sense that I was working my way through layers of secrecy and caution:

> This is so much like peeling an onion! No wonder no one does research on teachers' culture – it's so difficult to unveil and penetrate. (13 November 1987)

Entry to Rosemont School was superficially easier. Again, I worked through the head teacher, Dave Andrews, to whom I had been introduced by Mrs Clarke. Having ascertained that this school would contrast in interesting ways with Hillview, and being reassured by the head's welcoming stance, I began visiting Rosemont about once a week from April 1988. As noted in Chapter 1, Rosemont was larger, more modern, and better equipped than Hillview, with a largely white middle-class rather than a mixed student population in terms of class and ethnicity. Its staffroom was much larger than Hillview's, and visitors and helpers could often be found there. The Rosemont staffroom lacked the backstage aura of Hillview's equivalent. Similarly, the head teacher's office door was usually open rather than closed as it was at Hillview. Nevertheless, appearances were deceptive. Rosemont's head teacher's door might be open, but to access the head teacher, one had to walk past the secretary's office down a corridor. The very silence of the head's office made one hesitant to interrupt. Thus, although the head was certainly a kind, caring individual, contact was much less spontaneous than with Mrs Clarke. Similarly, the staffroom at Rosemont was easy to enter, but one simply had the sense that the secret stories (Clandinin and Connelly, 1995) must be shared somewhere else.

THE RESEARCHER'S ROLE(S)

Like access negotiations, much of my 'presentation of self' was improvised and emergent. At Hillview, especially, I was always highly conscious that my presence could add one more source of strain to a difficult job. I thought that I had more to gain from being there than persons in the school. Thus I was motivated to please others and to help where possible. Many opportunities arose to do just that.

Certainly, if I had any idea of remaining cool and distant in the classrooms in order to improve the impartiality or accuracy of my observations, I soon lost it. The culture at Hillview, and to an extent at Rosemont, so emphasized pitching in, helping out, working together and so forth that it would have been quite counterproductive to have remained aloof. Moreover, contemporary writing in education about action research, research as praxis, and feminist research all seemed to point in the direction of active involvement. I was reminded of Ronald King, the 'man in the Wendy House' (1978, 1984), who described his strategies for avoiding conversation with the children and staying firmly in the observer role. Perhaps King, as a man among women teachers, found such a distance easier to assume, but for me, a woman in some ways much like those I was there to study, distance simply did not seem an option. Also it was clear that the teachers at Hillview needed the help. However good they were in the classroom, the demands of so many children, with such a large range of apparent abilities, confined in small spaces, challenged them all (see Chapters 3 and 4). After all, I was not only an education academic and a former teacher, but a mother myself. I also fit into the category of 'sensible adult', a most desirable acquisition for any trips outside the school grounds.

Rosemont needed me less, as it had a larger bank of parents who could be 'sensible adults' for such purposes and frequently also help in the classroom. Yet in both schools, an adult who could move around the classroom (as the teachers themselves did) helping the children when they were working as individuals or in small groups was very welcome.

The children were not particularly curious about what I was doing, although if they saw me taking notes they would sometimes ask what my notebook was for and I would explain. They were used to having adults around. Certain children at Hillview – almost always girls – would attach themselves to me, and in turn, I felt drawn to some of them. Sometimes they reminded me of my daughter, or perhaps there was just some inexplicable rapport. Other children I found disagreeable. Some children were very clinging, to the point of being irritating. During playground sessions, there would also be a small group, again mostly girls, clustered around each person on duty, seeking a kind of warmth (sometimes literally, as the days could be chilly and the children ill-dressed) or protection from their peers. Teachers had to work out how to be fair and show caring and kindness to all children when their natural reactions, like mine, were to favour some and dislike some others. They worked hard, I thought, at being professional in this regard.

My working with the children was useful in several ways. First, it meant that I could rehearse 'what it was like to be a primary school teacher' in a quasi-realistic manner. Second, it was appreciated by the teachers, which facilitated my research. Third, it meant that I knew the children well enough to engage in discussions with the teachers or understand the discussions they had among themselves. Fourth, it gave me a recognizable role in the classroom. Fifth, I felt good about making a real or at least an immediate contribution to the children and to the teachers.

Sometimes I played a role that I thought of as 'being Mrs Millerson'. Generally I used that name, my married name, around the school. All of the women teachers at Hillview went by 'Mrs', so it seemed to fit in better than 'Dr' or 'Ms'. Once introduced as Mrs Millerson, it was easier to continue that way. When in a classroom with one of the teachers, I could be useful as a kind of foil. For example, the teacher might say in rather exaggerated fashion, 'What do you think, Mrs Millerson? Is this the kind of behaviour we should be expecting from third-year juniors?' Or, when a child had done something particularly praiseworthy, 'Mrs Millerson, look at Daniel's number work – he has tried very hard this time.' 'Mrs Stevens' or 'Mrs Jones' or anyone else could play too; it was not only a role for visitors, although it was a role for adults. Outside the classroom, first names were the norm. But in this classroom world, there was a faint sense of irony in the 'Mrs Millerson' role – we would often smile during these exchanges (except when its use was disciplinary, when we would look stern) and sometimes the child would also pick up the humour.

about Hillview. We amused ourselves, sitting in her garden over wine coolers, thinking that the rest of the world would think our shared obsession quite mad. In interacting with the head and the teachers, I had to be sensitive about what I said or reported. Sometimes teachers told me things that they wanted me to tell Mrs Clarke. 'If you could just suggest, maybe say . . .' I do not think this strategy meant that they felt unable to raise the issues themselves, rather that with my support they might have more chance of getting whatever it was that they wanted. I did my best to oblige and also raised issues or put forward ideas that came independently from my observations or conversations. The advantage of being an outsider (however integrated I was becoming) was that I still saw conventions or ways of doing things that I could imagine being done differently. Teachers and the head seemed to like my suggestions, whether or not anything came of them. It simply meant that I was a participating adult in the life of the school. People used me as a sounding-board. A teacher might try out on me her ideas about what to do about a particular child. The head might outline her thoughts about staffing for next session. I rarely had the sense that I was seen as an expert 'from the university', but rather as another concerned adult in a good position to help.

In these everyday interactions, it was not usually too difficult not to repeat gossip or critical comments. But it might be difficult not to listen to it. Like other ethnographers, I had to tread a fine line between being fully absorbed in the culture I was studying, and being too distant from its everyday preoccupations and interactions to be trusted or to grasp what was going on. I developed a few rules of thumb. For example, if I had to participate in a discussion in which someone expected me to tell them what someone else said or thought, I would only report positive things. Also I would try to be authentic, in that I would not disguise my own views or refuse to give them in conversations. That did not mean that I would be vociferous about my opinions, however. Generally that meant keeping quiet more than I would in my own workplace and deferring to others' views, at least on school-related matters. This was not as hard as it may seem, for I was always conscious that in this setting, others did know more than I did. Now and again, for example when Mr Benton (Dennis Bryan's predecessor as deputy head) told me that girls are not as naturally good at mathematics as boys, I did have difficulty striking a balance between deference and my own views or expertise. In that case, I knew he was about to leave the school, so I did not bother to make an issue of his views.

Perhaps what was most difficult for me was accepting the changes of plan that so frequently occurred, especially when I was counting on doing an interview or watching a particular teacher. I simply had to learn to accept that an appointment might not be honoured because something else came up, or that a meeting could be cancelled, and if it were, chances were that nobody would let me know. One teacher at Rosemont failed to turn up for a scheduled interview during lunch-time until twenty minutes before the afternoon bell, explaining on her return that she needed to go to the hairdresser. I took it that she was not keen to be interviewed. But mostly it was simply a case of priorities, and given the myriad of other things to be juggled, my schedule was not high on the list, however much I was liked and appreciated. Like the helping in the classroom, this aspect of doing the research was the research itself: I was learning about what it was like to be a primary school teacher, where it sometimes seemed that nothing very much could be counted on to happen as planned. Those who, like myself, preferred order and predictability had to learn to live with something different.

I have described the most obvious roles I played at Hillview – classroom helper, 'sensible adult', 'Mrs Millerson', sounding-board, conduit, commentator – but they did not exhaust my versatility and the school's need. I found myself playing the piano (on a few occasions) for assembly or for lessons given by the violin teacher. When I was in the office, I became an all-purpose 'gopher', running errands, answering the telephone, proofreading letters to parents or school documents, photocopying, reminding the head of things she had said or meetings she had agreed to, even taking prospective parents on tours of the school. After I began attending staff meetings, I took minutes, freeing up the deputy head from a distracting job and giving me field notes into the bargain. At a parents' evening I took notes on the discussion and typed them up for the head teacher. I could also provide information about programmes at the university and occasionally books on a particular topic for someone in the school who might be writing a paper for a course or who wanted something for classroom use. At Rosemont, I was more conventional, and mainly helped in the classroom and acted as a sounding-board, principally for the deputy head, Alison Holly. I was comfortable there, but never as intensely involved as I was at Hillview.

TECHNICAL DECISIONS

Decisions and dilemmas are integral to all research and perhaps more problematic for ethnographic research than other types of projects. I had to make broad plans – how much time to spend in each school over a period of time, which days to attend and whom to observe – and such plans were continuously revised as circumstances changed. I had to work around my university obligations, which had to take first place in cases of conflict. The school terms extended before and after the university ones, which generally meant some concentrated school time in September and July and during other breaks in the university timetable. Much of my own teaching was at night, which helped clear spaces. But I would often be flying (so it seemed) back and forth between venues. I might be at the university in the morning, at a school in the afternoon, and back in the university for an evening course. Hillview, with its older buildings, was often cold, while the university could be overheated, so I would dress in layers and add and subtract as necessary. Often I felt like Wonder Woman, as if I would change my clothes and my personality with a few magic words or spins *en route* to one or the other venue. It must also have been Wonder Woman who managed to do the research on top of having a full-time university job and a family.

How to dress for success(ful) research is a topic raised in some books on ethnography and not always easy to decide upon. It seemed most reasonable to me to dress like the teachers, at least in my initial days in the school. In many cases, and in line with the relative social and economic status of the community surrounding each school, the women teachers at Rosemont wore more expensive clothes and accessories than those at Hillview. In both schools, women teachers usually wore skirts and blouses with sweaters, or dresses. Hillview's head teacher would wear a dress or a suit. On a day containing 'games' or swimming, teachers might change into a tracksuit. I began by wearing similar clothing – finding it much easier at Hillview to feel appropriately garbed, where as the research proceeded, I was eventually more comfortable wearing trousers than a skirt.

I gave great thought to the notebooks I bought. I generally liked those with hard covers, not spiral bound, that would fit into my handbag or pocket. Of course, I had to think about what, when and where to write in these notebooks. I became adept at scribbling a few notes that I could decipher and expand later. In the evenings, I would read through the notes and type up extended field notes, adding comments, thoughts, things to check on and so forth. After about a year and half, I found I could not face the typing any longer, and instead switched to bigger notebooks and worked to make my handwriting more legible. By that point, I no longer needed such detailed notes, and my presence in the schools was so taken for granted that a larger notebook was not intrusive. Unfortunately this work was done before I learned to use a computer, so I cannot pull up my field notes on the computer at will, but must retype as necessary. I made several photocopies of field notes, keeping them in safe places.

I decided that the jokey references in the methods books to the ethnographer's frequent trips to the toilet to generate field notes were written by people who had not spent much time in a school lavatory. Hillview's teachers' lavatory could only take one inhabitant at a time, which precluded lengthy stays (a second one was off the side of the head teacher's office, and could also be used on occasion, but lacked privacy as it opened on to a clockroom used by ancillary staff). Luckily, however, there were opportunities in the classrooms and in the office and sometimes over lunch to fill in notes in my notebook. The regular coffee breaks were slightly more problematic. Hillview had a break of about 20 minutes mid-morning, after the assembly and during the children's playtime (two teachers on a rotating basis would be on playground duty). In one sense a coffee break was a good opportunity to catch up on my notes, but I also wanted to participate in the general conversation and learn things by listening to the teachers.

It is clear that my research was qualitative, an approach well suited for investigating a setting in depth. Ideally, perhaps, I would have been a full-time participant in the school, rather than moving back and forth to my university responsibilities. The model for ethnographic work is one of immersion, in the tradition of the anthropologists who learned languages and chronicled the rituals and habits of distant peoples. However, sociological ethnographers often have to make compromises, given that they are typically not in foreign lands and may have commitments beyond the research. My lack of total immersion was compensated for by my extended period of research, and also had the advantage of allowing me when out of 'the field' to contemplate what was going on and catch up on typed field notes. In typical ethnographic tradition, I combined three main techniques: participant observation, in-depth interviewing and the collection of documents. I have already described my participant observation in Chapter 1 and earlier in this appendix. Document collection meant in practice that I acquired copies of or photocopied such items as school brochures, communications with parents, staff meeting minutes, government or local education authority circulars. I also took photographs of Hillview school events and of the school itself as an *aide-mémoire*.

Interviews took several forms. Most were taped. Some of the interviews were specifically about the Middle Junior (and later the Older Junior) Unit. With all of the teachers at Hillview (with the exception of new teachers who arrived during the period of research and those who left in my first term) and two-thirds of those at Rosemont, I conducted an interview that covered their views on teaching in general, some aspects of their lives outside school, their past and anticipated future careers and (the main body of the interview) 'teaching here': descriptions of the children, parents, teachers, head teacher and other features of the school, as well as the teacher's own roles, records, responsibilities and routines. Interviews with the head teachers covered these matters as well as other items such as the history of the school and their plans for it.

Interviews provided an interesting counterpart to the participant observation. Some teachers were less comfortable speaking on tape than in conversation. Sometimes what was said on tape did not exactly match my observations, or was undermined by subsequent events during the research. Interview tapes gave me the comfort of quotable segments that were accurately recalled, but observation produced a more nuanced view of events in context. In looking at recently published books on schools and teachers in Britain, it is striking how often interviews are the main mode of data collection and how rarely field notes are quoted, even where some observational time is said to have been a part of the study. I wonder if the pressure to publish more quickly, spurred by the Research Assessment Exercises which have shaped the production of research at British universities in the 1990s (where departmental funding depends on ratings of research productivity), has made it difficult to invest the extended time required for ethnographic work, or whether difficulties of gaining access into schools already troubled by rapid changes, government requirements and intrusive inspections have worked against potential ethnographic studies.

Qualitative data can be analysed in a variety of ways and, in fact, the process is more idiosyncratic than many textbooks would have us believe. At the heart of the analysis is the task of reading and rereading field notes, including the memos and comments written at the time, and interview transcripts, and identifying themes that provide an organizing structure for the data. My preference was to go for broad themes, such as 'change'. Although in some cases, I went through my notes marking a number of themes, I discovered that I worked better pursuing one theme at a time. For example, I could mark in the margins all of the incidences related to 'change' using an orange highlighter, and then go through again, deciding what the subcategories of change appeared to be. Then I would prepare an index so that under each subheading I could find the occurrence of that theme (date and page) with a few words to remind me of the specific context, perhaps including an asterisk for a particularly significant example. Some of the themes became articles or conference papers; others were not pursued further; and new ones emerged as I worked with the data.

As I wrote the chapters, I sent most of them in draft form to Debbie Stevens and Liz Clarke. Their feedback was helpful, and both were gracious about answering questions when I wanted to make sure factual details were correct. Debbie was able to share some extracts with two of the other teachers. However, none of the teachers read the entire study in advance.[2] I think my 'readers' found it strange to have their movements catalogued in such detail; with their current lives pressing ahead, it seemed rather like a dream to recall the Hillview of several years ago.

ETHICAL DILEMMAS

Coffee and tea breaks, as well as informal occasions such as parties, presented the dilemma of whether to regard everything heard as fair game for the research. Once at Rosemont I was trying to scribble down a run of impromptu jokes made after a child (no one's favourite) had sliced off a bit of his finger while going through a door he wasn't supposed to open. A quick-thinking teacher had saved the piece of finger, preserving it with a bag of frozen peas to keep it cold, and he was rushed to hospital. Humour, of course, is a resort when under tension and this event was followed by a series of jocular remarks. However, someone noticed that I was writing down the jokes, and made a comment that made me uncomfortable. After that, I was careful not to write down things people said or did as they happened, but if necessary try to commit them to memory and write a note later. Peshkin (1984) has remarked that 'deception is a *sine qua non* of field work' (p. 257). I was not deceiving anyone about my purpose in the school, but whenever I took notes after private conversations, telephone calls, or parties, I did wonder if people knew I was 'the researcher' as well as 'Sandy' on those occasions. I did decide that I would respect confidences and not, for example, write anything using personal comments one teacher might make about another. But sometimes such comments helped me understand more about one or other of those teachers.

Other ethical dilemmas arose from time to time, although none so serious as to truncate or seriously affect the research. An Easter assembly at Hillview in 1988 posed a problem for me, as a Jewish woman, when I thought that what I was hearing could be interpreted by the children as possibly reinforcing harmful stereotypes about Judaism. As a school committed to a multicultural perspective, with children from a number of ethnic groups, Hillview made special efforts to explain and celebrate rituals of different faiths, but little attention had been paid to Judaism. Hesitantly, I raised the issue with Liz Clarke. She agreed that I had a point and said that the children probably did not know that Jesus himself was Jewish. A further difficulty arose, however, when she raised the issue with the teacher who had organized the assembly; essentially, I had placed myself in the role of critic, just the position I had been trying to avoid.

As with access negotiations, ethics pose continuous dilemmas, which even the strictest ethical review form cannot anticipate. As I write, I continue to make decisions about what examples to use, what to highlight and what to ignore.

BECOMING AN INSIDER?

Despite the books that warn, in that rather unpleasant phrase, about 'going native' in ethnographic work, I found it not a clear-cut in-or-out experience. I could never be fully immersed, be 'one of them', but I could come pretty close. I rarely completely lost the sense that I was 'the researcher', but now and again it happened. For example, my notes record one such time in the staffroom at Hillview, when several of us started demonstrating dance steps we knew, and I showed off the jitterbug my mother had taught me. The teachers knew about my family and I knew about theirs. I counted several of them among my good friends by the time the research was completed. At times, it made for a pretty emotional experience (Ellis, 1991). Even now, going through my notes from several years ago, I can re-live events. On the tapes, I can hear actual voices. I can be moved to tears by memories.

A more problematic consequence of my involvement at Hillview was the sense of alienation I was developing from my university. In one sense, Hillview was helping me cope with my disappointment with certain events there. It was also helping me cope with a bereavement I had recently experienced. It was so alive! In contrast, the School of Education seemed quiet, dead, lacking in children's voices and movement and excitement. The government's cuts to universities and other initiatives were changing the university culture in very evident ways. Whatever we did was becoming rationalized, intensified, increasingly judged by narrow output measures. A scramble to bring money into the School, a preoccupation with 'survival' was (it seemed) changing many of the values I had found attractive years earlier (see Acker, 1995b). The way in which Hillview's head teacher went out of her way to express appreciation to her colleagues, both to individuals and to the group – a bottle of sherry in the staffroom after a play or concert; a note of thanks; a sentimental speech – impressed me greatly. The contrast was the beginning of my return to a gender analysis in this study. What was there about a workplace culture made up of a small number of (mostly) women, working with children, that produced this warmth? Why did the large, bureaucratic, university department produce such a contrasting culture? I realized, too, that my being female was important to the research: it gave me easy access to informal situations and empathy with aspects of women teachers' lives. I think it would have been far more difficult for a man to have the lengthy phone conversations I had with some of the teachers and to develop the degree of intimacy I had with a few. Of course, further dilemmas can arise if it seems that very intimacy is a research tool (Stacey, 1991).

There were, however, some dangers for me as a researcher in this seductive culture. Often, I wanted to be absorbed into the culture of the school. I wanted to bask in the warm glow of Mrs Clarke's approval and the teachers' friendship. When my suggestion for a way to diagram the curriculum plans was adopted, I felt proud. But if my name was forgotten when a list was made up – say for Christmas dinner at a restaurant, or when copies of a document were made for the teachers – I was hurt. My position was something like the part-time teachers in the school, who often missed out on important information and, I think, shared the sense (and were frequently told) that important things were happening when we weren't there. And, of course, I couldn't *be* a primary school teacher. When I went into the school, I had half-thought about changing careers. I was going through a period of regret for the musical career I had not pursued, and I toyed with several ideas about changing directions before it was 'too late'. But I soon learned that as much as I admired what the teachers were doing, I did not really want their job, partly because I had different skills and different preferences for working styles, but also because it was breathtakingly difficult – physically, mentally and emotionally. I hope I have conveyed some of this difficulty in this book. On behalf of the teachers and the school (and other teachers and other schools) I feel angry at the lack of widespread appreciation and understanding of what they do, the special but shadowed status of their craft (Lortie, 1975, p. 10).

Some readers may wonder whether my attachment to the school impedes my 'objectivity'. Here, of course, one answer is that in ethnographic research, subjectivity is integral. The researcher's main 'instrument' is himself or herself. There is no way that my observations, and my account, can be unfiltered through my respect for the school and the teachers. However, that does not mean that I always romanticized what they did, or suppressed the less heroic moments. It is important to realize that this kind of study is not meant to be an evaluation of a school. Some comments will inevitably carry a note of evaluation, but it is not the purpose of the study. I wanted to dig out the underlying themes that make sense of what goes on among teachers in the schools, not to give gold stars or letter Fs.

FINISHING THE STUDY

Given my rather hesitant start to the project, I rather slid into doing the research and did not enjoy the funding or team support that many other research projects have. The positive consequence of being a solo researcher without funding was that I was not responsible to government or a funding body and could follow my own judgement as to how the research should develop (subject to the wishes of the schools). On the negative side, I had no computer, no secretary to transcribe my interviews, no released time. I did qualify for a small amount of money from a Bristol School of Education research fund, which allowed me to pay for someone to teach one of my summer term courses and to buy a transcribing machine, for which I was very grateful and which enabled me to transcribe parts of the Hillview interviews.

Once in Canada, I also received some money through a small-scale grant from the Ontario Institute for Studies in Education (now Ontario Institute for Studies in Education of the University of Toronto) which paid for typing of some of the Rosemont transcripts, and later on the services of an OISE/UT graduate student assistant, Lisa Richards, who transcribed some of the other tapes and also helped with library work. Another graduate assistant, Amy Sullivan, helped me figure out how to merge chapters together into a single file and solve other small technical problems. It is likely that the lack of substantial funding extended the writing of this volume. It was also held up by conflicting priorities, including beginning other research in Canada and teaching new courses, and by my worries that it would be seen as out-of-date because it was not primarily about consequences of the 1988 Education Reform Act, which appeared to be fast becoming the core of British educational research. Eventually I decided that it was not necessarily a virtue to focus narrowly on the impact of recent reforms, and that I would try for an account of primary school teachers' work and cultures that would transcend the particular preoccupations of the day.

REFLECTIONS: DOING THINGS DIFFERENTLY?

Given the extended time between beginning the study and completing this book, it was bound to be the case that time and place – briefly discussed in Chapter 12 – brought certain changes in my theoretical framework and literature base, and to some extent the focus of interest, although there was a lot of stability here too. As outlined in Chapter 2, I began with a framework drawn from symbolic interactionism. I was interested in teacher culture. I saw the teacher workplace culture in the school as a joint product of understandings and interpretations, one that is never entirely stable or entirely unstable, but based on negotiations among the participants. There is always a context to reckon with. So, for example, when the government changes the curriculum (as it did, and continues to do), the way in which the change is understood and implemented will be somewhat different in every school because it goes through a process of collective interpretation and mediation. I also had a notion that the picture of teacher isolation and individualism painted in the literature, especially from the USA, might not so inevitably be the case in British primary schools, and my study bore this suspicion out, as the culture was collaborative and collegial.

I started out with a hunch that teaching should be understood as work, one quickly validated when I spent time in the school. However much teachers cared for the children, or loved teaching, what they did could not be understood as natural nurturing or an extension of motherhood. It was hard work, too. Yet there is more than a little irony in my argument that teachers should be seen as workers. What I had in mind was work as opposed to non-work; or hard work as opposed to easy, natural actions. When I began to argue that teaching was work, I was influenced by writers such as Michael Apple (1986, 1988) who saw it as subject to some of the same processes such as deskilling and intensification that afflicted other occupations. I did not see teachers as workers in the industrial sense, though analogies were possible. The irony lies in the fact that while I might have seen it as necessary to convince scholars and the reading public that teachers were workers, governments have been all too ready to see teaching as work and teachers as workers. They have passed legislation to control, regulate and inspect teachers with little regard, except at rhetorical level, for teacher claims to professionalism.

When I began the research I was feeling somewhat jaded about gender as a topic and convinced my institution would never reward that kind of research (see Acker, 1994). But given that much of my previous writing and research was on gender and education, perhaps it was bound to surface as a major theme. When I looked at career patterns and at caring relationships among the staff or the way in which Liz Clarke or Debbie Stevens carried out their management roles, I could see gender at work. At the same time, I wanted to be careful not to essentialize 'the woman teacher' or 'woman head teacher' either. At several points I have warned against too simple an equation of femininity with caring or devotion to duty.

A poststructuralist feminist approach might suggest that perhaps I did not pay enough attention to differences among the women (teachers) while I was doing the study. The differences among Hillview women that emerged most clearly were related to whether or not they were parents and to their generation. The two women without children were both actively seeking promotions. The women with children were juggling, or had juggled, extremely complicated commitments in that respect. The older women teachers usually had interrupted their careers for childrearing and tended not to be overtly ambitious. The younger women took minimal time out of the labour market, coming back after maternity leaves and using various creative methods for child care. Social mores had changed, but so had the teacher labour market; there were no guarantees of getting back in once one left.

The Hillview teacher who was black and male was obviously 'different' from the others in those respects, and these characteristics mattered in terms of his career chances (very good, at least in urban schools) and his commitments to be a role model for black children. Otherwise he was in many ways like the other teachers in his generation. He also had young children and talked about them in the staffroom. I have worried about whether even to mention his race, as it could make the school more easily identifiable. Also I resisted thinking of him as a 'black male' when after a long association I simply thought of him as 'Dennis'. But how could I leave it out, equally? Troyna (1994) has argued that the dominant deracialized discourse in the literature has led to studies of teachers either focusing specifically on ethnic minority teachers, or ignoring race and thereby naturalizing whiteness, leaving readers to assume whiteness is the natural state for teachers. Advantages teachers might gain from whiteness are not problematized (see also Fine, Weis, Powell and Wong, 1997). The logic is that instead of singling out Dennis as 'black', I could have looked into the nuances of what 'being white' meant for the other teachers. During the research, I paid relatively little attention to class and ethnicity among the (white) women teachers. White women seemed more ethnically homogenous in England than they do in multicultural Toronto. Two of the women were from Wales, which had some effects, e.g. on their accents and when the school noted St David's Day. The others were from various regions in England. Regional origin makes subtle differences, but they did not seem to intrude in any obvious way.

Similarly, there were some variations I could point to in class origins, although they had been smoothed out, in a sense, by all of the teachers having gravitated towards a teaching career, whether that meant upward, downward, or no mobility. I was intrigued by the way in which the economic positions of the women differed, however, despite their all doing a similar job within a fairly restricted salary range. The difference related to husbands' occupations. The teacher married to an electrical fitter simply had a different lifestyle than the one married to a lawyer. There was a kind of school effect in who was drawn to each setting. Judging from their dress, speech and where they lived, teachers at upper-middle-class Rosemont seemed more economically advantaged than those at Hillview. I think it would have been possible to probe more directly for class and ethnic origins but I did not do so. No teacher in either school was known as gay or lesbian although there may have been some who were; all the literature I have read suggests teachers find it important to hide this facet of identity. There was no easy way I could have asked about it, either.

So, with hindsight, I might have done a few things differently, to make more use of the developing theoretical frameworks I encountered in Canada. Yet in my experience of ethnography, the method itself has a magnetism, drawing us into its magic even when our theories simultaneously question how we can possibly represent the thoughts, lives, worlds of others. Seen in that sense, my title becomes ironic: the *realities* of teachers' work are just what we cannot fathom because of the elusiveness of 'the real' (Britzman, 1995). I doubt if the teachers would object. Perhaps they would like to add a word: 'the *harsh* realities of teachers' work'. Semantic squabbles and poststructuralist postures will not help us to convince the public of the daily struggle with '*realities*' involved for teachers, nor the humour, solidarity and optimism with which they look on the bright side and comment with a rueful smile: '*Never a dull moment!*'

NOTES

1. Lareau (1989) describes similar difficulties in her study of American elementary schools.
2. While the book was in press, Liz Clarke was able to read the manuscript in full. She wrote that she was glad to have this record of what she was trying to do at Hillview and of the reality of being a primary school teacher in the closing decades of the twentieth century.

References

Abbott, D. (1996) Lessons from lessons: Constraints on teaching and learning. In P. Croll (ed.), *Teachers, Pupils and Primary Schooling: Continuity and Change* (pp. 102–18). London: Cassell.

Acker, S. (1983) Women and teaching: A semi-detached sociology of a semi-profession. In S. Walker and L. Barton (eds), *Gender, Class and Education* (pp. 123–9). Lewes: Falmer Press.

Acker, S. (1987) Primary school teaching as an occupation. In S. Delamont (ed.), *The Primary School Teacher* (pp. 83–99). Lewes: Falmer Press.

Acker, S. (1988) Teachers, gender and resistance. *British Journal of Sociology of Education*, 9(3), 307–22.

Acker, S. (ed.) (1989a) *Teachers, Gender and Careers*. Lewes: Falmer Press.

Acker, S. (1989b) Rethinking teachers' careers. In S. Acker (ed.), *Teachers, Gender and Careers* (pp. 7–20). Lewes: Falmer Press.

Acker, S. (1990a) Managing the drama: The head teacher's work in an urban primary school. *Sociological Review*, 38(2), 247–71.

Acker, S. (1990b) Teachers' culture in an English primary school: Continuity and change. *British Journal of Sociology of Education*, 11(3), 257–73.

Acker, S. (1991) Teacher relationships and educational reform in England and Wales. *The Curriculum Journal*, 2(3), 301–16.

Acker, S. (1992) Creating careers: Women teachers at work. *Curriculum Inquiry*, 22(2), 141–63.

Acker, S. (1994) *Gendered Education: Sociological Reflections on Women, Teaching and Feminism*. Buckingham: Open University Press.

Acker, S. (1995a) Carry on caring: The work of women teachers. *British Journal of Sociology of Education*, 16(1), 21–36.

Acker, S. (1995b) Unkind cuts: Reflections on the UK university experience. *Ontario Journal of Higher Education*, 55–74.

Acker, S. (1995/96) Gender and teachers' work. In M. Apple (ed.), *Review of Research in Education* 21 (pp. 99–162). Washington, DC: American Educational Research Association.

Acker, S. (1997) Primary school teachers' work: The response to educational reform. In G. Helsby and G. McCulloch (eds), *Teachers and the National Curriculum* (pp. 34–51). London: Cassell.

Acker, S. and Feuerverger, G. (1996) Doing good and feeling bad: The work of women university teachers. *Cambridge Journal of Education*, 26, 401–22.

Alexander, R.J. (1984) *Primary Teaching*. London: Holt, Rinehart and Winston.

Alexander, R.J. (1995) *Versions of Primary Education*. London: Routledge.

Alexander, R.J. (1997) *Policy and Practice in Primary Education*. Second edition. London: Routledge.

Alexander, R.J., Rose, J. and Woodhead, C. (1992) *Curriculum Organization and Classroom Practice in Primary Schools: A Discussion Paper*. London: Department of Education and Science.

Apple, M. (1986) *Teachers and Texts: A Political Economy of Class and Gender Relations in Education*. New York: Routledge.

Apple, M. (1988) Work, class and teaching. In J. Ozga (ed.), *Schoolwork* (pp. 99–115). Milton Keynes: Open University Press.

Apple, M. (1993) *Official Knowledge*. NY: Routledge.

Atkinson, P. (1983) The reproduction of the professional community. In R. Dingwall and P. Lewis (eds), *The Sociology of the Professions: Lawyers, Doctors and Others* (pp. 224–41). London: Macmillan.

Ball, S.J. (1987) *The Micro-politics of the School*. London: Methuen.

Ball, S.J. (1990) *Politics and Policy Making in Education*. London: Routledge.

Ball, S.J. (1992, April) *Changing Management and the Management of Change: Educational Reform and School Processes, an English Perspective*. Paper presented at the Annual Meeting of the American Educational Research Association, San Francisco, CA.

Ball, S.J. and Goodson, I. (eds) (1985) *Teachers' Lives and Careers*. London: Falmer Press.

Ball, S.J., Bowe, R. and Gewirtz, S. (1995) Circuits of schooling: a sociological exploration of parental choice of school in social class contexts. *Sociological Review*, 43(1), 52–78.

Ball, S.J., Hull, R., Skelton, M. and Tudor, R. (1984) The tyranny of 'the devil's mill': Time and task at school. In S. Delamont (ed.), *Readings on Interaction in the Classroom* (pp. 41–57). London: Methuen.

Bangar, S. and McDermott, J. (1989) Black women speak. In H. DeLyon and F. Migniuolo (eds), *Women Teachers: Issues and Experiences* (pp. 135–53). Milton Keynes: Open University Press.

Bascia, N. (1994) *Unions in Teachers' Professional Lives*. New York: Teachers College Press.

Belenky, M.F., Clinchy, B.M., Goldberger, N.R. and Tarule, J.M. (1986) *Women's Ways of Knowing*. New York: Basic Books.

Bennett, S.N., Wragg, E., Carre, C.G. and Carter, D.S.G. (1992) A longitudinal study of primary teachers' perceived competence in, and concerns about, national curriculum implementation. *Research Papers in Education*, 7(1), 53–78.

Berlak, A. and Berlak, H. (1981) *Dilemmas of Schooling: Teaching and Social Change*. London: Methuen.

Best, R. (1983) *We've All Got Scars: What Boys and Girls Learn in Elementary School*. Bloomington: Indiana University Press.

Beynon, J. and Atkinson, P. (1984) Pupils as data-gatherers: Mucking and sussing. In S. Delamont (ed.), *Readings on Interaction in the Classroom* (pp. 255–72). London: Methuen.

Biklen, S.K. (1995) *School Work*. Albany, NY: State University of New York Press.

Blackmore, J. (1989) Educational leadership: A feminist critique and reconstruction. In J. Smyth (ed.), *Critical Perspectives on Educational Leadership* (pp. 93–130). London: Falmer Press.

Bowe, R. and Ball, S., with A. Gold (1992) *Reforming Education and Changing Schools*. London: Routledge.

Brehony, K. (1990) Neither rhyme nor reason: Primary schooling and the national curriculum. In M. Flude and M. Hammer (eds), *The Education Reform Act, 1988: Its Origins and Implications* (pp. 107–31). London: Falmer Press.

Brehony, K. (1992, April). *Just 'a Body of Philanthropic Ladies': The Froebel Movement and English Elementary Schooling*. Paper presented at the Annual Meeting of the American Educational Research Association, San Francisco, CA.

Britzman, D. (1995) 'The question of belief': Writing poststructural ethnography. *Qualitative Studies in Education*, 8(3), 229–38.

Broadfoot, P. and Abbott, D., with Croll, P., Osborn, M. and Pollard, A. (1991) *Look Back in Anger? Findings from the PACE Project Concerning Primary Teachers' Experiences of SATs*. Unpublished paper, School of Education, University of Bristol, Bristol.

Broadfoot, P. and Osborn, M. (1988) What professional responsibility means to teachers: National contexts and classroom constraints. *British Journal of Sociology of Education*, 9(3), 265–87.

Broadfoot, P. and Osborn, M. (1993) *Perceptions of Teaching: Primary School Teachers in England and France*. London: Cassell.

Brown, P. (1990) The third wave: Education and the ideology of parentocracy. *British Journal of Sociology of Education*, 11(1), 65–85.

Bryk, A., Lee, V. and Holland, P. (1993) *Catholic Schools and the Common Good*. Cambridge, MA: Harvard University Press.

Burgess, R. (1983) *Experiencing Comprehensive Education*. London: Methuen.

Butt, R., Raymond, D., McCue, G. and Yamagishi, L. (1992) Collaborative autobiography and the teacher's voice. In I. Goodson (ed.), *Studying Teachers' Lives* (pp. 51–98). London: Routledge.

Campbell, R.J. (1985) *Developing the Primary School Curriculum*. London: Holt, Rinehart and Winston.

Campbell, R.J. (1988) *The Routledge Compendium of Primary Education*. London: Routledge.

Campbell, R.J. and Neill, S.R.StJ. (1994) *Primary Teachers at Work*. London: Routledge.

Casanova, U. (1996) Parent involvement: A call for prudence. *Educational Researcher*, 25(8), 30–6.

Casey, K. (1993) *I Answer with My Life*. New York: Routledge.

Chard, S. (1994) The national curriculum in England and Wales. In P. Grimmett and J. Neufeld (eds), *Teacher Development and the Struggle for Authenticity* (pp. 101–20). New York: Teachers College Press.

Chessum, L. (1989) *The Part-time Nobody: Part-time Women Teachers in West Yorkshire*. Bradford: WYCROW, University of Bradford.

Chubb, J. and Moe, T. (1990) *Politics, Markets and America's Schools*. Washington, DC: The Brookings Institution.

Clandinin, D.J. (1986) *Classroom Practice: Teacher Images in Action*. London: Falmer Press.

Clandinin, D.J. and Connelly, F.M. (1986) Rhythms in teaching: The narrative study of teachers' personal practical knowledge of classrooms. *Teaching and Teacher Education*, 2, 377–87.

Clandinin, D.J. and Connelly, F.M., with C. Craig, A. Davies, M.F. He, P. Hogan, J. Huber, K. Whelan and R. Young (1995) *Teachers' Professional Knowledge Landscapes*. New York: Teachers College Press.

Clarke, K. (1991) Primary education: A statement by the Secretary of State for Education and Science, 3 December 1991, London, Department of Education and Science.

Clerkin, C. (1985) What do primary heads actually do all day? *School Organization*, 5(4), 287–300.

Cogger, D. (1985) *Women Teachers on Low Scales*. Unpublished M.Ed. thesis, University of Wales, Cardiff.

Cole, A. (1991) Relationships in the workplace: Doing what comes naturally? *Teaching and Teacher Education*, 7(5/6), 415–26.

Connell, R.W. (1985) *Teachers' Work*. Sydney: George Allen and Unwin.

Connelly, F.M. and Clandinin, D.J. (1990) Stories of experience and narrative inquiry. *Educational Researcher*, 19(5), 2–14.

Connelly, F.M. and Clandinin, D.J. (1993) Cycles, rhythms, and the meaning of school time. In L. Anderson and H. Walberg (eds), *Timepiece: Extending and Enhancing Learning Time* (pp. 9–14). Reston, VA: National Association of Secondary School Principals.

Cortazzi, M. (1991) *Primary Teaching How It Is: A Narrative Account*. London: David Fulton.

Cortazzi, M. (1993) *Narrative Analysis*. London: Falmer Press.

Coulter, R. (1995) Struggling with sexism: Experiences of feminist first-year teachers. *Gender and Education*, 7(1), 33–50.

Croll, P. (ed) (1996) *Teachers, Pupils and Primary Schooling: Continuity and Change*. London: Cassell.

Cunnison, S. (1989) Gender joking in the staffroom. In S. Acker (ed.), *Teachers, Gender and Careers* (pp. 151–67). Lewes: Falmer Press.

Dale, R. (1994) Marketing the education market and the polarisation of schooling. In D. Kallos and S. Lindblad (eds), *New Policy Contexts for Education: Sweden and the United Kingdom*. Umea: Umea University.

Damianos, M. (1998) *Substitute Teachers in Elementary Schools and Their Professional Discourses*. Unpublished M.A. thesis, Ontario Institute for Studies in Education of the University of Toronto, Toronto.

David, M.E. (1980) *The State, the Family and Education*. London: Routledge and Kegan Paul.

David, M.E. (1984) Women, family and education. In S. Acker *et al.* (eds), *World Yearbook of Education 1984: Women and Education* (pp. 191–201). London: Kogan Page.

David, M.E. (1985) Motherhood and social policy – a matter of education? *Critical Social Policy*, 12, 28–44.

David, M.E. (1993) *Parents, Gender and Education Reform*. London: Polity Press.

David, M.E. (1996) Choice and markets in education: A critique of some key texts. *Discourse*, 17(3), 417–21.

David, M.E., Davies, J., Edwards, R., Reay, D. and Standing, K. (1997) Choice within constraints: Mothers and schooling. *Gender and Education*, 9(4), 397–410.

David, M.E., Edwards, R., Hughes, M. and Ribbens, J. (1993) *Mothers and Education: Inside Out? Exploring Family-education Policy and Practice*. London: Macmillan.

David, M.E., West, A. and Ribbens, J. (1994) *Mother's Intuition? Choosing Secondary Schools*. London: Falmer Press.

Davies, B. (1982) *Life in the Classroom and Playground: The Accounts of Primary School Children*. London: Routledge and Kegan Paul.

Davies, L. (1984) *Pupil Power: Deviance and Gender in School*. Lewes: Falmer Press.

Davies, L. (1990) *Equity and Efficiency? School Management in an International Context*. Lewes: Falmer Press.

Davis, J. (1992) Cultures and subcultures in secondary schools. In A. Hargreaves, J. Davis, M. Fullan, R. Wignall, M. Stager and R. Macmillan, *Secondary School Work Cultures and Educational Change* (pp. 147–66). Toronto: Ontario Institute for Studies in Education.

Dearing, R. (1993). *The National Curriculum and Its Assessment, Final Report*. London: School Curriculum and Assessment Authority.

Deem, R., Brehony, K. and Heath, S. (1995) *Active Citizenship and the Governing of Schools*. Buckingham: Open University Press.

Dehli, K. (1996). Travelling tales: Education reform and parental 'choice' in postmodern times. *Journal of Education Policy*, 11(1), 75–88.

Dehli, K. (1997) Shopping for schools: The future of education in Ontario? Unpublished paper, Ontario Institute for Studies in Education of the University of Toronto.

Dehli, K., with I. Juanario (1994) *Parent Activism and School Reform in Toronto*. Research Report prepared for the Ontario Ministry of Education and Training. Toronto: Ontario Institute for Studies in Education, University of Toronto.

Delamont, S. (1983) *Interaction in the Classroom*. Second edition. London: Methuen.

Delamont, S. (ed.) (1984) *Readings on Interaction in the Classroom*. London: Methuen.

Delamont, S. (ed.) (1987) *The Primary School Teacher*. Lewes: Falmer Press.

Delpit, L. (1993) The silenced dialogue: power and pedagogy in educating other people's children. In L. Weis and M. Fine (eds), *Beyond Silenced Voices: Class, Race and Gender in United States Schools* (pp. 119–39). Albany, NY: State University of New York Press.

Denscombe, M. (1985) *Classroom Control: A Sociological Perspective*. London: George Allen and Unwin.

Densmore, K. (1987) Professionalism, proletarianization and teacher work. In T.

Popkewitz (ed.), *Critical Studies in Teacher Education* (pp. 130–60). London: Falmer Press.

Department for Education and Employment (1996) *Statistics of Education: Teachers – England and Wales*. London: HMSO.

Department for Education and Employment (1998) *Teachers: Meeting the Challenge of Change* (Government Green Paper). London: HMSO.

Department of Education and Science (1992) *Statistics of Education: Teachers in Service, England and Wales, 1989 and 1990*. London: DES.

Dove, L. (1986) *Teachers and Teacher Education in Developing Countries*. London: Croom Helm.

Doyle, W. and Ponder, G.A. (1977) The practicality ethic in teacher decision-making. *Interchange*, 8, 1–12.

Dreeben, R. (1970) *The Nature of Teaching*. Glenview, IL: Scott Foresman.

Durkheim, E. (1964) *The Division of Labour in Society*. (G. Simpson, trans.) New York: The Free Press of Glencoe. (Originally published in 1893; published in English by Macmillan, 1933).

Ellis, C. (1991) Emotional sociology. In N. Denzin (ed.), *Studies in Symbolic Interaction*, 12 (pp. 123–45). Greenwich, CT: JAI Press.

Epstein, J. (1995, May) School/family/community partnerships. *Phi Delta Kappan*, pp. 701–12.

Evans, T. (1988) *A Gender Agenda*. Sydney: Allen and Unwin.

Evetts, J. (1989) The internal labour market for primary teachers. In S. Acker (ed.), *Teachers, Gender and Careers* (pp. 187–202). Lewes: Falmer Press.

Evetts, J. (1990) *Women in Primary Teaching: Career Contexts and Strategies*. London: Unwin Hyman.

Feiman-Nemser, S. and Floden, R. (1986) The cultures of teaching. In M. Wittrock (ed.), *Third Handbook of Research on Teaching* (pp. 505–26). London: Macmillan.

Ferguson, K. (1984) *The Feminist Case against Bureaucracy*. Philadelphia: Temple University Press.

Feuerverger, G. (1997) On the edges of the map: A study of heritage language teachers in Toronto. *Teaching and Teacher Education*, 13(1), 39–53.

Fine, M. (1991) *Framing Dropouts: Notes on the Politics of an Urban High School*. Albany, NY: State University of New York Press.

Fine, M. (1993) [Ap]parent involvement: Reflections on parents, power and urban public schools. *Teachers College Record*, 94(4), 682–710.

Fine, M., Weis, L., Powell, L. and Wong, L.M. (eds) (1997) *Off White: Readings on Race, Power, and Society*. New York: Routledge.

Foster, M. (1993a) Othermothers: Exploring the educational philosophy of Black American women teachers. In M. Arnot and K. Weiler (eds), *Feminism and Social Justice in Education: International Perspectives* (pp. 101–23). New York: Falmer Press.

Foster, M. (1993b) Resisting racism: Personal testimonies of African-American teachers. In L. Weis and M. Fine (eds), *Beyond Silenced Voices: Class, Race, and Gender in United States Schools* (pp. 273–88). Albany, NY: State University of New York Press.

Fullan, M., with S. Stiegelbauer (1991) *The New Meaning of Educational Change.* New York: Teachers College Press.

Fullan, M. and Hargreaves, A. (1991) *What's Worth Fighting for in Your School?* Toronto: Ontario Public Schools Teachers Federation.

Fuller, B. and Elmore, R., with G. Orfield (eds) (1996) *Who Chooses? Who Loses? Culture, Institutions, and the Unequal Effects of School Choice.* New York: Teachers College Press.

Galloway, S. and Morrison, M. (eds) (1994) *The Supply Story: Professional Substitutes in Education.* London: Falmer Press.

Galton, M. (1989) *Teaching in the Primary School.* London: David Fulton.

Galton, M. (1995) *Crisis in the Primary Classroom.* London: David Fulton.

Galton, M., Simon, B. and Croll, P. (1980) *Inside the Primary Classroom.* London: Routledge.

Gewirtz, S., Ball, S.J. and Bowe, R. (1995) *Markets, Choice and Equity in Education.* Buckingham: Open University Press.

Gilligan, C. (1982) *In a Different Voice.* Cambridge, MA: Harvard University Press.

Gipps, C. (1994) What we know about effective primary teaching. In J. Bourne (ed.), *Thinking Through Primary Practice* (pp. 22–39). London: Routledge.

Goldring, E. and Chen, M. (1993) The feminization of the principalship in Israel: The trade-off between political power and cooperative leadership. In C. Marshall (ed.), *The New Politics of Race and Gender* (pp. 175–82). Washington, DC: Falmer Press.

Goodson, I. (1991) Sponsoring the teacher's voice: Teachers' lives and teacher development. *Cambridge Journal of Education*, 21(1), 35–45.

Gore, J. (1993) *The Struggle for Pedagogies.* New York: Routledge.

Grace, G. (1987) Teachers and the state in Britain: A changing relation. In M. Lawn and G. Grace (eds), *Teachers: The Culture and Politics of Work* (pp. 193–228). Lewes: Falmer Press.

Grace, G. (1995) *School Leadership: Beyond Education Management.* London: Falmer Press.

Grant, R. (1989) Women teachers' career pathways: Towards an alternative model of 'career'. In S. Acker (ed.), *Teachers, Gender and Careers* (pp. 35–50). Lewes: Falmer Press.

Griffin, P. (1991) Identity management strategies among lesbian and gay educators. *Qualitative Studies in Education*, 4(3), 189–202.

Griffith, A. and Smith, D.E. (1991) Constructing cultural knowledge: Mothering as discourse. In J. Gaskell and A. McLaren (eds), *Women and Education* (pp. 81–97). Calgary: Detselig.

Grossman, P. and Stodolsky, S. (1994) Considerations of content and the circumstances of secondary school teaching. In L. Darling-Hammond (ed.), *Review of Research in Education* 20 (pp. 179–221). Washington, DC: American Educational Research Association.

Grumet, M. (1988) *Bitter Milk: Women and Teaching.* Amherst: University of Massachusetts Press.

Hall, V. (1996) *Dancing on the Ceiling: A Study of Women Managers in Education.* London: Paul Chapman.

Hargreaves, A. (1984) Contrastive rhetoric and extremist talk. In A. Hargreaves and P. Woods (eds), *Classrooms and Staffrooms: The Sociology of Teachers and Teaching* (pp. 215–31). Milton Keynes: Open University Press.

Hargreaves, A. (1994) *Changing Teachers, Changing Times: Teachers' Work and Culture in the Postmodern Age*. London: Cassell.

Hargreaves, A. (1996) Revisiting voice. *Educational Researcher*, 25 (1), 30–6.

Hargreaves, A. and Macmillan, R. (1995) The balkanization of secondary school teaching. In L.S. Siskin and J.W. Little (eds), *The Subjects in Question* (pp. 141–71). New York: Teachers College Press.

Hargreaves, A. and Tucker, E. (1991) Teaching and guilt: Exploring the feelings of teaching. *Teaching and Teacher Education*, 7(5/6), 491–505.

Hargreaves, A. and Woods, P. (eds) (1984) *Classrooms and Staffrooms*. Milton Keynes: Open University Press.

Hargreaves, D. (1972) *Interpersonal Relations and Education*. London: Routledge and Kegan Paul.

Hargreaves, D. (1980) The occupational culture of teachers. In P. Woods (ed.), *Teacher Strategies: Explorations in the Sociology of the School* (pp. 125–48). London: Croom Helm.

Harvey, C.W. (1986) How primary heads spend their time. *Educational Management and Administration*, 14, 60–8.

Hayes, D. (1994) A primary headteacher in search of a collaborative climate. In G. Southworth (ed.), *Readings in Primary School Development* (pp. 69–88). London: Falmer Press.

Heath, S.B. (1983) *Ways with Words: Language, Life, and Work in Communities and Classrooms*. Cambridge: Cambridge University Press.

Hellawell, D. (1992) Structural changes in education in England. *International Journal of Educational Reform*, 1 (4), 356–65.

Helsby, G. (1999) *Changing Teachers' Work: The 'Reform' of Secondary Education*. Buckingham: Open University Press.

Helsby, G. and McCulloch, G. (eds) (1997) *Teachers and the National Curriculum*. London: Cassell.

Henry, M. (1996) *Parent–School Collaboration*. Albany, NY: State University of New York Press.

Hill, T. (1989) *Managing the Primary School*. London: David Fulton.

Hilsum, S. and Cane, B. (1971) *The Teacher's Day*. Slough: NFER.

Hirschman, A.O. (1970) *Exit, Voice and Loyalty*. Cambridge, MA: Harvard University Press.

Hofkins, D. (1992) Barking up the wrong dogma. *Times Educational Supplement*, 31 January, p. 11.

Holtom, V. (1988) *Primary School Headteachers' Conceptions of Their Professional Responsibility in England and France*. Unpublished M.Phil. thesis, University of Bristol School of Education.

Hoyle, E. (1974) Professionality, professionalism and control in teaching. *London Educational Review*, 3, 13–19.

Hughes, M. and Kennedy, M. (1985). *New Futures: Changing Women's Education*. London: Routledge and Kegan Paul.

Intriligator, B.A. (1983) Leadership theory revisited. *Journal of Educational Equity and Leadership*, 3(1), 5–17.

Jackson, P. (1968) *Life in Classrooms.* New York: Holt, Rinehart and Winston.

Johnson, D. (1990) *Parental Choice in Education.* London: Unwin Hyman.

Johnson, S.M. (1990) *Teachers at Work: Achieving Success in Our Schools.* New York: Basic Books.

Jones, G. and Hayes, D. (1991) Primary headteachers and ERA two years on: The pace of change and its impact upon schools. *School Organisation,* 11(2), 211–21.

Kainan, A. (1994) *The Staffroom: Observing the Professional Culture of Teachers.* Aldershot: Avebury.

Kandiyoti, D. (1988) Bargaining with patriarchy. *Gender and Society,* 2(3), 274–90.

Kidder, T. (1989) *Among Schoolchildren.* Boston: Houghton Mifflin.

King, R. (1978) *All Things Bright and Beautiful?* Chichester: John Wiley.

King, R. (1983) *The Sociology of School Organization.* London: Methuen.

King, R. (1984) The man in the Wendy house: Researching infants' schools. In R.G. Burgess (ed.), *The Research Process in Educational Settings: Ten Case Studies* (pp. 117–38). Lewes: Falmer Press.

Lacey, C. (1977) *The Socialization of Teachers.* London: Methuen.

Lampert, M. (1985) How do teachers manage to teach? *Harvard Educational Review,* 55, 178–94.

Langford, R. (1997) Child development knowledge and the socialization of early childhood education students. Unpublished paper, Department of Sociology and Equity Studies in Education, Ontario Institute for Studies in Education of the University of Toronto.

Lanier, J. and Little, J.W. (1986) Research on teacher education. In M. Wittrock (ed.), *Handbook of Research on Teaching* (pp. 527–69). New York: Macmillan.

Lareau, A. (1989) *Home Advantage: Social Class and Parental Intervention in Elementary Education.* Philadelphia: Falmer Press.

Lareau, A. (1992) Gender differences in parent involvement in schooling. In J. Wrigley (ed.), *Education and Gender Equality* (pp. 207–24). Washington, DC: Falmer Press.

Lareau, A. and Shultz, J. (1996) *Journeys Through Ethnography: Realistic Accounts of Fieldwork.* Boulder: Westview Press.

Lawn, M. (1996) *Modern Times? Work, Professionalism and Citizenship in Teaching.* London: Falmer Press.

Leggatt, T. (1970) Teaching as a profession. In J. Jackson (ed.), *Professions and Professionalization* (pp. 153–77). Cambridge: Cambridge University Press.

Lepkowska, D. (1998) Shake-up of funding back in spotlight. *Times Educational Supplement,* 27 February, p. 9.

Lieberman, A. (ed.) (1990) *Schools as Collaborative Cultures: Creating the Future Now.* New York: Falmer Press.

Lightfoot, S.L. (1978) *Worlds Apart: Relationships Between Families and Schools.* New York: Basic Books.

Lightfoot, S.L. (1983a) *The Good High School: Portraits of Character and Culture.* New York: Basic Books.

Lightfoot, S.L. (1983b) The lives of teachers. In L. Shulman and G. Sykes (eds), *Handbook of Teaching and Policy* (pp. 241–60). New York: Longman.

Little, J.W. (1987) Teachers as colleagues. In V. Richardson-Koehler (ed.), *Educators' Handbook: A Research Perspective* (pp. 491–518). London: Longman.

Little, J.W. (1990) The persistence of privacy. *Teachers College Record*, 91, 509–36.

Little, J.W. (1992) Opening the black box of professional community. In A. Lieberman (ed.), *The Changing Contexts of Teaching: Ninety-first Yearbook of the National Society for the Study of Education* (pp. 157–78). Chicago: NSSE and University of Chicago Press.

Little, J.W. and McLaughlin, M. (eds) (1993) *Teachers' Work: Individuals, Colleagues, and Contexts*. New York: Teachers College Press.

Lortie, D.C. (1973) Observations on teaching as work. In R.M.W. Travers (ed.), *Second Handbook of Research on Teaching* (pp. 474–97). Chicago: Rand-McNally.

Lortie, D.C. (1975) *School-teacher: A Sociological Study*. Chicago: University of Chicago Press.

Lubeck, S. (1985) *Sandbox Society*. Lewes: Falmer Press.

Lyons, N. (1983) Two perspectives: On self, relationships, and morality. *Harvard Educational Review*, 53, 125–45.

Mac an Ghaill, M. (1992) Teachers' work: Curriculum restructuring, culture, power and comprehensive schooling. *British Journal of Sociology of Education*, 13(2), 177–99.

McCall, A. (1995) The bureaucratic restraints to caring in schools. In D. Dunlap and P.A. Schmuck (eds), *Women Leading in Education* (pp. 180–96). Albany, NY: SUNY Press.

McCallum, B., McAlister, S., Brown, M. and Gipps, C. (1993) Teacher assessment at Key Stage 1. *Research Papers in Education*, 8 (3), 305–27.

McLellan, D. (1980) *The Thought of Karl Marx*. Second edition. London: Macmillan.

McPherson, G. (1972) *Small Town Teacher*. Cambridge, MA: Harvard University Press.

Markowitz, R. (1993) *My Daughter the Teacher: Jewish Teachers in the New York City Schools*. New Brunswick, NJ: Rutgers University Press.

Marshall, C. and Mitchell, B. (1989) *Women's Careers as a Critique of the Administrative Culture*. Paper presented at the Annual Meeting of the American Educational Research Association, San Francisco.

Menter, I., Muschamp, Y., Nicholls, P., Ozga, J. and Pollard, A. (1997) *Work and Identity in the Primary School: A Post-Fordist Analysis*. Buckingham: Open University Press.

Metz, M. (1989) Teachers' pride in craft, school subcultures, and societal pressures. In L. Weis, P. Altbach, G. Kelly, H. Petrie and S. Slaughter (eds), *Crisis in Teaching* (pp. 205–25). Albany, NY: State University of New York Press.

Middleton, S. (1989) Educating feminists: A life-history study. In S. Acker (ed.), *Teachers, Gender and Careers* (pp. 53–68). Lewes: Falmer Press.

Mortimore, P., Sammons, P., Stoll, L., Lewis, D. and Ecob, R. (1988) *School Matters: The Junior Years*. Wells: Open Books.

Munn, P. (ed.) (1993) *Parents and Schools: Customers, Managers or Partners?* London: Routledge.

Murnane, R.J., Singer, J.D., Willett, J.B., Kemple, J.J. and Olsen, R.J. (1991) *Who Will Teach? Policies That Matter*. Cambridge, MA: Harvard University Press.

Nelson, M. (1992) The intersection of home and work: Rural Vermont schoolteachers, 1915–1950. In R. Altenbaugh (ed.), *The Teacher's Voice* (pp. 26–39). London: Falmer Press.

Nias, J. (1987) One finger, one thumb: A case study of the deputy head's part in the leadership of a nursery/infant school. In G. Southworth (ed.), *Readings in Primary School Management* (pp. 30–53). London: Falmer Press.

Nias, J. (1989) *Primary Teachers Talking.* London: Routledge.

Nias, J., Southworth, G. and Yeomans, R. (1989) *Staff Relationships in the Primary School.* London: Cassell.

Noddings, N. (1984) *Caring: A Feminine Approach to Ethics and Moral Education.* Berkeley: University of California Press.

Noddings, N. (1992) *The Challenge to Care in Schools.* New York: Teachers College Press.

Office for Standards in Education (OFSTED) (1994) *Teacher Supply: The Work of Part-time and Returning Teachers.* London: HMSO.

Ogbu, J. (1974) *The Next Generation: An Ethnography of Education in an Urban Neighborhood.* New York: Academic Press.

Osborn, M. (1996a) Identity, career and change: A tale of two teachers. In P. Croll (ed.), *Teachers, Pupils and Primary Schooling* (pp. 53–68). London: Cassell.

Osborn, M. (1996b) Teachers mediating change: Key Stage 1 revisited. In P. Croll (ed.), *Teachers, Pupils and Primary Schooling* (pp. 35–52). London: Cassell.

Osborn, M. and Black, E. (1994) *Developing the National Curriculum at Key Stage 2: The Changing Nature of Teachers' Work.* Birmingham: National Association of Schoolmasters and Union of Women Teachers.

Osborn, M. and Black, E. (1996) Working together in primary schools: Changing relationships at key stage 2. In R. Chawla-Duggan and C. Pole (eds), *Reshaping Education in the 1990s: Perspectives on Primary Schooling* (pp. 50–64). London: Falmer Press.

Ozga, J. and Lawn, M. (1988) Schoolwork: Interpreting the labour process of teaching. *British Journal of Sociology of Education*, 9(3), 323–36.

Peshkin, A. (1984) Odd man out: The participant observer in an absolutist setting. *Sociology of Education*, 57 (4), 254–64.

Peshkin, A. (1986) *God's Choice: The Total World of a Fundamentalist Christian School.* New York: Teachers College Press.

Pietrasik, R. (1987) The teachers' action, 1984–1986. In M. Lawn and G. Grace (eds), *Teachers: The Culture and Politics of Work* (pp. 168–89). Lewes: Falmer Press.

Pollard, A. (1985) *The Social World of the Primary School.* London: Cassell.

Pollard, A. (1996) *The Social World of Children's Learning.* London: Cassell.

Pollard, A., Broadfoot, P., Croll, P., Osborn, M. and Abbott, D. (1994) *Changing English Primary Schools? The Impact of the Education Reform Act at Key Stage One.* London: Cassell.

Prentice, A. and Theobald, M. (1991) The historiography of women teachers: A retrospect. In A. Prentice and M. Theobald (eds), *Women Who Taught* (pp. 3–33). Toronto: University of Toronto Press.

Purvis, J.R. and Dennison, W.F. (1993) Primary school deputy headship – Has ERA and LMS changed the job? *Education 3–13*, 21(2), 15–21.

Reay, D. (1996) Contextualising choice: Social power and parental involvement. *British Educational Research Journal*, 22(5): 581–96.

Reforms and regrets (1998, January 16) *Times Educational Supplement*, p. 23.

Reynolds, C. (1990) Hegemony and hierarchy: Becoming a teacher in Toronto, 1930–1980. *Historical Studies in Education*, 2(1), 95–118.

Reynolds, C. (1995) Feminist frameworks for the study of administration and leadership in educational organizations. In C. Reynolds and B. Young (eds), *Women and Leadership in Canadian Education* (pp. 3–17). Calgary: Detselig.

Riddell, S. (1989) 'It's nothing to do with me': Teachers' views and gender divisions in the curriculum. In S. Acker (ed.), *Teachers, Gender and Careers* (pp. 123–38). Lewes: Falmer Press.

Rossman, G., Corbett, H. and Firestone, W. (1988) *Change and Effectiveness in Schools: A Cultural Perspective*. Albany, NY: State University of New York Press.

Rutter, M., Maughan, B., Mortimore, P. and Ouston, J. (1979) *Fifteen Thousand Hours: Secondary Schools and Their Effects on Children*. London: Open Books.

Sadker, M., Sadker, D. and Klein, S. (1991) The issue of gender in elementary and secondary education. In G. Grant (ed.), *Review of Research in Education*, 17 (pp. 269–334). Washington, DC: American Educational Research Association.

School Teachers' Review Body (1993) *Second Report*. London: HMSO.

Seddon, T. (1991). Teachers' work: A perspective on schooling. In R. Maclean and P. McKenzie (eds), *Australian Teachers' Careers* (pp. 45–67). Hawthorn, Victoria: Australian Council for Educational Research.

Shakeshaft, C. (1989) *Women in Educational Administration*. Newbury Park, CA: Sage.

Sikes, P., Measor, L. and Woods, P. (1985) *Teachers' Careers: Crises and Continuities*. Lewes: Falmer Press.

Siskin, L.S. (1991) Departments as different worlds: Subject subcultures in secondary schools. *Educational Administration Quarterly*, 27 (2), 134–60.

Siskin, L.S. (1994) *Realms of Knowledge: Academic Departments in Secondary Schools*. Philadelphia: Falmer Press.

Smith, D.E. (1987) *The Everyday World as Problematic: A Feminist Sociology*. Milton Keynes: Open University Press.

Smith, D.J. and Tomlinson, S. (1989) *The School Effect: A Study of Multi-Racial Comprehensives*. London: Policy Studies Institute.

Smith, L. and Geoffrey, W. (1968) *The Complexities of an Urban Classroom*. New York: Holt, Rinehart and Winston.

Smith, L. and Keith, P. (1971) *Anatomy of Educational Innovation: An Organizational Analysis of an Elementary School*. New York: Wiley and Sons.

Smulyan, L. (1996) Gender and school leadership: Using case studies to challenge the frameworks. In R. Chawla-Duggan and C. Pole (eds), *Reshaping Education in the 1990s* (pp. 169–91). London: Falmer Press.

Southworth, G. (1994a) Headteachers and deputy heads: Partners and cultural leaders. In G. Southworth (ed.), *Readings in Primary School Development* (pp. 29–47). London: Falmer Press.

Southworth, G. (1994b) Trading places: Job rotation in a primary school. In G.

Southworth (ed.), *Readings in Primary School Development* (pp. 48–66). London: Falmer Press.

Southworth, G. (1995) *Looking into Primary Headship: A Research Based Interpretation*. London: Falmer Press.

Spencer, D.A. (1986) *Contemporary Women Teachers: Balancing School and Home*. New York: Longman.

Squirrell, G. (1989a) In passing . . . teachers and sexual orientation. In S. Acker (ed.), *Teachers, Gender and Careers* (pp. 87–106). Lewes: Falmer Press.

Squirrell, G. (1989b) Teachers and issues of sexual orientation. *Gender and Education*, 1(1), 17–34.

Stacey, J. (1991) Can there be a feminist ethnography? In S. Gluck and D. Patai (eds), *Women's Words: The Feminist Practice of Oral History* (pp. 111–19). New York: Routledge.

Steedman, C. (1987) Prisonhouses. In M. Lawn and G. Grace (eds), *Teachers: The Culture and Politics of Work* (pp. 117–29). Lewes: Falmer Press.

Stillman, A. (1994) Half a century of parental choice in Britain? In M. Halstead (ed.), *Parental Choice in Education: Principles, Policy and Practice* (pp. 19–35). London: Kogan Page.

Stone, C. (1993) Questioning the new orthodoxies. *School Organisation*, 11(3), 187–98.

Sussmann, L. (1977) *Tales Out of School*. Philadelphia: Temple University Press.

Talbert, J. (1993) Constructing a schoolwide professional community: The negotiated order of a performing arts school. In J. Little and M. McLaughlin (eds), *Teachers' Work* (pp. 164–84). New York: Teachers College Press.

Tierney, W. and Rhoads, R. (1993) Postmodern and critical theory in higher education: Implications for research and practice. In J. Smart (ed.), *Higher Education: Handbook of Theory and Research*, 9 (pp. 308–43). New York: Agathon.

Tomlinson, S. (1984) *Home and School in Multicultural Britain*. London: Batsford.

Troen, V. and Boles, K. (1995) Leadership from the classroom: Women teachers as a key to school reform. In D. Dunlap and P. Schmuck (eds), *Women Leading in Education* (pp. 358–79). Albany, NY: State University of New York Press.

Troyna, B. (1994) The 'everyday world' of teachers? Deracialised discourses in the sociology of teachers and the teaching profession. *British Journal of Sociology of Education*, 15 (3), 325–39.

Valentine, P. and McIntosh, G. (1991) Food for thought: Realities of a woman-dominated organization. In J. Gaskell and A. McLaren (eds), *Women and Education* (pp. 61–79). Second edition. Calgary: Detselig.

Vincent, C. (1996) *Parents and Teachers: Power and Participation*. London: Falmer Press.

Vincent, C. and Tomlinson, S. (1997) Home-school relationships: 'The swarming of disciplinary mechanisms'? *British Educational Research Journal*, 23 (3): 361–77.

Walkerdine, V. (1981) Sex, power and pedagogy. *Screen Education*, 38, 14–23.

Walkerdine, V. (1986) Progressive pedagogy and political struggle. *Screen*, 27(5), 54–60.

Walkerdine, V. and Lucey, H (1989) *Democracy in the Kitchen*. London: Virago Press.

Wallace, M. and McMahon, A. (1994) *Planning for Change in Turbulent Times: The Case of Multiracial Primary Schools*. London: Cassell.

Waller, W. (1965) *The Sociology of Teaching*. New York: Wiley and Sons. (Original work published 1932.)

Waters, S. (1995) At the core: 'Oh, to be in England'. In J. Bell (ed.), *Teachers Talk about Teaching: Coping with Change in Turbulent Times* (pp. 110–22). Buckingham: Open University Press.

Webb, R. and Vulliamy, G. (1996) *Roles and Responsibilities in the Primary School*. Buckingham: Open University Press.

Weber, M. (1978) The nature of charismatic domination. In W. Runciman (ed.), E. Matthews (trans.), *Weber: Selections in Translation* (pp. 226–50). Cambridge: Cambridge University Press (Original work published 1922.)

Weber, S. and Mitchell, C. (1995) *'That's Funny, You Don't Look Like a Teacher': Interrogating Images and Identity in Popular Culture*. London: Falmer Press.

Weiler, K. (1988) *Women Teaching for Change*. South Hadley, MA: Bergin and Garvey.

Wells, A.S. (1996) African-American students' view of school choice. In B. Fuller and R. Elmore with G. Orfield (eds), *Who Chooses? Who Loses? Culture, Institutions, and the Unequal Effects of School Choice* (pp. 25–49). New York: Teachers College Press.

West, A., Sammons, P., Hailes, J. and Nuttall, D. (1994) The Standard Assessment Tasks and the boycott at Key Stage 1: Teachers' and headteachers' views in six inner-city schools. *Research Papers in Education*, 9(3), 321–38.

Wideen, M., with I. Pye (1994) *The Struggle for Change: The Story of One School*. London: Falmer Press.

Wignall, R. (1992, June) *Building a Collaborative School Culture: A Case Study of One Woman in the Principalship*. Paper presented at the European Conference on Educational Research, Enschede, The Netherlands.

Wolcott, H. (1973) *The Man in the Principal's Office: An Ethnography*. New York: Holt, Rinehart and Winston.

Woods, P. (1979) *The Divided School*. London: Routledge and Kegan Paul.

Woods, P. (ed.) (1980) *Teacher Strategies: Explorations in the Sociology of the School*. London: Croom Helm.

Woods, P. (1983) *Sociology and the School: An Interactionist Viewpoint*. London: Routledge and Kegan Paul.

Woods, P. (1987) Managing the primary teacher's role. In S. Delamont (ed.), *The Primary School Teacher* (pp. 120–43). London: Falmer Press.

Woods, P. (1990) *Teacher Skills and Strategies*. London: Falmer Press.

Woods, P. (1995) *Creative Teachers in the Primary School*. Buckingham: Open University Press.

Woods, P. and Jeffrey, B. (1996) *Teachable Moments: The Art of Teaching in Primary Schools*. Buckingham: Open University Press.

Woods, P., Jeffrey, B., Troman, G. and Boyle, M. (1997) *Restructuring Schools, Reconstructing Teachers*. Buckingham: Open University Press.

Woods, P. and Wenham, P. (1995) Politics and pedagogy: A case study in appropriation. *Journal of Education Policy*, 10 (2), 119–41.

Wragg, E. (1989) Parent power. In F. Macleod (ed.) *Parents and Schools: The Contemporary Challenge* (pp. 123–45). London: Falmer Press.

Wragg, E. (1993) *Primary Teaching Skills*. London: Routledge.

Wright, C. (1992) *Race Relations in the Primary School*. London: David Fulton.

Young, B. (1992) On careers: Themes from the lives of four Western Canadian women educators. *Canadian Journal of Education*, 17(2), 148–61.

Young, B. (1995) Postscript: Where do we go from here? In C. Reynolds and B. Young (eds), *Women and Leadership in Canadian Education* (pp. 243–52). Calgary: Detselig.

Author Index

Subject Index